Graham Greene's Thrillers and the 1930s

In *Graham Greene's Thrillers and the 1930s* Brian Diemert examines the first and most prolific phase of Graham Greene's career, demonstrating the close relationship between Greene's fiction and the political, economic, social, and literary contexts of the period. Situating Greene alongside other young writers who responded to the worsening political climate of the 1930s by promoting social and political reform, Diemert argues that Greene believed literature could not be divorced from its social and political milieu and saw popular forms of writing as the best way to inform a wide audience.

Diemert traces Greene's adaptation of nineteenth-century romance thrillers and classical detective stories into modern political thrillers as a means of presenting serious concerns in an engaging fashion. He argues that Greene's popular thrillers were in part a reaction to the high modernism of writers such as James Joyce, Gertrude Stein, and Virginia Woolf, whose esoteric experiments with language were disengaged from immediate social concerns and inaccessible to a large segment of the reading public.

Graham Greene's Thrillers and the 1930s investigates some of Greene's best-known works, such as *A Gun for Sale*, *Brighton Rock*, and *The Ministry of Fear*, and shows how they reflect the evolution of Greene's sense of the importance of popular culture in the 1930s.

BRIAN DIEMERT is assistant professor of English, Brescia College.

Graham Greene's Thrillers and the 1930s

BRIAN DIEMERT

McGill-Queen's University Press
Montreal & Kingston • London • Buffalo

© McGill-Queen's University Press 1996
ISBN 0–7735–1432–5 (cloth)
ISBN 0–7735–1433–3 (paper)

Legal deposit third quarter 1996
Bibliothèque nationale du Québec

Printed in Canada on acid-free paper

This book has been published with the help of grants from the Humanities and Social Science Federation of Canada, using funds provided by the Social Sciences and Humanities Research Council of Canada, and Brescia College.

McGill-Queen's University Press is grateful to the Canada Council for support of its publishing program.

Canadian Cataloguing in Publication Data

Diemert, Brian, 1959–
    Graham Greene's thrillers and the 1930s
    Includes bibliographical references and index.
    ISBN 0–7735–1432–5 (bound)
    ISBN 0–7735–1433–3 (pbk.)
    1. Greene, Graham, 1904–1991 – Criticism and interpretation.
    2. Greene, Graham, 1904–1991 – Political and social views.
    3. Political fiction, English – History and criticism. I. Title.
    PR6013.R44Z6324 1996   823'.912   C96-900319-6

This book was typeset by Typo Litho Composition Inc. in 10/12 Palatino.

Contents

Acknowledgments

Like any work that has been created over the course of years, this one could not have been written without the advice and support I received from a host of people who gave generously of their time and ideas. Most notably, I wish to thank Allan Gedalof and Michael Groden at the University of Western Ontario for their careful reading of the manuscript and many helpful criticisms. I am also grateful to Judith Adamson, whose commentary on the manuscript and knowledge of Greene and his work led me to clarify much of my thinking about Greene's politics in the 1930s and so made this a better book. I owe a debt of gratitude as well to Tom Carmichael, Alison Lee, and Carole Farber for their many valuable comments.

It is not possible to name all of those whose insights, encouragement, and friendship assisted me in the development of this book, but I particularly want to thank D.M.R. Bentley, Jim Snyder, Tracy Ware, Richard Costello, and Sr Corona Sharp of Brescia College. I must also thank Kim Morningstar, who ably assisted me in preparing a legible typescript by word-processing what were often nearly illegible handwritten revisions. During the early stages of my work on Greene, I was fortunate to have the support of a Social Sciences and Humanities Research Council fellowship. This book has been published with the help of grants from the Social Science Federation of Canada and from Brescia College. Lastly, my greatest debts are owed to my parents, Marvin and Barbara Diemert, and to my wife, Dr Monika Lee, whose love, encouragement, and patience made this book possible. She is my best critic and a constant source of inspiration. This book is for her and our daughter, Anna.

Portions of my commentary on *It's a Battlefield* have already appeared in *PLL: Papers on Language and Literature*, vol. 30, no. 3 (summer 1994) and are reprinted by permission of the publisher, the board of trustees of Southern Illinois University at Edwardsville. My comments on *Brighton Rock* have previously appeared, again in altered form, in *Twentieth Century Literature*, vol. 38, no. 4 (winter 1992).

Abbreviations

Graham Greene's Thrillers and the 1930s

1 Graham Greene and the 1930s

Prompted by the publication of *The End of the Affair*, *Time* magazine claimed in a 1951 cover story that Graham Greene's stories are "as gripping as a good movie ... The people who have made Graham Greene the popular success he is today are, by and large, people who like the movies – people who go for a 'good thriller' ... he is now seriously discussed as possibly 'the finest writer of his generation.' No other writer in England enjoys Greene's combination of popular and critical success" ("Shocker" 62).

In many ways, these remarks epitomize the critical consensus on Greene's work over the past forty years, for, until his death on 3 April 1991, Graham Greene was routinely referred to as "our greatest living novelist" and praised for his ability to weld popularity to critical acceptance. Indeed, as Roger Sharrock remarks, "Greene's great technical achievement has been the elevation of the form of the thriller into a medium for serious fiction" (12). The story of how and why Greene's fiction developed in this way is the subject of this book.

To call any author "our greatest novelist" or, as Sharrock does, "our most distinguished novelist" (12), however glowing the praise, ultimately raises questions about the ground upon which such epithets stand. Certainly there is no denying Greene's continuing popularity, as is clear from the fact that all but two of his forty or so books remain in print and available in paperback editions.[1] Equally certain is that his popularity stems in part at least from his ability to write exciting, suspenseful stories – many of which have been filmed – that continue to entertain a broad spectrum of readers.

Many literary critics, however, view popularity with suspicion and seldom see it as the mark of a writer's literary worth. Greene, himself, aware of this attitude, none the less was able to mock it in *The End of the Affair* when the novelist Bendrix anticipates the critic's assessment of his own work: "Patronizingly in the end he would place me – probably a little above Maugham because Maugham is popular and I have not yet committed that crime – not yet, but although I retain a little of the exclusiveness of unsuccess, the little reviews, like wise detectives, can scent it on its way" (148). Greene's popularity, as David Lodge observes, has often been seen as reason to doubt the quality of his work ("Graham" 2). Indeed, a strong critical bias within the academy has in the past separated popular culture from high culture and so condemned popular works and popular forms or subgenres such as science fiction, crime fiction, the western, and historical romance novels.[2] At its most extreme, as in the cases of F.R. Leavis, Q.D. Leavis, and José Ortega y Gasset, this bias has seen popularity and artistic quality as mutually exclusive. More recently, owing to the work of critics such as Leslie Fiedler, Northrop Frye, Dennis Porter, William Stowe, Janice Radway, and Catherine Belsey and to structuralist and post-structuralist theorists such as Umberto Eco, Tzvetan Todorov, Roland Barthes, and Jacques Derrida, and, of course, to authors such as Greene, the bias against the serious analysis of popular forms and popular texts is openly questioned, particularly when the issue of canon formation is discussed by Marxist, feminist, minority, and interdisciplinary commentators. In many respects, the whole idea of a "great tradition" of English literature (which is to be read, studied, and taught) has crumbled as troubling assumptions behind the canonization of literary texts are increasingly exposed; as Terry Eagleton remarks, "The unquestioned 'great tradition' of the 'national literature' has to be recognized as a *construct*, fashioned by particular people for particular reasons at a certain time. There is no such thing as a literary work or tradition which is valuable *in itself*" (*Literary Theory* 11). Yet, the question of literary value has not disappeared either from critical debate or from the reading public's imagination. As an issue of *Esquire* magazine demonstrated some few years ago (July 1989), publishers continue to employ a critical apparatus that maintains a hierarchy of authors and texts in bookstores and in those periodicals, magazines, and newspapers from which the majority of readers get their literary news.

Because he has received both acclaim and scorn for his use of the thriller format in many of his texts,[3] the reaction to Greene's work exposes a host of biases – against popular fiction, against genre fiction, and against realistic fiction – to which critics are now opening their eyes. What renders this issue even more complex is that, although Greene is undoubtedly a popular writer, the same media that most strongly preserve the hierarchical distinctions between "serious" literature and "popular" literature also hailed Greene before his death as the "best living novelist" writing in English.[4]

To study Greene's fiction in light of his use of the popular form of the thriller, then, is to explore indirectly, through an examination of the strategies for reading that Greene develops in his texts, the twin concepts of canon formation and critical authority, of privileging certain types of literary texts – for whatever reasons – over others, and also to consider one kind of response after 1930 to the innovations of the high modernists in the previous decade. In this regard, the whole question of Greene's attraction to the thriller as a form and the subsequent distinction between "entertainment" and "novel" that he applied to his work prior to 1969 must be brought into focus.[5] As well, the structure of the thriller, and its relation to the detective-fiction formula, needs to be viewed as a metaphor for the activity of reading because intelligent reading is now, as it was in the 1930s, the first line of intellectual self-defence that citizens can adopt in order to ensure the development and maintenance of a free society.

This chapter focuses particularly on the first and most prolific phase of Greene's career, the years from 1929 to 1943. It begins by portraying Greene's use of the thriller as part of a widespread response to the literature and criticism of high modernism, which emerged during and after the First World War, and to the political, socio-economic, and military crises of the 1930s. Donat O'Donnell made the point well when he wrote in 1947 that "far more than the left-wing militancy of such poets as Auden and Spender … the thrillers of Mr. Greene reflect the state of the West European mind in the 'thirties," and that, as a result, Greene is "the most truly characteristic writer of the 'thirties in England, and the leading novelist of that time and place" (25, 28). After briefly discussing the "entertainment" label that Greene attached to his thrillers, the chapter examines the formation of Greene's attitudes to popular literature and art within the context of critical opinion in the 1930s. Crucial to its approach is a consideration of the place of detective fiction within Greene's aesthetic.

"ENTERTAINMENTS" AND "NOVELS"

In the 1970s Greene said that, between 1936 and 1969, he applied the label "entertainments" to those of his books that deliberately made use of the popular form of the thriller, the point of the term being to distinguish those writings from his "more serious work" (*WE* 78). *A*

Gun For Sale (1936) was the first to be labelled an "Entertainment," and five subsequent texts share this subheading: *The Confidential Agent* (1939), *The Ministry of Fear* (1943), *The Third Man* (1950), *Loser Takes All* (1956), and *Our Man in Havana* (1958). These books were "entertainments" because, as Greene told the *Paris Review* in 1953, "they [did] not carry a message" (Shuttleworth 32). But the issue of how Greene employed this designation calls for some comment when we consider other incidents of its use. *Stamboul Train* (1932), his fourth published novel, was not originally called an "entertainment" in its first editions but was given this heading after 1936, and critics now routinely group it with the six other entertainments. "The Basement Room" (1935) was also called an "entertainment" but only when it was reprinted as "The Fallen Idol" (after the title of the film version) and published, after 1950, by Heinemann and later Penguin with *The Third Man*.[6] Greene even considered *The Quiet American* (1955) an entertainment when he was working on it (Allain 148–9), and indeed it is a book that shares a great deal with the thrillers of the 1930s. *Brighton Rock* (1938) is a more difficult case because it was called an entertainment in its first American edition but not in its first British edition published a month later, and subsequent American reprintings removed the subheading.

This vacillation suggests that the issue of what constitutes an entertainment and Greene's use of the term is not as straightforward as it is sometimes made to appear. Despite the growing volume of critical commentary that Greene has inspired, much of it offers brief and dismissive treatments of those works he chose to call "entertainments." And, although Philip Stratford's *Faith and Fiction*, Judith Adamson's *The Dangerous Edge*, and Elliott Malamet's dissertation offer good discussions of all or some of these texts, only Peter Wolfe's 1972 study, *Graham Greene: The Entertainer*, treats them exclusively.[7] Recent studies by Henry Donaghy, Neil McEwen, and R.H. Miller, among others, continue to slight the "entertainments" with brief comment. On the other hand, as an anonymous reviewer has noted, Greene's "novels," particularly the so-called Catholic novels (*Brighton Rock* [1938], *The Power and the Glory* [1940], *The Heart of the Matter* [1948], *The End of the Affair* [1951], and *The Burnt-Out Case* [1961]) receive most of the critical attention for three main reasons: they offer easily isolated themes and a certain guaranteed seriousness; Catholic critics have been quick to offer Catholic explanations and interpretations; and Greene's distinction between "novels" and "entertainments" "encouraged critics to take his best work lightly" ("GG: Man Within" 11).

To be sure, Greene's selective use of the label "entertainment" implies a difference between two kinds of texts. What is more, critics often see this difference as both generic and qualitative; that is, the "entertainments" are considered "pot-boilers" (Atkins 30) and "lighter" or "lesser" fare since they are more obvious in their attempts to reach a large audience through their explicit use of the thriller's conventions. By contrast, the novels are deemed "serious work" (Atkins 30) both in theme and in form. Hence, in the 1950s and 1960s it was fashionable to dismiss *A Gun For Sale* (1936), *The Confidential Agent* (1939), and *The Ministry of Fear* (1943) as "trial run[s]" (Lewis 240) for the more significant novels that followed each: *Brighton Rock*, *The Power and the Glory*, and *The Heart of the Matter*. For R.W.B. Lewis, these latter texts make up a "trilogy" exploring an explicitly religious theme.[8]

Attempts to downplay down the distinction between "novel" and "entertainment" also run into difficulties because the label continues to be seen as a mark of genuine difference. For instance, Robert O. Evans calls Greene's distinction "superficial" but follows a commonly held position that sees the "entertainment" label as a mark of the supposedly small degree to which these texts deal with the seriousness of life (Evans, "Introduction" vii)[9]; consequently, the entertainments are conceived of as less important, and Evans' selection of critical essays reflects this assumption. Similarly, John Atkins, Richard Kelly, David Pryce-Jones, and Martin Turnell all question the distinction, but each implicitly validates the practice of designating some texts entertainments and others novels by treating the label as a mark of genuine difference. This approach to Greene's work is widespread. Most readers, including those who admire the "entertainments" above the "novels" (such as W.W. Robson, Gavin Lambert, and, to an extent, David Lodge), have largely accepted the idea that Greene's texts are of two kinds, that Greene writes in two distinct genres.

One problem is that many commentators still accept the definition of the "entertainment" genre that was proposed in 1951 by Kenneth Allott and Miriam Farris in the first book-length study of Greene's fiction.[10] They suggested that the entertainments were distinguished from the novels by a comparative lack of character development, by the wilful use of an interesting background for its own sake, and by the free use of coincidence and improbabilities to link aspects of the plot (78–9). Others have added to this definition by claiming that the entertainments possess melodramatic story-lines (particularly in their use of violence) (Kunkel 157), rapidly paced action moving "in short, sharp, cinematographic flashes" which give the reader little time to weigh probabilities (Kunkel 105), and relatively happy endings (Sharrock 12, 72) or, at least, "solution[s] with resolution" in contrast to the novels' resolutions without solutions (R.H. Miller 10). On a more thematic level, A.A. De Vitis argues that the novels express "the serious preoccupation with religious and ethical problems" while the "secular" entertainments subordinate these concerns to "plot, action, and melodrama" (27). For De Vitis and others, this emphasis ensures that the "entertainments are not the thought-provoking documents that the novels are," though "any writer of thrillers or light fiction would be proud to have written" them (53).

In one sense, De Vitis and others who share his view of the entertainments cannot be blamed for seeing them as less important work. As already noted, Greene himself seemed to express this opinion in a number of places, among them a 1955 radio interview in which he commented: "In one's entertainments one is primarily interested in having an exciting story as in physical action, with just enough character to give interest in the action … In the novels I hope one is primarily interested in the character and the action takes a minor part" (cited in Pryce-Jones 62; Wolfe 32; and Silverstein 24). Yet, although it is always tempting and sometimes useful to do so, anyone who quotes Greene for support does so at his or her peril[11]: in a later interview with Anthony Burgess, Greene expressed his concern over the kind of thing that happens when critics separate his fiction into the serious novels – therefore, important work – and the not-so-serious entertainments (thrillers) – therefore, escapist or minor work: "The more I think of it, the more I worry about this division of literature into the great because hard to read, the not so great – or certainly ignoble by scholars – because of the desire to divert, be readable, keep it plain. You don't find Conan Doyle dealt with at length in the literary histories. Yet he was a great writer. He created several great characters – … Something ought to be done about this double standard" (Burgess 22–3). Similarly, in an extended conversation with Marie-Françoise Allain, Greene noted that he originally employed the distinction to escape melodrama (by which he means "a measure of violence in the action" [Allain 37]), but that after *The Ministry of Fear* the "novels and entertainments resembled each other more and more" so that he "abandoned the dichotomy once and for all with *Travels With My Aunt*, for it served no further purpose" (Allain 148). Curiously, however, he had confessed earlier in the interview that he "only avoided melodrama in one or two books, *The End of the Affair* and *Travels With My Aunt*" (37), which suggests that if the "entertainments" were written to purge, through an imaginative process, "the temptation of melodrama" (Stratford, "GG" 67), they must have failed in their objective.

In considering the differences between "entertainments" and "novels," we face the difficulty of generic classification, and so terminology itself becomes a problem because "genre" is often used in two distinct ways. On the one hand, it describes the broad classifications of form such as novel, short story, novella, play, poem, epic, lyric, and so on into which we place literary texts. On the other hand, "genre," in the sense of genre fiction for instance, describes particular types of narrative such as detective fiction, science fiction, or the western which can be found in any text regardless of its form as novel, film, play, or whatever. For critics of Greene's work, these differing uses raise potential difficulties since, with the two exceptions of "The Fallen Idol," a short story, and *Loser Takes All*, a novella, Greene's entertainments are also novels. The distinction between "entertainment" and "novel," however, is usually treated as a generic difference in the term genre's second sense; the "entertainment" is seen as a type of genre fiction and so is generally accorded less respect. (To avoid confusion, I use "genre" in the second sense of the term, although other critics might use terms such as type, mode, or subgenre to describe the distinction between "entertainment" and "novel.") But whether one treats "entertainment" as a modal or a generic term hardly matters since the second use of "genre" includes all other possible distinctions (type, kind, mode, form, subgenre) that might be applied in the classification of texts. In this way one can speak of thrillers, mysteries, detective stories, spy stories, police-procedural novels (to name five closely related forms) as distinct genres, although a more precise typology might describe them as subgenres of the novel or types of crime fiction – itself a variety of the mode of romance – or even as forms of the "entertainment."

The chief difficulty, despite Tzvetan Todorov's warning that genres are constantly being transformed (*Genres* 15), lies in seeing genre as a "natural" or prescriptive entity and in viewing Greene as working in distinct genres. On a general level, this presumption leads critics to make "entertainment" the marginalized term in the Greenian binary opposition of "entertainment"/"novel" (thus the entertainments are treated separately and/or differently from the novels). More specifically, however, such thinking has led to some remarkable charges against Greene which seem to miss the point of his work because critics assume that genres cannot be mixed.

For instance, one influential critic in this regard, R.W.B. Lewis,[12] thinks Greene guilty of generic confusion in his early novels, because they display "an apparent failure to distinguish between various fictional genres ... [and] the confusion of purpose and the blurry handling of the elements are rooted in a failure to disentangle the *mystery* of the mystery, to separate it out from the contingencies of melodrama and the staged surprises of the brain-twister" (239–40). For

Lewis, the early novels fail because they do not conform easily to standards of decorum for generic conventions: Greene, it seems, does not know how to write a proper thriller because he has mixed seriousness of purpose with the artificial constructions of the genre. The text that demonstrates this confusion most clearly for Lewis is *Brighton Rock*, which, although it effectively exploits the "confusion" of genres, still "betrays an initial confusion between what Greene calls an 'entertainment' and what he finally offered as tragedy" (239). André Maurois is similarly critical of *Brighton Rock* and does not rank it high among Greene's texts because he finds that the detective-story element in the novel (Ida Arnold's pursuit of Pinkie Brown) holds a disproportionate place in the story (Maurois 387). By way of contrast, David Lodge admires *Brighton Rock* precisely for its use of the crime story (Lodge/Gregor 165).

What Lewis and Maurois, among others, demonstrate is the power of expectations surrounding the concept of genre. In recognizing that genre signals control reader response, they rely on an understanding of genre similar to Frederic Jameson's formulation that "genres are essentially literary *institutions*, or social contracts between a writer and a specific public, whose function is to specify the proper use of a particular cultural artifact" (*Political Unconscious* 106). Here, the idea of genre as a contract suggests that reading is permitted by a kind of legitimate, legal, authority and that a particular text can be properly or improperly used, just as the book can be improperly shelved. A label such as "entertainment", however, raises questions about genre since it is a commentary superimposed on the text by the text, yet, as Jacques Derrida notes, it is not of the text ("Law of Genre" 61). For Derrida, "genre" (like "presence," "centre," "speech," and so on) is the privileged term in a structure of binary opposition (hence, presence/absence, centre/periphery, speech/writing, or, in Greene's terms, novel/entertainment) that marks the boundary of two conceptual fields by defining an edge. To do this, however, Derridian logic dictates that genre must contain within it "a principle of contamination, a law of impurity," which involves "a sort of participation without belonging – a taking part in without being a part of, without having membership in a set." Derrida calls this aspect of genre "the law of the law of genre" (55).

Evidence for the "law of the law of genre" is found in the individual trait that marks genre within a text. The mark that a set of texts shares distinguishes that group from other texts, but in itself the mark (or "re-mark" since it is repetition that renders a trait a mark of genre) evinces the contamination of a generic distinction. Hence, any text, whether a newspaper editorial or a novel, indicates by means of a mark, even if it is not explicitly designated as such, that it is an article of the genre newspaper editorial or novel. This mark of genre is crucial to our understanding of a text, and to condemn a text for openly declaring its generic allegiance raises serious problems. As Todorov notes, the text generally considered literature is traditionally seen as the text that breaks generic boundaries, and so it must essentially be seen as a genre unto itself. The best example of a popular form, by contrast, most clearly shows its generic membership because it conforms exactly to the strictures of generic formula; to improve upon the formula is to write literature (*Poetics* 43). It is this view of literature that is at the heart of the critical prejudice against genre fiction. Yet, if it were truly the case that the text of literature broke completely from generic patterning to become a genre unto itself, then the text would be incomprehensible. Instead, any text teaches us how it is to be read by putting forward generic signals – by re-marking on the mark of genre within it – that appeal to our experience of reading because they are the traces of what we already know, of what has already been read. As Northrop Frye never tired of teaching, "all fiction is conventionalized" (45).

The "entertainment" label, then, like other subheadings ("novel," "mystery," "romance," and so on), is only one of many forms the mark of genre may take. In Greene's texts, we can say with Derrida that the designation "entertainment" "places within and without the work, along its boundary, an inclusion and exclusion with regard to genre in general, as to an identifiable class in general" (61). But such a "remark of belonging need not pass through the consciousness of the author or the reader, although it often does so. It can also refute this consciousness or render the explicit 'mention' mendacious, false, inadequate, or ironic according to all sorts of overdetermined figures" (60). Nor need the mark of genre be a theme or the thematic component of the work: the mark exists and is re-marked upon in the text even in the absence of a subheading. The status of the subheading is, thus, severely undermined, since it is only *one* form of self-comment that the text possesses. The designation "commits one to nothing. Neither reader nor critic nor author are bound to believe that the text preceded by this designation conforms readily to the strict, normal, normed, or normative definition of the genre" (Derrida 62–3). Equally damaging to the label's status is that its effacement "leav[es] a trace that, inscribed and filed away, remains as an effect of supplementary relief which is not easily accounted for in all of its facets" (63). Hence, Greene's abandonment of the designation in 1969 has not stopped people from continuing to see texts that were once called "entertainments" as entertainment. Ultimately, attempts to make a clear distinction between "entertainment" and "novel" are destined to fail because such a determination turns on the very question of what literature is; that is, why is one piece of fiction accepted as literature and another piece, specifically a work that uses the form of a popular genre, dismissed as insignificant fiction destined to be forgotten? In a Derridian analysis, serious literature and popular literature inscribe each other: each is crucial to the survival of the other.

We cannot, then, think of the "entertainment" label as a formal description marking some of Greene's books as different from his others. Instead, it is more important for us to recognize how Greene's texts comment on their generic qualities. Indeed, Greene's texts exist on and investigate the border or the frontier of genre. Whether "entertainments" or not, they embody a process of reflexive investigation that scrutinizes critical distinctions, between entertainment and novel, popular genre and literary genre, popular fiction and canonical literature, by challenging our methodology of reading.

Still, because Greene did adopt the subtitle "entertainment" for several of his books, it has acquired a certain generic authority that, like similar terms – "a mystery," "a romance," or "a history" – structures a set of expectations against which the text is measured and judged, and directs us in how we read and in what we take from our reading. As a mark of genre, the label invokes what Roland Barthes calls the "already read" (*s/z* 19), which is that part of the reading experience with which we are already familiar before we come to the text.

The question becomes, then, why did Greene seek to invoke this kind of reading experience? The answer, I think, lies in the critical milieu of the 1930s and Greene's response to it. In the years between the publication of *Stamboul Train* (1932) and *England Made Me* (1935), Greene became increasingly uneasy with the idea that cultural production could be separated into categories of high, meaning serious or élite, art and low, meaning escapist or popular, art. In his criticism and in his fiction he developed ways to bridge this "great divide," as Andreas Huyssen calls it. (One thinks, for instance, of the hilarious and rather pointed scene in *The Third Man*, in which Rollo Martins, a writer of westerns under the pseudonym of Buck Dexter, is confused with a more literary author with the similar name of Benjamin Dexter, and consequently ends up giving a lecture on contemporary literature to the British Cultural Relations Society [68–75]. The scene's importance for Greene is emphasized by the fact that Calloway opens and closes his narrative with references to the episode.) The fact that Greene's early entertainments resemble his early novels explains why he abandoned the "entertainment" subtitle in 1969 when he came to write *Travels With My Aunt*. Indeed, in that novel the marriage of popular and serious fiction is clearly allegorized in the concluding scene when Henry Pulling interrupts his aunt Augusta as she dances a slow waltz with her one true love, Mr Visconti, a name taken from Marjorie Bowen's *The Viper of Milan*, with the news that "Wordsworth's dead" (264). When we consider that only books published between 1936 and 1958 were called "entertainments" (*Stamboul Train*, as we have observed, was belatedly given this title) and that the label was allowed to stand until 1969, we can see that its use was tied to a specific historical period. More particularly, if we take into account Greene's comment that the novels and entertainments began to resemble each other more and more after *The Ministry of Fear*, it becomes apparent that the label was most important, for him at least, in the years from 1936 to 1943 and perhaps slightly beyond. Greene's own comments from this period, found in his essays and film reviews, are particularly illuminating in this regard.

Greene considered "melodrama ... one of [his] working tools" because it enabled him "to obtain effects that would be unattainable otherwise" (Shuttleworth 39–40); one of these effects was to excite his readers by getting them "involved in the story." For Greene, the work's effect upon the reader was always crucial: "If you excite your audience first," he wrote in a 1936 review of *Rhythm on the Range*, "you can put over what you will of horror, suffering, truth" (*PD* 94); and more than thirty years later, he said that "this is still true and applies to the novel as well as to the film. By exciting the audience I mean getting them involved in the story. Once they are involved they will accept the thing as you present it" (Phillips, "GG: On Screen" 172–3). What this comment suggests is that, in the same year that he first decided to use the term "entertainment" to describe *A Gun For Sale*, Greene saw the thriller form as tendering more than an outlet for melodramatic creative impulses or a short cut to financial success. What it offered was a means of putting ideas, specifically political ideas, across to readers who would otherwise not be reached by more conventional political discourse. As Carolyn Scott notes in her fine discussion of the entertainments, there is a "political emphasis" in these books that is less well marked in the other, more theologically oriented work (2). This suggestion of a political emphasis in the "entertainments" provides a clue to Greene's use of the thriller form and to his decision to adopt the "entertainment" label.

The 1930s was Greene's formative period as a novelist and the period in which he was most prolific.[13] In these years Greene, like many writers of his generation, developed a sense of art's social role that shaped his view of what the novel should be and of the place of popular culture in society. His growing awareness of the value of the popular in the arts arose out of more than personal loyalty to the beloved authors of his youth; it was a part of the response of second-generation modernists – that is, the writers who emerged in the 1930s – to the high modernists of the previous generation who had emerged during and after the First World War. For many of the younger writers of the crisis-filled 1930s, literature and art had to align themselves with social concerns, and, acting on this belief, numerous critics and authors from both the Left and the Right sought to redefine literature's role within the culture. Although George Woodcock sees Greene's "aloofness" from the party politics of the 1930s' generation of writers as the key to his survival (129), Greene's fiction and his decision to use popular forms of discourse demonstrate that he shared his generation's view of the modernism of the twenties. They also mark him as sympathetic to the concerns of the Left but also sceptical enough to avoid the traps of dogmatic positions; consequently, Greene was equally critical of both the established order of the Right and of the excesses of the Left (Webster 106). Like Auden and his followers, Greene believed that the artist could be, had to be, serious without being "highbrow," and it is in this context that his thrillers and his decision to use the "entertainment" label have their place.

THE MELODRAMATIC IMAGINATION

It has been suggested that the "entertainment" label reflects Greene's "squeamishness" about melodramatic elements in some of his novels and that, accordingly, the subtitle is some sort of apology to critical fashion (Davis 47; Lambert 138). Greene, however, was not shy about his affection for what Orwell, borrowing from G.K. Chesterton, called "good bad books" and their authors. Indeed, Greene's love of melodramatic forms of literature such as detective fiction and adventure stories is clearly seen not only in autobiographical reminiscences but also in his contributions to a bibliography of Victorian detective fiction and to an edition of four Victorian mysteries.[14] Greene was never comfortable with the critical "double-standard" that casually dismisses popular art and popular forms, such as the thriller, as the inferior cultural products of a mass consumer-oriented society, and in reviews he was just as apt to praise the work of Arthur Conan Doyle, H. Rider Haggard, Anthony Hope, or John Buchan as he was that of more "literary" figures such as Henry Fielding, Henry James, Joseph Conrad, or James Joyce. It is not that Greene was uncritical of popular writing or the products of popular culture, for he certainly was.

Popular authors, such as Charles Morgan and Mrs Parkinson Keyes, are frequently taken to task for careless writing. Similarly, he reproduces on one level the hierarchical structures he challenges on another level when he applies Ford Madox Ford's distinction between "novels" and "nuvvels" to film in a 1937 review, suggesting that films could be classified as either cinema or movies, with the former approaching the condition of art and the latter pandering to popular taste and fashion (*PD* 186).[15]

In part, Greene's preference for the thriller was deeply rooted in his early experience of reading. Most prominently in "The Lost Childhood" (after remarking that the first book he recalls ever reading was *Dixon Brett: Detective*), he cites Rider Haggard, Percy Westerman, Stanley Weyman, M.R. Ballantyne, Anthony Hope, Captain Gilson, and Marjorie Bowen's *The Viper of Milan* as shaping influences on his own fiction (*CE* 13–18).[16] Elsewhere he adds figures such as John Buchan (*CE* 167) and A.E.W. Mason (*CE* 157) to this list of now largely forgotten authors. Childhood and the importance of formative experiences are recurring concerns in Greene's writing, and the profound influence of the romantic-adventure tales he read while young is insisted upon throughout his autobiographical work:

Perhaps it is only in childhood that books have any deep influence on our lives ... in childhood all books are books of divination, telling us about the future, and like the fortune-teller who sees a long journey in the cards or death by water they influence the future. I suppose that is why books excited us so much. What do we ever get nowadays from reading to equal the excitement and the revelation in those first fourteen years? Of course, I should be interested to hear that a new novel by Mr E.M. Forster was going to appear this spring, but I could never compare that mild expectation of civilized pleasure with the missed heartbeat, the appalled glee I felt when I found on a library shelf a novel by Rider Haggard, Percy Westerman, Captain Brereton or Stanley Weyman which I had not read before. (*CE* 13)

The corollary of this emphasis on childhood reading is Greene's sense that "the creative writer perceives his world once and for all in childhood and adolescence, and his whole career is an effort to illustrate his private world in terms of the great public world we all share" (*CE* 83). Greene's private world, as is readily apparent in his fiction, is composed out of the images and romance patterns of the books he loved as a boy. As his often quoted remarks about *The Viper of Milan* make clear, Greene sees the moral universe of his own fiction rooted in the romance world of Bowen's book, which, he says, provided him with his subject:

As for Visconti [the villainous Duke of Milan], with his beauty, his patience, and his genius for evil, I had watched him pass by many a time ... His name was Carter. He exercised terror from a distance ... Goodness has only once found a perfect incarnation in a human body and never will again, but evil can always find a home there. Human nature is not black and white but black and grey. I read all that in *The Viper of Milan* and I looked round and I saw that it was so.

There was another theme I found there ... the sense of doom that lies over success – the feeling that the pendulum is about to swing. That too made sense; one looked around and saw the doomed everywhere ...

One had lived for fourteen years in a wild jungle country without a map, but now the paths had been traced and naturally one had to follow them ... [Bowen] had given me my pattern – religion might later explain it to me in other terms, but the pattern was already there – perfect evil walking the world where perfect good can never walk again, and only the pendulum ensures that after all in the end justice is done. (*CE* 16–17)

Such remarks offer a well-travelled way into Greene's fiction: Here we see Greene's theological interest, his attraction to romance, auto-biographical information, and his moral vision of a world infected by some "aboriginal calamity" (a phrase of Cardinal John Henry Newman's that Greene is fond of quoting [*LR* vii]). Equally telling is the metaphor he uses to describe his life before writing. The journey through "a wild jungle country" is the stuff of boy's adventure tales by Haggard, Buchan, or Kipling and of accounts by explorers such as David Livingstone or Henry Stanley. As well, Greene observes that he "naturally" had to follow the path previously traced by earlier writers of romantic adventure; and, while *Journey Without Maps* (1935) may be a literal expression of the search for personal and socio-political origins, much of Greene's fiction continues to repeat and rework patterns found in these nineteenth-century romances, which are in one sense the origins of his work. The model for all of Greene's books, as John Spurling points out, "is the Victorian adventure story, but translated to a world in which the Victorian adventure hero cannot rely on the values that once supported him" (65).

In these respects, the thriller became an apt genre for Greene to write in: not only had much of his early reading consisted of thrillers and adventure stories, but the importance he placed on origins found its corollary in detective fiction's emphasis on discovering the origins of crime. The thriller easily accommodated itself to Greene's sense of a morally ambiguous universe and to the pattern of romance (one element of which is a concern with the hero's origins) that Greene found so appealing in Bowen's novel and then used in various forms throughout his career.[17] As well, the archetypal struggle between Visconti and della Scala in Bowen's novel is precisely the conflict that W.H. Auden sees as informing the "superior" thriller (to add Greene's qualification [*PD* 260]), wherein the battle between good and evil takes place under the cover of everyday reality and the reader is made to feel partisan to one side ("Guilty Vicarage" 147; "Heresy" 43). Yet, while we do find ourselves sympathetically located in Greene's novels, the issue of partisanship is always problematic. Human nature cannot be so neatly polarized, and so the writer, as Greene says, must be able "to write from the point of view of the black square as well as of the white" (*Why?* 32). Hence, Raven and Pinkie are made sympathetic, but they are also cold-blooded murderers; both D. and Rowe at the end of their respective novels are in positions that on one level seem to offer the reader happy endings, but at another level these endings open only onto uncertainty.[18]

For Greene, the elemental nature of the romance conflict is best seen in the action of the thriller and not in the leisurely meditation of the detective story: "Action has a moral simplicity which thought lacks" (*Reflections* 79). This is the thriller's appeal which Greene cites in *Journey Without Maps* (1936):

Today our world seems peculiarly susceptible to brutality. There is a touch of nostalgia in the pleasure we take in gangster novels, in characters who have so agreeably simplified their emotions that they have begun living again at a level below the cerebral. We, like Wordsworth, are living after a war and a revolution, and these half-castes fighting with bombs between the cliffs of skyscrapers seem more likely than we to be aware of Proteus rising from the sea. It is not, of course, that one wishes to stay for ever at that level, but when one sees to what unhappiness, to what peril of extinction centuries of cerebration have brought us, one sometimes has a curiosity to discover if one can from what we have come, to recall at which point we went astray. (21)

Implicitly, the passage argues for the thriller as the genre best suited to the contemporary situation. What is also striking in Greene's remarks is his linking of the thriller's plot structure to the quest for origins both at a socio-political level, where he seeks the cause of society's and humanity's failings, and at a personal level, where he searches for the roots of his own character.[19] Ultimately, the origin that the thriller and Greene seek lie in an understanding of the "calamity" in which all humanity is implicated.[20]

From an early point in his career, however, Greene's attraction to romance was tempered by an equally strong attraction to realism in the depiction of political and social situations. To be sure, the moral or "religious sense" of fiction (*CE* 91) remained a crucial element in Greene's understanding of what the novel should be, and in his own fiction, as we will see, the romance pattern of the thriller allowed an elemental presentation of religious or moral conflict. In choosing the thriller over the detective story, however, Greene selected the form that is better able to accommodate realism to the structures of romance. But he must transform the thriller. The basic objective of the 1930s generation of writers was to bring a sense of social and political realism into their work, and this objective was a driving force, as Raymond Chandler observed, behind the development of the hard-boiled detective novel best exemplified in the work of Dashiell Hammett. The hard-boiled detective novel remains the story of a detective "in search of a hidden truth" (Chandler, "Simple" 21), but the degree to which this quest is successful is tempered by, among other things, a sense of reality. Both the thriller, as Greene writes it, and the hard-boiled detective novel are characterized by their preoccupation with the grit of the real world.[21]

THE SITUATION OF THE 1930S

Histories of detective fiction routinely refer to the 1920s and 1930s as the "golden age" of the genre. Not only did the number of detective novels published annually increase enormously in the period, but formal patterns quickly took shape as many of the genre's most familiar practitioners – Agatha Christie, Dorothy Sayers, Marjorie Allingham, Hammett, Chandler, and a host of others – emerged. As well, essays and reviews by Sayers, S.S. Van Dine, Ronald Knox, T.S. Eliot, Auden, and, at Greene's request, Herbert Read, to name a few, created a critical discourse that gave the genre some measure of respectability. By 1932, Graves and Hodge tell us, popular reading was dominated by detective fiction (300).

The tremendous popularity of detective fiction in the period following the First World War defies any single explanation. On the most facile level, the genre's allure may have stemmed from a desire for imaginative escape from the memory of the war, the hardships of economic depression, and the fear of another war. Auden's suggestion that detective stories appeal to those with a sense of sin also tempts us as an explanation since we might then see, as Edmund Wilson did, their proliferation as reflecting a collective desire to exorcise a sense of guilt arising from the war ("Why Do People" 236). Similarly, one might argue that the seeming randomness of killing is given a significance and order in the ritualized world of the detective story that it does not possess in real life (Cunningham, *British Writers* 75).

And if we were more cynical we might, as Wyndham Lewis does in *The Apes of God* (1931) and *Left Wings Over Europe* (1936), link the blood-lust of the Great War with a general "blood-psychosis" that covertly manifested itself in the prevailing political climate and in the popularity of thrillers until it openly surfaced in the Second World War (Cunningham, *British Writers* 74). As is readily apparent, each of these explanations turns on the centrality of the war to the experience of life in the 1920s and 1930s.

The effects of the Great War were complex; on those men who were too young to have fought, the war inspired ambivalent feelings of revulsion at its brutality and waste, of guilt for not having fought, and of envy of those who had (Hynes, *Auden* 21). George Orwell recalled feeling "a little less than a man" for having missed it ("My Country" 537–8), and Christopher Isherwood confessed: "Like most of my generation, I was obsessed by a complex of terrors and longings connected with the idea 'War.' 'War,' in this purely neurotic sense, meant The Test. The test of your courage, of your maturity, of your sexual prowess: 'Are you really a Man?' Subconsciously, I believe, I longed to be subjected to this test" (75–6). The psychological effort to come to terms with these feelings led Isherwood to "the pages of adventure stories designed for boys of twelve years old" (78) and to day-dreams of heroism, as he and others translated the war into the domestic concerns of university life (*Lions* 77–8). Greene said much the came thing when he looked back on his youth in *Ways of Escape* (1980): "We were a generation brought up on adventure stories who had missed the enormous disillusionment of the First World War, so we went looking for adventure" (37). Such comments suggest that at least part of the imaginative appeal of adventure stories and of thrillers for male writers in the 1930s stemmed from a confused sense of having missed out on some "great adventure." The search for adventure explains the attraction of travelling and the consequent vogue in travel writing (Hynes, *Auden* 229), and it also helps to account for the enormous popularity of thrillers. Eliot and Auden's published remarks on detective fiction as well as certain of Eliot's poems and plays ("Macavity: the Mystery Cat," "Sweeney Agonistes," [1927], *Murder in the Cathedral* [1935], and *The Family Reunion* [1939]) and of Auden's poems ("The Secret Agent" and "Detective Story," to name two) reflect the thriller's importance for writers at this time. Similarly, C. Day Lewis, one of the poets most closely associated with Auden, expressed his affection for the genre by writing his own series of detective stories and thrillers under the pseudonym of Nicholas Blake. Still, the interest in adventure stories that the war reawakened in the young male writers of the thirties was not the same kind of interest they had possessed as children or adolescents; the war made sure of that.

Paul Fussell observes in his fine study of the experience of the Great War that "every war is ironic because every war is worse than expected" (*Great War* 7). When Britain, joining France and Russia, declared war on Germany on 4 August 1914, few politicians thought that the conflict would go beyond Christmas. Yet by the year's end both sides had dug themselves in and they soon lined the western front with a complex series of trenches separated by a no man's land that made advances by either side nearly impossible. In 1915 the British army suffered 300,000 casualties (Thomson 39). By 1916 the number of volunteers had dropped off so much so as to render conscription necessary through the Military Services Act. Also in 1916 British forces endured 400,000 casualties over a five-month period at the battle of the Somme (Thomson 39). Things were no better in 1917 at Passchendaele where, beginning on 31 July and continuing over the next three and a half months, a series of Allied offences exchanged 370,000 casualties for an advance of only five miles (Fussell, *Great War* 16). The events at the Somme and Passchendaele were echoed many times over the more than four years of fighting.

The scope of these and other disasters seems incredible, and there has been no shortage of blame hurled at Allied officers and governments. As Fussell observes, the catastrophes were exacerbated by a class bias permeating the British army which led officers to assume that the ordinary soldier was incapable of attacking at night or without close regimentation; as well, surprise attacks and evasive action were considered unsporting and so rarely occurred (13). By the armistice on 11 November 1918, over eight and a half million people had been killed in the war, with Allied losses accounting for over five million of those lost.

The experience of the war exploded the traditional virtues of what Patrick Howarth calls "the Newbolt man," who was the hero in books by Weyman, Hope, Buchan, Haggard, Edward Oppenheim, Rudyard Kipling, and others (Howarth 13–14) and whose qualities were celebrated in the popular poetry of Rupert Brooke, Kipling, and, of course, Henry Newbolt. No longer could a strong sense of institutional loyalty, a belief in a moral right to empire, an ungrudging acceptance of service and duty, and a belief in a natural power to command and achieve worldly success be unequivocally accepted by writers of the post-war generation. The war's seemingly meaningless slaughter and the sharp contrast between official government accounts of the war's progress and the reality of the front put an end to these illusions for the writers who emerged after 1918.

Nevertheless, as Martin Green argues, the impact of those writers who celebrated the Newbolt man, and of Kipling especially, was felt by all the writers of Greene's generation. In his reading of the history of literary modernism, Martin Green suggests that a changing scheme of literary values in the 1880s narrowed a division within English fiction between serious work that was domestic and largely written by and for women (the Brontës, Mrs Gaskell, George Eliot) and adventure stories that, stimulated by Benjamin Disraeli's rhetoric of imperialism, sought to address a largely male audience by dealing with national questions such as those of empire (*English Novel* xvi, 10) and by defining a particular code of masculinity.[22] Of the practioners of this latter type of fiction, it was Kipling who, because he achieved enormous critical success with professors, popular reviewers, and Henry James, brought literature and adventure together. Prior to Kipling, Green argues perhaps somewhat reductively, moral and aesthetic seriousness from Daniel Defoe to Samuel Richardson to Jane Austen was the prerogative of domestic fiction and, though the serious novel expanded to include industrialism, politics, and cultural change, it did not give up its domestic centre. By contrast, stories of adventure such as *Robinson Crusoe* fell into disrepute among literary intellectuals because of ambivalent feelings about colonialism and empire (*Dreams* 63–5); all the while, however, they were read by "ordinary" men, though it was felt that they were intended mainly for boys, who were, after all, the future rulers of the empire (*English Novel* 12–13).[23] With Kipling's success, and the popularity of figures such as Robert Louis Stevenson, Haggard, Conan Doyle, and Buchan, the adventure novel assumed an influential place in literature before the war despite its not being taken seriously by men of intellect (15). Afterwards, however, the xenophobia of William Le Queux or Buchan no longer had its appeal, and a reaction against the ideologies of Kipling and other adventure-story writers came to dominate literature, a development that "to some degree separated literature off from the rest of life, for non-literary readers continued to like what they had liked before" (203). Nevertheless, Martin Green continues, post-1930 novelists in England such as Greene and Evelyn Waugh were more inspired by adventure writers (even if they reacted against them) than they were by the more serious writers of domestic fiction (15).

Although Martin Green's reading of literary history is debatable, Graham Greene, as a 1947 book review suggests, also saw the history of the English novel as following two distinct paths, one of which stemmed from Austen and the other from Defoe (*Reflections* 109–10). Similarly, the attention Auden, Isherwood, Orwell, and Greene all gave to "boy's weeklies," the adventure stories of Haggard, and the thrillers of Buchan and Conan Doyle tends to support Martin Green's conclusions while again demonstrating the powerful hold popular authors had on the imaginations of writers in the thirties.

This situation gave rise to feelings of ambivalence in writers such as Greene and Waugh, since the authors they enjoyed reading in their youths, though ideologically discredited by the events of the war, continued to fascinate. Greene recognized that "all writing for schoolboys is propaganda for the established order" (*PD* 150), yet he continued to admire Haggard, Westerman, Frederick Brereton and Weyman. Paradoxically, as Richard Johnstone states, an "exaggerated consciousness of origins" led the thirties' writers to recognize "the inadequacy in the modern world of values inherited from another age," but "an instinctive faith [instilled by the public school system] in those values – the values, in short, of the English gentleman – ... prevented their complete abandonment" (133). In Greene's fiction this ambivalence towards childhood authors and traditional values is integral to all of his novels, but particularly *England Made Me* and *The Ministry of Fear*, where the pre-war attitudes are simultaneously longed for and rejected.[24] The challenge was to develop a popular form of writing that avoided becoming "propaganda for the established order" while yet enjoying broad appeal.

The British public school and its traditions held a nostalgic fascination for many writers. Isherwood and Auden romanticized their school days as a time of heroic resistance that coloured their view of the world; Auden wrote in 1934, "The best reason I have for opposing Fascism is that at school I lived in a Fascist state" ("Honour" 9). For others, such as Cyril Connolly and Greene, the experience of school was traumatic and, in Greene's case, the source of a personal mythology that reverberates throughout his work. Connolly, a relentless critic of public-school values, speculated that preparatory schools and public schools fostered a kind of "permanent adolescence" that affected "the greater part of the ruling class" (*Enemies* 271). The results of this fascination with the traditions of the public school were twofold: on the one hand, the values and beliefs that the war discredited for writers and intellectuals continued to have great currency within the wider society and especially among politicians; and, on the other hand, many of those who recognized the failures of public-school values continued to have a schoolboy's attitude towards the world and an idealistic, even naïve, view of revolutionary change, typified for Orwell by Auden's poem "Spain 1937." As the decade wore on, this outlook dissolved into pragmatism or apathy (Orwell, "Inside" 516; Johnstone 9–10).

Ultimately, many of the writers who are seen as characteristic of the
1930s – Auden, Stephen Spender, Day Lewis, Louis MacNeice – can
all be criticized for being politically insular and naïve (which is
Greene's view ["While Waiting" 14; Couto 207]). They were, in Virginia Woolf's phrase, part of "the leaning tower" generation who
were the beneficiaries of the very social order they sought to change.
Each of the writers mentioned, and Greene as well, grew up in a
middle-class environment that fostered traditional liberal-humanist
values and Arnoldian ideals of culture. Politically, their alignment
with the Left was slow in coming. Auden, Isherwood, and Greene all
defied the strikers during what Isherwood called "the tremendous
upper-middle-class lark" (*Lions* 177) of the 1926 General Strike. With
the onset of the Depression, however, these same figures became
"acutely tower conscious" (Woolf 171). Inherited national and cultural loyalties were divided or supressed by the crises of the times
(Sharrock 17), and, though "trapped by their education [and] pinned
down by their capital" (Woolf 176), British intellectuals in the 1930s
developed a social conscience that to varying degrees committed
them to the Left.[25] In some cases, as with Auden, this commitment
was later apologetically abandoned and largely disowned. Day Lewis
and Spender embraced the Communist Party, while Greene remained
politically ambivalent, sympathetic to ideals of social change but re-
luctant to tie himself to any single political platform. In later years,
Greene's commitment to the Left, which solidified after visits to Viet-
nam in the 1950s, was to be considerably stronger than that of his contemporaries in the thirties (Adamson, *Edge* 117, 133). Yet, whatever
the future was to hold, the 1930s writers' allegiance to the Left and
their admiration for communism expressed a widespread feeling
among many, but not all, intellectuals in the decade. In literary history, the 1930s quickly became associated with the rejection of high
modernism as it had developed after the war and with a renewed
dedication to realism and political commitment. These two intellectual currents were related and both, by and large, were associated
with the emergence of the Left as an influential force among young
writers; as Stephen Spender recalls, "The moment Thirties' writing
became illustrative of Marxist texts or reaction to 'history' … it ceased
to be part of the modern movement" (*30s* 14).

The roots of this intellectual departure can be traced back to the
1920s. Though the Great War may have signalled the death of the old
imperial order in Europe, Germany's defeat, relative economic prosperity, and the lack of a strong European rival conspired to mask
numerous and growing social problems. Some of these problems surfaced in the General Strike, but the strike's failure and the victory of

the "Poshocracy" (Isherwood, *Lions* 180) contributed to an illusory sense of British inviolablilty and of the permanence and rightness of the governing classes and the dominant ideology. This is not to say that British society emerged from the war unscathed: for many, postwar Britain resembled Eliot's "waste land" and the strike clearly pointed to tears in the social fabric.

The Great Depression fully exposed these fissures, revealing British capitalism's vulnerability and its failure. While real national income continued to rise from 1925 and the index of production increased from 1929 onwards (factors responsible for a consumer boom [Miles and Smith 17]), the overall economy in the 1930s steadily shrank in amount and value (Thomson 130). Traditionally relying on four main bases – textiles, coal, heavy metals, and shipbuilding – the British economy suffered badly from greater American competition and the world economic downturn. Unemployment, which had remained high throughout the 1920s, became extreme, especially in centres that relied most heavily on the traditional bases of economic support. While the whole of Great Britain experienced unemployment at the rate of 16.9 per cent between 1929 and 1936, rates in specific areas varied considerably: unemployment in the northeast ran at 22.7 per cent, in the Northwest at 21.4 per cent, in Scotland at 21.8 per cent, and in Wales at 30.1 per cent (Miles and Smith 17). Some individual communities, such as the shipbuilding town of Jarrow, experienced unemployment as high as 80 per cent (Symons, *Thirties* 56). But London (8.6 per cent), Coventry (5.1 per cent), and St Albans (3.9 per cent) continued to prosper and remained largely unaware of the plight of the more depressed regions (Harrison 371). The result was a widening gap between prosperity and depression in the country that followed the old division of north and south. At the Depression's height, three million people were unemployed and even in 1939, when rearmament had substantially lowered this figure, between 1.8 and 1.9 million people were still listed on the official registers of the unemployed (Thomson 182).

Although it wasn't much, the unemployed and the poor did receive some government assistance. Yet they also found themselves hurt by a 10 per cent cut in benefits in September 1931 and by the introduction of a means test, which had the effect of throwing the poor back on themselves. That is, a person might not qualify for benefits if he or she or another member of his or her family was deemed to have the means to offer support. Several government attempts to improve levels of assistance, such as the establishment of the Unemployment Assistance Board, which transferred assistance from local authorities to a statutory committee, and the Special Areas Act, which directed relief to particularly hard-hit areas, accomplished little. In this atmosphere of economic despair, typified by hunger marches such as the Jarrow Crusade of October 1936, both the communist and fascist movements rapidly gained supporters, whose several clashes with each other in 1934 led to extended police powers through 1934's Incitement to Disaffection Act and 1936's Public Order Act (Thomson 148). Meanwhile, a growing number of foreign crises further aggravated the political and economic crises at home and made it apparent that Britain would once again be at war. The rise of fascism in Europe, Germany's rearming, the League of Nations' failure, Japan's invasion of Manchuria, Italy's invasion of Ethiopia, the Spanish Civil War, and Stalin's purges all contributed strongly to the sense of crisis which everyone seemed to feel but about which little was done. As David Thomson writes, "The essence of the spirit of the thirties was not apathy but inertia: an incorrigible *immobilisme* in State and society, a structural resistance to change, and especially to any radical improvement" (181).

The consequence of all of this for the period's writers was a shared feeling that political commitment was unavoidable. Looking back on these years in his introduction to *England Made Me*, Greene wrote, "I think of those years between 1933 and 1937 as the middle years of my generation, clouded by the Depression in England ... and by the rise of Hitler. It was impossible in those days not to be committed ... as the enormous battlefield was prepared around us" (*WE* 29). Virginia Woolf expressed a similar view of the thirties' writers in "The Leaning Tower" (172), and George Orwell argued that "the invasion of literature by politics was bound to happen ... [since writers had developed] an awareness of the enormous injustice and misery of the world, and a guilt-stricken feeling that one ought to be doing something about it" ("Writers" 408–9). This mentality made the 1930s the decade of "serious purpose" ("Inside" 510). Orwell, however, also viewed the movement towards an ill-defined communism on the part of Auden, Spender, and company as symptomatic of a deeper need to believe in something in the face of the debunked and discredited values of patriotism, religion, and empire (514–15). According to Orwell, the old values of imperialism were replaced by the equally inadequate values of communism and/or religious orthodoxy, and certainly there was no shortage of writers who declared their allegiance to the Communist Party or who developed a strong sense of religious devotion.

In the judgments of Woolf, Orwell, and many others, the period's literature was severely weakened by its attachment to political ideology, yet this attachment was formed by writers who were well aware that political orthodoxy hurt literature: Cyril Connolly saw politics as one of the "enemies" of a writer's "promise," and Spender argued in "Poetry and Revolution" that poetry could not be political. Nevertheless, the decade's ruling passion in fiction was, as Greene declared in 1934, "political consciousness" ("Seed Cake" 523). Like his compatriots, Greene could "imagine no prose, critical, religious or philosophical, which does not suffer by its divorce from social consequences" (521). Whether orthodox or not, politics implicitly became a point of reference in Greene's and other writing from the period.

While Greene clearly saw the importance of a political awareness in literature, on a personal level he was careful not to align himself formally with any one ideological or political group. (Later he felt that this made him suspect in the eyes of both the literary and Catholic establishments [Couto 207].) In 1925, as a joke, he briefly became a Communist Party member and then for a short time in 1933 he was a member of the Independent Labour Party (a Leftist faction that broke off from the Labour Party in 1932), but, notwithstanding these associations, Greene believed that the writer had to remain free of rigid ideological positions; he or she must claim the privilege of "disloyalty" and "act as the devil's advocate ... to elicit sympathy and a measure of understanding for those who lie outside the boundaries of State approval" ("Virtue of Disloyalty" 609). Because he saw sympathy as the ground out of which commitment arose, it is no surprise that Greene aligned himself with the emerging Left on the political spectrum (Couto 206).[26] Equally, it is no surprise that Orwell found Greene, despite his Catholicism, to be "a mild Left with faint CP [Communist Party] leanings." Orwell went on to say that Greene "might become our first Catholic fellow-traveller, a thing that doesn't exist in England but does in France, etc .... [In] books like *A Gun for Sale*, *England Made Me*, *The Confidential Agent* and others ... there is the usual left-wing scenery. The bad men are millionaires, armaments manufacturers etc. and the good man is sometimes a Communist" ("Letter" 496).

The degree of Greene's commitment to the Left in the thirties, however, is open to question. Roger Sharrock, in his fine study of Greene's work, offers the commonly held view that "Greene was a man of the 1930s who to a large extent continued to maintain after the war the political allegiances of that period" (17). More recently, however, Judith Adamson has argued that Greene "wanted real social change ... but was completely opposed to the Left and highly suspicious of any form of state intervention" (50). She takes the position that in the 1930s he kept politics at "a sceptical distance in the name of objectivity" (11). None the less, Adamson is still able to argue that "his novels at the time were intensely political in that they recorded the pressure of immediate events on individual's lives, but nowhere do they suggest a future. Their characters are caught ... in the ideological assumptions which grounded ... society" (26). Greene's attitude in these years is described by Adamson not as a challenge to the capitalist system but as an attempt to come to terms with its apparent collapse (55). Surprisingly, she argues that it was only in the 1950s that Greene began to develop a true understanding of and commitment to the Left and communism (133).

Certainly Greene was not blindly supportive of the Left in his fiction of the 1930s. *It's a Battlefield* (1934), which he described as his "first overtly political novel" (Allain 87), is as critical of the self-deluding and ineffectual efforts of the Communist Party, headed in the book by Mr Surrogate, as it is of a British political and judicial system that brutally oppresses dissent. Similarly, in *The Confidential Agent*, both sides in the war (the Spanish Civil War, though this is not explicitly stated) are guilty of similar crimes – as D. remarks in the novel: "It's no good taking a moral line. My people [the communists] commit atrocities like the others" (60).[27] Greene believed that the crises of the 1930s could not be overcome with the simplistic solutions of political parties because their roots lay deeper than economics, and so he rejected party allegiance and declared his "distrust of any future based on what we are" (*Journey* 20). Ultimately, he was convinced that the world of the thirties had to end in destruction because only violence could "satisfy that moral craving for the just and reasonable expression of human nature left without belief" (*CE* 334).[28]

Nevertheless, despite seeing the destruction of the Blitz as a "just and poetic" (*CE* 336) expression of inherent human failings, Greene remained concerned in his fiction about social injustice and the possibilities for social change (Allain 88). "His political purpose ... was to expose, to shake people out of their indifference" (Adamson 64); and, in this respect, Greene's novels in the 1930s, even with their seeming political "objectivity," *can* be seen as socialist novels insofar as they do what Frederick Engels felt the socialist-based novel must do.[29] The main theme of *It's a Battlefield* may be the "injustice of men's justice" (*WE* 28) and injustice in the novel may be given, as critic Grahame Smith points out, "a universal dimension ... inseparable from basic human processes" (117), but injustice also has specific and local causes since "the laws were made by property owners in defence of property" (*It's a Battlefield* 169). Similarly, in "*Brighton Rock* evil and violence wear a social face" (Sharrock 83). What we see in Greene's work is a mixing of moral or religious and political beliefs that develops into a sympathy for both Catholicism and communism. As Orwell noted, it is unusual for such sympathies to coexist in an English writer, yet Greene was throughout his life an advocate of Catholic-Marxist dialogue in the interests of social justice.

Always uncomfortable with critics' attempts to label him as one or another kind of writer, Greene denied the view of John Le Carré, Denis Donoghue, and others that he was strictly a thirties' man (Allain 133). Similarly, he was uneasy with being called a political novelist or a Catholic novelist (Allain 80, 159). But his assertion that "politics are in the air we breathe, like the presence or absence of a God" (Allain 87) and his suggestion that he is "more a political writer than a Catholic writer" (Burstall 676) demonstrate the continued power of the "political consciousness" he developed in the 1930s and the profound mark that the decade left on those who experienced it ("Man of Mystery" 442).

THE REJECTION OF MODERNISM

The belief in the necessity of political commitment led many thirties' writers to reject the high modernism of the twenties initially on ideological and then on certain formal grounds. In the 1930s, criticism of modernist writing came largely from the Left and quickly focused on the overtly subjective and apolitical qualities of the experimental literature of the late 1910s and early 1920s. (An older generation of realists – Arnold Bennett, H.G. Wells, John Galsworthy and, in their tradition, Hugh Walpole and J.B. Priestley – continued their opposition to the aesthetics of high modernism for slightly different reasons.[30]) The American critic Edmund Wilson, who otherwise praised the modernists, identified as early as 1931 a number of shortcomings in the writings of W.B. Yeats, Eliot, James Joyce, Marcel Proust, Gertrude Stein, and, by extension, D.H. Lawrence, Woolf, Forster, and others: "They have tended to overemphasize the importance of the individual ... been preoccupied with introspection sometimes almost to the point of insanity, [and] ... endeavoured to discourage their readers, not only with politics, but with action of any kind" (Axel's Castle 297–8). In the 1930s' atmosphere of crisis, these tendencies were deemed major flaws.

Marxist commentators such as Philip Henderson and Ralph Fox intensified the criticism of modernist writing as introspective, abstract, and ahistorical.[31] And even less radical commentators such as Connolly and Orwell joined in this critique. Orwell called the 1920s "the golden age of the *rentier*-intellectual, a period of irresponsibility such as the world had never before seen" ("Inside" 509). He found it astonishing that the writers of the twenties seemingly ignored every important event in Europe; even the best of them demonstrated "too Olympian [an] attitude" and too great a readiness to wash their hands of practical problems (508–10). Equally damning for the younger writers was that, for the most part, the public politics of the high modernists were authoritarian, or at least conservative; figures such as Yeats, Lawrence, Ezra Pound, and Wyndham Lewis openly flirted with and admired fascism,[32] though one might argue that they misunderstood fascism and never grasped its brutal, more sinister nature. And, in a climate of increasingly shrill political rhetoric, it quickly came about that those who did not openly support the aims of the Communist Party were declared fascists. Since the existing capitalist system was assumed to be in its death throes, all political questions were reduced, particularly by the Left, to a choice between fascism and communism. Michael Roberts' 1933 "Preface" to the *New Country* anthology of poetry, the *Left Review*'s "Authors Take Sides" campaign in 1937, and Henderson's book *The Novel Today* – wherein he writes, "The central issue of our age is that of a society divided against itself in the struggle of capital and labour, the class-struggle, which, in the last resort, is the struggle between fascism and communism" (17) – all reflected this undeniably simplistic and reductive approach to political issues in the decade.

Primarily, the rejection of high modernism arose out of a profound discomfort with modernist assumptions about the nature of art and its audience. As Martin Green notes, the disillusionment that had followed the Great War contributed greatly to a shift away from the earlier models of Edwardian and Georgian literature, and to an extent this shift separated literature from the rest of life (*English Novel* 203). What the modernists offered, Connolly wrote, was "a religion of beauty, a cult of words, of meanings understood only by the initiated at a time when people were craving such initiations. The world had lived too long under martial law to desire a socialized form of art, for human beings in the mass had proved but a union of slaughterers. There was more hope and interest in extreme individuality" (*Enemies* 67). High modernist art stressed formal experimentation and a language of metaphor. Earlier conceptions of reality as an absolute, as something "out there" that was experienced in the same way by everyone, and of the self as integral and continuous shattered under the weight of the war and the growing currency of the ideas of Henri Bergson, Albert Einstein, and Sigmund Freud. Formally, in the realm of the novel, the result was a turn from the "formal realism" Ian Watt describes (35) to an exploration of new modes of discourse capable of presenting life as it is uniquely experienced. In this regard, Virginia Woolf's statements in "Modern Fiction" (1919) and "Mr. Bennett and Mrs. Brown" (1924) articulated the modernist approach to the novel and are most often cited as declarations of modernist aims.

In the first of these, Woolf expresses the new sense of reality in the post-war period. Life is experienced as an "incessant shower of innumerable atoms ... not [as] a series of gig lamps symmetrically arranged; life is a luminous halo, a semi-transparent envelope surrounding us from the beginning of consciousness to the end" (150). The modern novelist's task, then, is a mimetic one: to "record the atoms as they fall upon the mind in the order in which they fall ... [to] trace the pattern, however disconnected and incoherent in appearance, which each sight or incident scores upon consciousness" (150). As Woolf also writes in her diary, even "one incident – say the fall of a flower – might contain it all [the life of a character, in this case Clarissa Dalloway] ... the actual event practically does not exist – nor time either" (*Writer's* 105). Following from this, Woolf emphasizes in the second essay, are both the necessity of the modern writer's focus on character and the creation of character through the recording of responses to outside stimuli. The result is the highly subjective, highly self-conscious fiction of Proust or of Woolf herself wherein "exterior objective reality ... is nothing but an occasion" for the release of inner events (Auerbach 541). The outside world is reduced and subordinated to the experience of the individual, however narrow that experience may be.[33]

In these essays Woolf clears a space within the dominant mode of fictional discourse – typified for her by the work of Bennett, Galsworthy, and Wells – for a discourse of her own which claims to present a truer representation of reality. She is reacting both to the "doctrines, sing songs, [and] ... celebrate[d] glories of the British Empire" ("Mr Bennett" 97) found in the work of Kipling and company and to the fictional representation of reality which transfers the reader's interest from character to "something outside" the book. With the analogy of Mrs Brown in the railroad carriage, Woolf demonstrates how the Edwardian writers would treat the scene by shifting their interests from Mrs Brown to the world around her, whether that world be one of gentility and manners or one of drudgery and long hours, or, as Woolf alleges is the case with Bennett's work, the world of the carriage itself in all its particulars. None, in Woolf's estimation, would explore Mrs Brown herself because the character is identified only with surface detail.

Although we must be careful not to see modernism as a monolithically uniform entity, the high modernist writers, for the most part, violently broke from the outmoded conventions of an older realism to create a form for literature that struggled to remain true to the sense of reality as it is perceived and experienced by individuals. Thus, these writers fulfilled what Ian Watt sees as the growing tendency from the Renaissance onwards "for individual experience to replace collective tradition as the ultimate arbiter of reality" (15). The writers of the 1930s, however, retreated from the modern's rarefied perception of experience and instead turned back to a variant of the realist prose which preceded the moderns in order to emphasize a common and collective social experience. This turn was executed on two fronts, and Woolf was the figure most often cited on both.

In the first place, modernist writing was thought to negate history and attenuate reality. Those openly Leftist, such as Philip Henderson, charged Woolf – despite her support of the Labour Party[34] – with a refusal to acknowledge the fact that the world consists of more than Mrs Dalloway shopping in Bond St and giving parties in Westminster. For Henderson, it was imperative that the writer turn from Mrs Brown to look at the world of poverty and misery outside the carriage window (26). Greene's response to Woolf was similar. He saw her characters (and Forster's as well) as "cardboard symbols" in a "paper-thin" world (CE 91) and her novels as reducing the outside world to "a charming whimsical rather sentimental prose poem" (92). That world, in this case Regent St, "has a right to exist; it is more real than Mrs. Dalloway" (92).

The conviction that Bond St or Regent St has a right to exist was partially responsible for a return to the realist mode of discourse in the work of thirties' prose writers.[35] Greene, picking up Woolf's image of the railroad carriage in a 1938 review of Dorothy Richardson's Pilgrimage, referred to "stream of consciousness" as an "embarrassing cargo" and remarked that the method which "must have seemed in 1915 a revivifying change from the tyranny of the 'plot'" proved itself sterile[36]: "After twenty years of subjectivity, we are turning back to the old dictatorship, to the detached and objective treatment" (CE 114–16).

Certainly the extreme subjectivity of a Woolf or a Richardson could not adequately present the socio-political environment of the 1930s, but, then, "the detached and objective treatment" could not be the confident realism of the pre-war period characterized by an omniscient narrator who exercises complete authority within the text (Fox 103). As Watt explains, the novel as a form most fully reflects a particular named individual's relationship with a particular society at a particular time in history. The individualist emphasis on the representation of consciousness is, in both literary and ideological terms, a recognition of liberal-bourgeois individualism, which has at its heart a belief in the individual's essential freedom and in his or her ability to know the world through the senses (Watt 12–13). Hence, formal realism, the mode of discourse most often associated with the novel, is the vehicle for a fundamentally liberal-bourgeois outlook[37] because it embodies a carefully described spatial and temporal environment and so purports to be an authentic account of the actual experiences of individuals (Watt 35). Peter Widdowson argues that the fiction writers of the 1930s, aware of a crisis in liberal-bourgeois ideology, felt constrained by the individualist emphasis of the novel form (162); consequently, as Stephen Spender remarked, "There are two approaches to the contemporary political scene: the one is direct, or partially satiric, external presentation; the other is fantasy or allegory" (quoted in Laing 142). Formally, the sense of constraint resulted in the period's diversity of fictional modes, such as formal realism, documentary reportage, fable, allegory, satire, dystopia, and the continuation of the structural and textual discoveries of modernism (Widdowson 134). Each of these attempted to address the "fantastic realities" of the everyday world.[38]

For writers of the Left in the 1930s, the realist mode offered the possibility of revolutionary art because it could represent both the ideas of the rising class and the situation of individuals within a web of social, political, economic, and military forces that not only marginalized them but also endangered their freedom and, ultimately, their lives. The novel's traditional focus, the individual and his or her relationship to society, is thus displaced. In the case of Greene, this displacement is enacted in two ways: first, Greene's characters (D., Pinkie, and Raven) are in some way marginalized (by nationality, by class, and by physical deformity), degraded and made to seem insignificant, interesting not for themselves but for what they endure; secondly, Greene defines the form of the individual's relationship to society not as a negotiation but as a war – his dominant metaphor for society is the battlefield (seen most clearly in *It's a Battlefield* but equally present in all of the novels through to *The Ministry of Fear*) on which the class war is fought and the individual is hunted by "rapacious capitalism" (Widdowson 154). Greene's use of the thriller, in short, ideally suits Widdowson's reading of the thirties' response in fiction to the crisis affecting the dominant ideology: the thriller offers realism in a popular form. But there is another way in which the realism of the 1930s departs from the traditional realism of the nineteenth-century novel.

Julian Symons believes that the writers of the 1930s "attempted to deny utterly the validity of individual knowledge and observation"

(*Thirties* 142), and certainly this view is supported by the rejection of the high modernist mode of discourse which made individual perception and subjectivity the governing means of representing the world. Other attempts to represent a "true" reality by John Grierson in documentary film or by Tony Harrisson, Charles Madge, and Humphrey Jennings in the Mass Observation project equally attest to a desire in the decade to overthrow the interpretive authority of individual subjectivity and to replace it with a more objective authority based on a collective or shared sense of reality.[39] That said, however, the cult of facts that emerged in the period betrayed less a scientific faith than a loss of all faith (Thomson 183). In fiction, a complete return to the standards of nineteenth-century realism, to the old dictatorship of the detached and objective treatment, was impossible because such a return would imply the substitution of one form of individualist subjectivity, identified with the presentation of consciousness in Woolf, Richardson, or Proust, for example, with another equally individualistic authority found in what Colin MacCabe calls the "meta-language" (35) of the omniscient narrator in George Eliot, William Thackeray, or Charles Dickens. (Something of this sort happens in the documentary film where Grierson's typical use of voice-over narration ultimately replaces one monological authority with another.) Faced with this dilemma, the writers of the 1930s endeavoured to overcome the constraints of the novel form to which Widdowson draws attention.

For the Left, realism was, unavoidably, the necessary means of presenting the complexity of social relations, but its links to a liberal-bourgeois ideology made it equally necessary to undermine the structures of authority implicit in realist discourse.[40] Documentary reportage, as Isherwood uses it in *Goodbye to Berlin* (1939) – "I am a camera with its shutter open, quite passive, recording, not thinking" (11) – or as Orwell does in *Down and Out in Paris and London* (1933) and *The Road to Wigan Pier* (1937), attempts to free the text, more or less, from the kind of interpretive meta-language which had been the traditional prerogative of the omniscient narrator. In reportage, the "objective partisanship" of the text ensures that facts alone will shake people from their indifference (Eagleton, *Marxism* 47), though the necessary selectivity involved in observation and the force of juxtaposition fails to eliminate an interpretative frame from the text. Satire, fable, and allegory also offer ways of undermining the authority of realist discourse by their construction of fantasy worlds which distance the narrative and the narrator's authority: Rex Warner's *The Wild Goose Chase* (1937) and *The Aerodrome* (1941), Edward Upward's "The Railway Accident" (written in 1928, published in 1949), Aldous

Huxley's *Brave New World* (1932), and Orwell's *Animal Farm* (1945) and *Nineteen Eighty-Four* (1949) are just some of the texts that use these methods. More important for a consideration of Greene's work is the technique of replacing the individual who stood at the centre of the novel with a kind of collective hero, as John Sommerfield did in his novel *May Day* (1936),[41] or else with a variety of figures none of whom comes to dominate the text. Although it has practical limitations, this last method is the one Greene employed in both *Stamboul Train* and *It's a Battlefield* before he fully realized that the thriller – with its plot of an individual's pursuit by agents of a socially legitimate authority, its themes of betrayal and violence, its formal self-consciousness, and its use of interpretative and interrogative structures derived from the classical detective story – presented another way of discrediting not only the constitution of mass society but also the authority of realist discourse.

The second point on which modernism was rejected by the young writers of the 1930s was that much of high modernist literature worked to exclude the masses from culture by addressing itself, as Connolly pointed out, to an initiated élite. The turning of literature away from life that Martin Green detects in the post-war period shifted the emphasis in modernist art from a revolution of the world to a revolution of the word. In "The Dehumanization of Art" (1925) Ortega praised the modernist movement for its ability to dehumanize art. Moreover, "Modern art," he observed, "will always have the masses against it. It is essentially unpopular; moreover, it is antipopular" (5). Consequently, the public was divided into two groups: the "vulgar" masses, who felt threatened by the new art because it seemed to belong to a privileged aristocracy, and the illustrious minority, who saw themselves as cultural guardians preserving an Arnoldian ideal of "the best that has been thought and known in the world" (*Culture and Anarchy* 70) against the rising tide of democracy.[42] Modern artists, argued Ortega, evince a "will to style" ("Dehumanization" 25); hence, seminal modernist commentators such as Eliot, I.A. Richards, the Leavises, and Ortega himself addressed and in various ways encouraged an élite who could appreciate an aesthetic pleasure based on the artistry of style.

Although recent studies by Huyssen, Lawrence Levine, and others have revealed the relationship between high modernism and mass culture to be more complicated than it has been generally understood, many of the high modernists and their defenders still sought to preserve in their art and especially in their criticism a cultural heritage that seemed increasingly threatened in the post-war world. Taking their cue from Otto Spengler's *Decline of the West* (1917), Eliot,

Richards, and the Leavises feared the collapse of moral, social, cultural, and aesthetic standards under the weight of both a growing, increasingly literate, population and an accelerating commercialism that they blamed on the Americanization of English life (Leavis, "Mass" 7) and on the proliferation of the products of popular culture itself.[43] This sense of a civilization in decay was shared by intellectuals, including Greene and Auden, across a broad spectrum from the far Right to the extreme Left, but the responses to the crisis were varied. The Leavises' response was to promote an élite responsible for maintaining cultural and aesthetic standards ("Mass" 5). As *Scrutiny*'s opening "Manifesto" declared in May 1932: "The general dissolution of standards is a commonplace ... for the majority neither the present drift of civilization nor the plight of the arts is a matter of much concern ... it is only a small minority for whom the arts are something more than a luxury product, who believe, in fact, that they are 'the storehouse of recorded values'" (1–3).

To this end of promoting a cultural élite, many of high modernism's defenders, particularly critics, condemned what were deemed escapist forms of art – music-hall songs, cinema and radio, magazine verse, bestsellers, and genre fiction[44] – and formulated theories of aesthetic value that, as Barbara Herrnstein Smith says, pathologized the "Other" (Smith 38). That is, those who did not share "the consensus of best qualified opinion," because they preferred popular forms of artistic expression, were seen as possessing some debility that was attributed to defective "organs" or defective "organization" (Richards 202) or to innate deficiencies that resulted in the inability to experience "adequate impulses" in response to aesthetic stimuli (Richards 202).

Also blamed were the mass media and the products of popular culture themselves. For Q.D. Leavis, the training provided to an individual by cinema, by looking through magazines and newspapers, and by listening to jazz created habits that were inimical to mental effort and thus prevented normal development (224).[45] Leavis likened the habit of reading popular literary forms, such as the detective story or the thriller, to drug addiction (7, 19, 152) and considered it equally destructive in that it, too, could lead to maladjustment in actual life by encouraging the habit of fantasizing (54). Individuals afflicted with these kinds of disabilities were deemed unable to have a full existence in the modern world. A person's preference for popular literature – Richards cited a sonnet by Ella Wheeler Wilcox as an example (200–1) – was seen as evidence of this inability and, consequently, of a kind of biological unfitness, for, to continue the quotation from *Scrutiny*'s "Manifesto": "There is a necessary relationship between the quality of an individual's response to art and his general fitness for humane existence" (3). In this context, literary criticism takes on a special function within the state, since it provides the best training for general intelligence ("Manifesto" 1).

The modernists' concern for the state of high culture in the 1920s and early 1930s marked the revival of what has come to be known as the mass-culture critique. There was nothing new in Richards's or the Leavises' critical statements: such ideas have their champions in any age. F.R. Leavis's pamphlet "Mass Civilization and Minority Culture" (1930) was essentially an updating of positions taken in Arnold's *Culture and Anarchy* (1868).[46] But in the 1930s the general concern for the state of culture easily evolved into an attack on all forms of popular culture with the publication of "Mass Civilization and Minority Culture," Q.D. Leavis's *Fiction and the Reading Public* (1932), and F.R. Leavis and Denys Thompson's *Culture and Environment* (1933), and with the founding of *Scrutiny* (May 1932). As well, Ortega's *The Revolt of the Masses*, originally published in 1930, appeared in an English translation in 1932, the same year that Dover Wilson's edition of *Culture and Anarchy* was published. A more forceful response to the crises of the period would be difficult to imagine. Fuelled by the regular publication of *Scrutiny* and by the appearance of those books just mentioned as well as many others, the prejudice against popular literary forms entrenched itself within the academy and, to a lesser extent, within literary circles.[47] No wonder, then, that the prevalent feeling in the early 1930s was against reading novels for pure "entertainment" (Graves 298). For the extreme Left, art had a social function, which was to engage political questions and make the reader aware of the world outside the text; for the conservative Right, to read for "entertainment" was to fiddle while civilization burned: literature had a serious moral purpose to fulfil and the best of readers were open to it.

For Leavis and his followers, the decline of literary, artistic, and cultural standards, and the consequent diminishing of the value of high art, was evinced in the growth of popular culture. Popular fiction, such as bestsellers, appealed to and reflected the instincts and desires of the herd, who denied distinctions between good and bad art ("Mass" 19; Q.D. Leavis 195). Bestsellers were further condemned because the prospect of large sales and financial success threatened to corrupt the talent of serious writers, who would seek to produce popular work by repeating the tried and true formulas of what had been commercially successful in the past. (Quin Savory in *Stamboul Train* is Greene's fictional version of such an author.) As well, the indiscriminate marketing of "serious" literature with popular work would expose the superior work to the great mass of the semi-aware and semi-literate, whose lazy reading habits and misunderstandings would debase and degrade the cultural heritage (Q.D. Leavis 136).

More or less shared, but for different reasons, by Richards, the Leavises, and Ortega, this condemnation of popular culture found a correspondence later in the decade in the views of certain segments of the Left, such as Theodor Adorno and Max Horkheimer of the Frankfurt School and, to a lesser extent, Walter Benjamin, who saw the artifacts of popular culture as the debasement of art into commodity. They argued that the products of mass culture – jazz, kitsch, bestsellers, genre-fiction – are the substitutions of commercial production for genuine art by a capitalist economic élite. Thus, mass culture was viewed as an imposed culture that reflects and conveys the dominant ideology of capitalist society. Instead of offering new possibilities and encouraging new modes of thought, mass culture presents a homogeneous blend of reassuring fantasy, wish-fulfilment, and the confirmation of prejudices and attitudes that are essential to the maintenance of the established order: "always new books, new programs, new films, news items, but always the same meaning" (Barthes, *Pleasure* 42).[48] Under the pressure of monopoly capitalism, culture and entertainment are fused, and, with the merging of advertising and the culture industry, mass culture becomes a procedure for manipulating the public (Bottomore 45).

Neither of these two views of popular culture sees it as a natural artistic expression arising out of the people. For both the Right and the Left, such an expression can occur only outside the present: for the conservatives, it is found in an idealized past where high art had an appreciative audience at all levels of society (Q.D. Leavis 84, 134, 226); for Adorno and Horkheimer, it is something that could emerge only once the influence of monopoly capitalism is removed. Attempts to find a middle ground between these two extremes by some analysts, such as Stuart Hall and Paddy Whannel, and by Greene himself, try to distinguish between genuinely popular or populist art and what might be termed mass culture or industrial culture. Although such a distinction to some extent unavoidably duplicates the original paradigm by seeing some forms of art as superior to others, it is useful in considering Greene, who was critical of many aspects of popular culture: Hollywood films, certain bestsellers by Priestley and others, the "metroland" world of Brighton, the insipidness of theatrical revues (*A Gun for Sale* 152), and the homogeneous housing developments of British suburbs (*GS* 44). Still, Greene's admiration for film as an art form, for music hall tunes, and for popular literary genres showed that he was certainly not of the same mind as either the Leavises or Adorno.

In fact, Greene's stance on the products of popular culture was paradoxical and marked by profound ambivalence stemming from his own education in Arnoldian notions of culture and literature. Taking his cue from Eliot's sense of the poetic dramatist's task,[49] Greene recognizes that the popular is not necessarily artistically valuable but the artistically valuable is necessarily rooted in the popular. Repeatedly in his criticism, particularly in his film reviews and in the short *British Dramatists*, he stresses the artist's need to be aware of an audience: "I doubt if the best work has ever been produced in complete independence of a public ... Popular *taste* makes a thoroughly bad dictator, but the awareness of an audience is an essential discipline for the artist" (*PD* 40). For Greene, the work of art fails when it is separated from the people by being too intellectual or too academic (*British Dramatists* 10). His own response to this situation is the one Eliot suggests, "to take a form of entertainment, and subject it to the process which would leave it a form of art" (*Sacred Wood* 70). The artist, Greene believes, must make use of forms which are popular, such as the thriller, but shape them so that they present "the truth as [the artist] sees it" (*Why?* 30).

As his remarks on film demonstrate, Greene saw popular forms as offering the possibility of a genuine art. In his judgment, genuinely popular film comes from the level of the people. The early work of Charlie Chaplin, the Marx Brothers' *Duck Soup*, and a few Laurel and Hardy films are popular art because they "convey a sense that the picture has been made by its spectators and not merely shown to them, that it has sprung ... from *their* level" (*PD* 94). Similarly, Greene rejects the common idea, which he imagines studio executives to have, that popular entertainment, such as *Rhythm on the Range*, should be soothing and gently amusing. Greene argues that the public does not ask to be soothed but to be excited to a mass feeling of collective strength (*PD* 94). This distinct sense of what the popular should be is at the root of Greene's complaints about "popular" novelists, such as Walpole, Priestley, Brett Young, Charles Morgan, or Parkinson Keyes, who "bring nothing new to their readers" and specialize in producing cliché-filled novels (Allain 147). Theirs are "crude minds representing no more of contemporary life than is to be got in a holiday snapshot" because – and here Greene echoes Arnold – a critical sense of life is missing from their work (*Reflections* 58–9, 61).

Of course, any attempt to distinguish between genuine popular art and the product of mass culture is plagued with the problem of determining difference: is or is not a certain phenomenon art? The area between the two becomes murky and ill-defined as attempts to draw distinctions easily modulate into lists of personally preferred texts or artifacts. It is the same dilemma that is involved in attempts to distinguish, in the general sense, "serious" literature (high art) from other literature (popular fiction), or, in the particular sense, Greene's novels from his "entertainments": each term in the opposition contaminates and inscribes the other.

Nevertheless, in the early 1930s, certain proponents of the emergent Left sought to challenge and debate the conservative assumptions and statements, associated particularly with the Leavises, by reinvesting the popular with aesthetic and cultural importance. They did so partly to preserve at least some of the cultural heritage in a time of decay, as Connolly wrote: "If culture is to survive it must survive through the masses; if it cannot be made acceptable to them there is no one else who will be prepared to guarantee it, since the liberal capitalist society who protected it will not be in a position to do so after another slump or a war. Much that is subtle in literature and life will have to be sacrificed if they are to survive at all; consequently it is necessary for literature to approach its future custodians in a language they will understand" (*Enemies* 81).

There thus occurred a shift in the dominant mode of fictional discourse from what Connolly called "the Mandarin style" to "the vernacular style." Long recognized as one of the literary characteristics of a democratic society,[50] the vernacular style, with its realism, simplicity, and colloquial tone, produces a relatively uniform prose style (85) but is also more popular with readers and, consequently, with writers. As Greene noted, being "hard to read" is no guarantee that a text is "great" literature (Burgess 22).

At the same time, the efforts made towards creating and using popular art forms, such as we see in Greene's fiction, were aimed at social change. Like Eliot, Richards, the Leavises, and Ortega, Greene and others recognized a widening gulf between what were seen as "high-brow" and "low-brow" tastes (Auden, "Poet's Tongue" 328). Yet, instead of retreating into the abbey of a cultural clerisy, many of the young writers of the 1930s turned to popular art forms in the hope of invigorating them with new life, freeing them from the pressures of commercial demands, and reaching through them a large audience. Auden summarized this approach in a 1933 review of three texts, by F.R. Leavis, F.R. Leavis and Denys Thompson, and L.C. Knights. Starting from the same premise as the "Scrutineers," he shifted the emphasis from focusing and organizing the minority to developing a critically alert majority: "We live in an age in which the collapse of all previous standards coincides with the perfection in technique for the centralized distribution of ideas; some kind of revolution is inevitable, and will as inevitably be imposed from above by a minority; in consequence, if the result is not to depend on the loudest voice, if the majority is to have the slightest say in its future, it must be more critical than it is necessary for it to be in an epoch of straightforward development" (Review 317).

Since the new mass media – radio, cinema, mass publishing – contained the potential for disaster (the "loudest voice" in Germany in 1933 was Hitler's and Mussolini's dominated Italy), writers such as Auden and Greene sought from their leaning tower to elevate the critical faculties of the majority in order to arm them against the rhetoric of totalitarianism. Rather than join the high moderns in promoting a cultured minority and in denigrating cultural forms considered popular or "low brow," they used these forms not only to combat fascism but also to instill in a large segment of the public that was disenfranchised by high modernism a sense of the value of the culture that all citizens shared. In this way, it was hoped, the gap between "highbrow" and "low-brow" art could be bridged and a new, more egalitarian, society might emerge. Hence, Auden attacked Richards's assumptions about bad art by asserting that "the secret of good art is ... to find out what you are interested in, however strange, or trivial, or ambitious, or shocking, or uplifting, and deal with that, for that is all you can deal with well" ("Poetry, Poets, and Taste" 360). The definitions of art and culture were broadened so that high art and high culture were not restricted to a canon defined by a minority; as Edgell Rickword noted, for the Left, culture included "not only music and science and philosophy [but also] games and dancing and popular songs" ("Political Pamphlet" 80). In poetry, Auden's anthology of light verse (1938) and his use of the ballad and other verse forms deriving from popular song and the tradition of the music hall attested to his desire to reach beyond the traditional audience for poetry and to break down artificial and elitist distinctions between the "difficult" poetry Eliot called for ("Metaphysical" 248) and, say, magazine verse. Indeed, Greene thought Auden "the finest living poet" precisely for this reason; he admired him as "a popular poet – as distinct from a popular versifier ... [who put] no barrier between himself and his public. The obscurity is where it should be, in the layers of suggestion under the lucid surface" (Comments 29).

Auden's was not the only voice in the 1930s, but it was an influential one heard not only by those closest to him (Spender, Day Lewis, MacNeice, Isherwood, and Edward Upward) but also by novelists such as Rex Warner, Orwell, and Greene. Auden's concluding remarks in "Poetry, Poets, and Taste" coupled Marxist thought and

Wordsworthian ideas of poetic revolution in order to identify popular forms in literature with Leftist causes; and, for Greene, the consequences of this identification were to use and rework, first, the realist mode of discourse, and, second, the thriller which, in this "golden age" of detective fiction, dominated popular reading.

Like other young writers in the 1930s, however, Greene had to confront the achievements of the high modernists; as Spender later remarked, the thirties' writers "were aware of having renounced values which we continued nevertheless to consider aesthetically superior in Joyce, Yeats, Eliot, Lawrence and Virginia Woolf" (*30s* 6). Eliot's influence, particularly, was profoundly felt by all who followed him, and Greene's vision of the modern world owes as much to *The Waste Land* as it does to anything else.[51] Similarly, as Elizabeth Davis and Harold Bloom have noted, Greene's own critical stance developed along lines traced by Eliot, who along with Herbert Read was one of "the two great figures of [Greene's] young manhood" (*WE* 33). It is not surprising, then, that Greene's early novels in the decade differ from those written after 1935 both in terms of formal techniques and, as we shall see in a consideration of *Stamboul Train* and *England Made Me*, in terms of the attitudes towards popular culture.

Formally, the influence of the high modernist prose writers is particularly apparent (as it is in Isherwood's first novel, *The Memorial* [1928]), in Greene's early work. Even as late as 1935 with *England Made Me* and the short story "The Bear Fell Free," Greene was experimenting with modes of presenting consciousness and of organizing time that were more familiar to and more comfortably handled by Joyce or Woolf. Similar experiments, coupled with clumsy attempts to construct fine prose, mar his first three novels – *The Man Within* (1929), *The Name of Action* (1930), and *Rumour at Nightfall* (1931) – which, as Kenneth Allott and Miriam Farris point out, fail as much for their self-conscious attempts to be "serious" literature as for their weak plots and unconvincing characterizations (73–4).[52]

A review by Frank Swinnerton opened Greene's eyes to the "defects of what [he] believed to be true art" (*WE* 17)[53]: looking back on *Rumour at Nightfall*, Greene concluded that he was "too much concerned with style and the style is bad and derivative ... All is vague, shadowy, out of focus – there are no clear images, but the same extravagant similes and metaphors as in *The Name of Action*" (*WE* 17). Like many in his generation, Greene turned from the deliberately literary and artificial (mandarin) prose to a more natural (vernacular) prose based on clarity, compression, and precision. In his first novels, he said that he was "too concerned with 'point of view' to ... know that the sort of novel I was trying to write, unlike a poem, was not made with words but with movement, action, character" (*SL* 144–5). Implicitly, Greene saw himself as consciously rejecting old-style fine writing and the experimental discourse of Woolf, Forster, and others in favour of a style similar to Robert Louis Stevenson's. What he wanted was for his novels "to be in a sense adventure stories" (Couto 216).

To suggest that "movement, action, [and] character" make up the novel acknowledges the referential capacity of the text. Greene assumes that the novel is to be a realistic, mimetic form which has as one of its primary concerns the presentation through a representational language of things as they are. "There have been no revolutions in the history of the novel," he writes in 1934, echoing James, "only technical discoveries with the object of making more perfect the illusion of life" ("Seed Cake" 517).[54] Although he is all too aware that words are all the novelist has to work with (Josipovici 122–4), Greene insists on "discrimination in one's words … not love of one's words (*SL* 145). Language must not draw attention to itself and become a barrier between the author and his public; rather it must render a true picture of the world through a lucid surface.

Greene's criticism from the 1930s emphasizes this view by arguing for clarity and economy in prose: "The danger to the novelist is that he should write with his mind on the subjective response of his readers instead of being concerned only to express his idea with the greatest accuracy and the greatest economy" ("Seed Cake" 518). The lyricism and introspection of high modernist discourse as it appears in a subjective novel by Virginia Woolf or Dorothy Richardson, for instance, leads only to self-indulgent and insular prose in which the emotions of the author blend into the emotions of the character; Richardson's Miriam "reads far too much significance into a cup of coffee, a flower in a vase, a fog, a sunset" because the character's insights, Greene says, are blurred with the author's (*CE* 116).

Greene's criticism of his own work and of the work of others identifies accuracy and clarity with truth. The novelist must "tell the truth as he sees it" (*Why?* 30), and so he or she must avoid using phrases and turns of speech that are not true because, as Orwell also argues in "Politics and the English Language", such usages muddle thought: poor writing leads to poor thinking (*Why?* 30). It is therefore to be expected that Greene should insist on the veracity of what critics since Arthur Calder-Marshall in 1940 have called "Greeneland" – the allegedly stylized and distorted milieu in which almost all of his fiction takes place (*WE* 60). The attempt to produce a transparent prose is problematic, however, since any language that appears referential, pointing innocently towards an objective world, can also be seen as opaque and self-reflexive; yet this attempt, as we have seen, is thoroughly rooted in the literary climate of the 1930s.

Having rejected one brand of high modernist discourse with oedipal fervour, Greene aligns himself with the earlier tradition of Joseph Conrad, Henry James, and Ford Maddox Ford – each of whom is "modern," though in ways that are distinct from Woolf's, Forster's, Richardson's, and Proust's modernism.[55] The difference between these two modernisms, however, is not solely one of technique since Conrad, James, and Ford are just as innovative as the later group of writers and, like them, just as attuned to the vagaries of perspective, consciousness, and the experience of time. Similarly, Woolf and the subjectivist writers of the post-war period are equally concerned with "making more perfect the illusion of life" ("Seed Cake" 517). Where the two camps differ is in their conceptions of reality, and in large measure this accounts for their differing approaches to fiction. As we have seen, for Woolf and those like her, including the Ford of "On Impressionism" (1913) and *The Good Soldier* (1915), reality is filtered through consciousness, and the world is experienced in a highly personal and subjective manner. Conrad and James, on the other hand, share a sense of reality that is also found in the young writers of the 1930s; the older writers, no matter how ironic or experimental they are, believe in history and in the presence of a "visible universe" that exists independently of the individual's experience. Nowhere, perhaps, is this belief more forcefully stated that in Conrad's "Preface" to *The Nigger of the Narcissus* when he asserts that "art itself may be defined as a single-minded attempt to render the highest kind of justice to the visible universe" (160) and that the novelist's task is, "by the power of the written word, to make you hear, to make you feel – it is, before all, to make you see. That – and no more, and it is everything" (162). Similarly, the work of James, which Greene says fulfils Conrad's definition of art (*CE* 29), shows an obsessive concern with point of view and with consciousness. Yet the consciousness James presents apprehends "a specified social and historical environment" (Bradbury 126),[56] whereas in Woolf consciousness overwhelms the environment and the discreteness of character so that the novel ultimately becomes a dramatization of the creative process itself (128–9, 125).[57]

Ford follows James in believing that fictional technique must answer to experience, not predetermine it; hence, subject matter is crucial since – and the panoramic scope of *Parade's End* (1924–28) bears this out – Ford believes that art's task is to register the temper of the age (Bradbury 135). But to fulfill this role properly the novelist has to be aloof, "rendering the world as he sees it, uttering no comments, falsifying no issues and carrying the subject – the Affair – he has selected for rendering, remorselessly out to its logical conclusion ... the story of a novel should be the history of an Affair" (*English Novel* 129–31). Ford's sense that the writer must be aloof from his subject – an idea taken from Gustave Flaubert and echoed in Joyce's *Portrait of an Artist as a Young Man* (1916) – finds a complement in the desire of writers' in the 1930s to produce a realistic fiction free of the ideological structures of the traditional novel; aloofness is crucial to "the detached and objective treatment" (*CE* 116) that Greene welcomed in the 1930s.

Although Greene learned a great deal about fictional technique from his study of Conrad, James, and Ford, their influences, particularly Conrad's and James's, were damaging to his own fiction. Greene stated that after the failure of *Rumour at Nightfall* he ceased to read Conrad because "his influence was too great and too disastrous" (*In Search* 42). He also says that he became so concerned with James's techniques, as outlined in Lubbock's *The Craft of Fiction*, that he could not present action convincingly (*SL* 144; *WE* 13). Accordingly, after 1931 he begins a movement towards a new mode of discourse that synthesizes the technical and aesthetic innovations of Conrad, James, and Ford with the action and excitement of the popular texts of Stevenson, Buchan, and Haggard. The resulting form has the potential to reach a large, albeit mostly male, readership and the ability to interrogate the political, social, and literary positions of the modernists by undermining the critical hierarchies that structure the canonization of particular texts and genres. Implicit in this procedure is a criticism of the social and class structures of society.

These are grand claims to make about Greene's texts and the measure of his success in light of these claims is difficult to judge. Certainly, the three novels published between 1932 and 1936's *A Gun for Sale* represent tentative gropings towards meeting the requirements of being realistic, popular, and critical. *Stamboul Train, It's a Battlefield,* and *England Made Me* are each attempts to reorient the values and ideology of the traditional realist novel while also working towards an understanding of how popular culture can and does function in mass society. And, although only *Stamboul Train* belatedly received the designation "entertainment" after 1936, each contains elements associated with the genre of the thriller. With *A Gun for Sale*, however, Greene fully develops what critics have oxymoronically called the "highbrow thriller."[58] This novel, since it is the first to be called an "entertainment," is also the first to challenge explicitly, though the previous three novels do so implicitly, the distinction between serious literature and popular fiction.

Traditional and modernist critics alike often forget Henry James's injunction that "the *effect* of a novel – the effect of any work of art – is to entertain" ("Alphonse Daudet" 93). Yet Greene himself recognized that entertainment and escape are not only valid and valuable effects of reading but also that such effects should not preclude a text from being considered art. "One is apt to forget that the literature of escape is literature just because it is a real escape; it contains a recognition of life as much as the action of a deserter contains the recognition on an enemy" (*PD* 240).[59] This view was in sharp contrast to that of the Leavises (who frequently used "entertain" as a pejorative term in descriptions of popular texts[60]), yet it was consistent with the position of Auden and others who saw popular forms as one means of creating a majority of people who are able to think critically.

And so thrillers and detective stories became doubly charged in the 1930s because they developed their potential to be both entertaining and serious. Indeed, defenders of detective fiction assert its kinship with all fiction, since any novel or story has operating within it what Roland Barthes calls in *s/z* the hermeneutic code. Ford noted in 1938 that the "superior intelligences of the day" were wrong not to apply themselves to mystery stories (one might argue that many did), because "the greatest novels of the world, whether of the romantic, the classical or the realistic modern schools, have all … been mystery stories" ("Detective Novel" 286).[61] The implication of Ford's remarks is obvious: distinctions between serious literature (high art) and popular literature (low, "escapist" art) are untenable. It is no wonder, then, that post-modern critics such as Stephano Tani and authors such as Peter Ackroyd in *Hawksmoor* use detective fiction to undercut epistemological structures and literary hierarchies that are perceived as being largely based on class.[62]

In turning to the thriller, Greene was more fortunate than other writers of the period who failed to achieve the same commercial success, though he too, despite *Stamboul Train's* early popularily, could not support himself solely with his fiction until after the publication of *The Heart of the Matter* in 1948 (*Yours* 214). Auden and the poets of the thirties who followed him failed to gain the wide readership they desired. Similarly, despite impressions to the contrary, the Left was not as strong or as cohesive a force as it presented itself (Cunningham, "Neutral?" 50); as Stephen Spender speculates, the sense of a cohesive Left in the 1930s was "perhaps due to the fact that Fascism itself gave anti-fascism a semblance of unity" (*30s* 15). Claud Cockburn points out that few publishers in Britain in the 1930s were willing to market Marxist fiction (179). As well, as Woolf observed in "The Leaning Tower," the Left's major writers were almost without exception from the upper and middle classes and so found themselves in an awkward position of being supported by the very society they attacked; and, to quote Spender again, "communism [did] not provide the young writers with a belief, but it did provide them with a bad conscience" ("Theme" 144).

In many ways, Auden and Isherwood's departure from England in 1939 and Auden's subsequent dismissal of the 1930s as "a low dishonest decade" ("September 1, 1939") signalled the decline of the Left's influence among writers, though in political terms the collapse of the Left had already been marked by a number of external events including Stalin's purges, Franco's victory in Spain, and the Nazi-Soviet pact of August 1939. Greene, because he refused to be identified with any specific position or party, continued to develop his own type of fiction based on the mixing of serious themes and popular forms. The political and literary concerns of *Stamboul Train*, which implicitly tie leftist political views to a popular literary form, echo throughout his work and find their fullest expression in those texts that are most obvious in their use of patterns derived from detective fiction. As Barry Meikoff notes, when Greene "adopted the detective novel and brought it into the twentieth century," he drew together those "aspects of the genre that concentrated almost exclusively on social criticism" (87). The means by which Greene was able to make a supposedly "inferior" form of literature the basis of a cultural and social critique is the subject of the following chapters.

2 Exploring the Popular in Two Early Novels: *Stamboul Train* and *England Made Me*

Most critics of Greene's work agree that *Stamboul Train* marks a definite shift in his approach to his fiction, but however great this shift is, Greene's movement towards the thriller as a way of addressing his political concerns in the 1930s was not sudden. In fact, none of the three novels preceding *A Gun for Sale* is a thriller in the way that *A Gun for Sale*, *The Confidential Agent*, *The Ministry of Fear*, or even *Brighton Rock* is, though this is not to say that the earlier books do not make use of certain elements of the thriller. Grünlich's murder of Kolber as well as Czinner's arrest and escape attempt in *Stamboul Train*, Conrad Drover's stalking and attempted assassination of the assistant commissioner in *It's a Battlefield*, and Krogh's shady business dealings and Anthony Farrant's murder in *England Made Me* are all melodramatic incidents that could find a place in the most conventional of thrillers. Yet we also find in these books, as we do in *The Ministry of Fear*, indications that Greene is wrestling with his own love of popular literary forms and his desire to produce works that can be taken as art while also reaching a large audience. What he is moving towards is a form that will allow him to achieve popularity and financial security for himself and to convey a particular moral and ideological vision to readers disenfranchised by modernist obscurity. *Stamboul Train*, he tells us, was a deliberate attempt to gain popularity (*WE* 22), and it, along with *It's a Battlefield* and *England Made Me*, introduces and illustrates elements of the aesthetic, political, and social critique that finds expression in Greene's later novels. Additionally, each of these works shows Greene exploring for himself critical distinctions between high culture, identified with modernist experimental art, and popular or, rather, populist culture. Through *Stamboul Train*, *It's a Battlefield*, and *England Made Me*, Greene discovers his own sense of the nature and function of literature by questioning differences between "serious" and light, or escapist, fiction. This process eventually results in him adopting the popular form of the thriller for *A Gun for Sale* and deciding to call that book an "entertainment" so as to foreground critical issues first raised in the previous three novels.

Greene's criticism of the established order emerges in *Stamboul Train*, *It's a Battlefield*, and *England Made Me* in a number of different ways. In each novel, he constructs a model of English society through the setting. In *Stamboul Train*, the train itself, with its own well-defined class system (first, second, and third classes), is used to stand for the capitalist social structure dominated by wealth. In *It's a Battlefield*, the city of London provides the containing structure for most of the novel's action and, again, class differences are sharply etched. In *England Made Me*, the English community in Stockholm, made up of Sir Ronald, Minty, the Davidges, Hall, and Kate and Anthony Farrant, is a microcosm of English society in the post-war period, cut off from traditional public-school values without any kind of replacement.

Greene's discontent with the dominant ideology and his criticism of twentieth-century capitalism in these novels is balanced by his recognition of the weaknesses and failings of a dogmatic alternative to the present order. In *Stamboul Train* Czinner, the communist revolutionary who brings the bulk of the novel's political content into the narrative, is ambiguously portrayed. Not only is his name a pun on "sinner," but he also travels first-class and finds the smell of the third-class passengers "too much for him" (116). Similarly, although he dreams of delivering a rousing courtroom defence (73), he is in practice inarticulate and ineffective, first in attempting to defend Coral Musker before Mr and Mrs Peters (109–10) and then in his own defence before Hartep where, "conscious of the artificiality of his words" (165), he falls back on slogans and clichés, "becoming a tub orator, no more" (166). In *It's a Battlefield*, which will be discussed in more detail in a later chapter, the Communist Party and its leaders, particularly the hypocritical Surrogate, are exposed as divided and incapable of taking action.[1] And in *England Made Me*, sympathy is extended to Krogh who, even though he heads a multinational corporation, finds himself isolated, "altered" from what he once was (158), and "[conditioned] by his career" (42). As Greene presents him, Krogh too is forced "out of his proper place" (158) by his success within a capitalist system that shapes and breaks individuals to the purpose of perpetuating itself. As Professor Hammarsten, a language teacher, points out, it is "impossible" for anyone, including Krogh, to do spontaneously what he or she would like to do (107).

Greene's ambivalence in these novels about political dogmatism works against the 1930s' tendency to polarize political opinions, but this does not make him "apolitical, or even right-wing," as Bernard Bergonzi claims (*Reading* 3). Despite his scepticism about the aims of the Left, there remains in Greene's work an avowed concern for social justice that later develops into his "dream ... of Communism with a human face" (Allain 95), a kind of ideal socialism able to guard and preserve the rights and dignity of the individual while also preparing the way for the "change of heart" of which Auden wrote.[2] Indeed, Greene declared in 1947 that a writer has the explicitly political task of working for the establishment of justice, which means protecting even his or her enemies from injustice and acting as "a piece of grit in the State machinery" by evoking sympathy for all; the novelist "is to draw his own likeness to any human being, the guilty as much as the innocent" (*Why?* 46, 48).[3] This attitude explains in part the measure of sympathy for Krogh that we sense in *England Made Me*, and it helps us to realize that Greene's novels, while showing "the nature of the class struggle in modern society," also "go beyond the Marxists to a realization of that even more fundamental struggle ... between the individual and the collective, the common man and the State" (Woodcock 143). And it is this aspect of Greene's work that is so well illustrated in his thrillers, where "the relation between the individual and society ... is concretely symbolized in the concept of crime and punishment, for this relationship becomes dramatic when either the individual or society transgresses against the other" (Hays 137). To see how Greene came to view a popular form as best suited to his political and aesthetic purposes in 1936, it is useful to contrast *Stamboul Train* with *England Made Me* in terms of how these texts deal with popular culture and its products.

In *Stamboul Train*, published in the same year as Q.D. Leavis's *Fiction and the Reading Public*, popular culture is by and large presented as either the impoverished and diminished reflection of high culture or as something imposed upon the lower classes in order to render them passive adherents to a dominant ideology. The first case is illustrated, as Neil McEwen notes, in the contrast between the two songs Czinner and Musker sing to pass the time while under arrest at the Subotica station (McEwen 29). Alongside Czinner's old and romantic folk-song about two lovers planning a midnight meeting, Musker's song from *Dunn's Babies* about the vicissitudes of modern love seems banal and trite (*ST* 168–70). The second case is of more interest, however, since it suggests a view similar to the one, described earlier, that

Adorno and Horkheimer of the Frankfurt School took later in the decade.

Coral Musker fruitlessly dreams of being mistaken for a lady in order to escape her life of poverty as a chorus girl (*ST* 107, 111). What fuels her dreams, in part, is her reading of women's magazines featuring "photographs of youngsters and of the daughters of the obscurer peers" (111). Such a practice encourages the magazine's readers to identify themselves with the peerage and so imagine themselves as members of a class higher than their own. For Musker, these magazines constitute a course of study in how to move up the social ladder, since they teach her "what accessories were being worn and what were the powders in favour" (111). The fact is, however, that it is impossible for her to leave her class behind. Even Myatt, on whom she pins her hopes of social elevation, sees her as little more than a common chorus girl, "a small alley, enticing a man's footsteps, but blind at the end with a windowless wall" (174); for him, Janet Pardoe, because of her class, beauty, wealth, lineage (her mother was Jewish), and, most important, connections to Myatt's own business, is "the kind of woman whom I should like to marry" (125).

The magazines that Musker reads reflect and are part of the dominant culture's attempt to preserve itself because they offer the illusion of social prestige to those without the hope of achieving it and discredit, through their emphasis on the "obscurer peers," those who seek to disrupt the social hierarchy. Musker's horrified response to the news that Czinner is a communist reflects the depth to which the prevailing capitalist ideology is able to impose itself even on those who are its victims.

"I've tried to make things different." He explained with an air of distaste for labels: "I'm a Communist." At once she exclaimed, "Why? Why?" watching him fearfully, unable to hide that she felt her faith shaken in the only man, except Myatt, able and willing to help her. Even the kindness he had shown her on the train she now regarded with suspicion

....

"It would take a long time to tell you why," he said. She took no notice, shutting her mind to the meaning of any words he uttered. She thought of him now as one of the untidy men who paraded on Saturday afternoons in Trafalgar Square bearing hideous banners: "Workers of the World Unite," "Walthamstow Old Comrades," "Belham Branch of the Juvenile Workers' League." They were the kill-joys, who would hang the rich and close the theatres and drive her into dismal free love at a summer camp, and afterwards make her walk in procession down Oxford Street, carrying her baby behind a banner: "British Women Workers."

"Longer than I've got," he said.

She took no notice. She was, for the moment in her thoughts, immeasurably above him. She was a rich man's mistress, and he was a workman. (145–6)[4]

Not only does the irony of the passage expose Coral Musker's misconceptions about communism, but it also draws attention to her pathetic attempts to deny the truth of her relationship with Myatt. She believes that a communist government would compel her to become sexually promiscuous, and the thought appals her. Complicating her response is her own attempt to rationalize her encounter with Myatt, to whom she feels she "owe[s]" (76) something because "he had been kind" (105). She denies both the reduction of herself to a commodity within the economy of their relationship and her own promiscuity on the grounds that she is "a rich man's mistress," (146) a status she has achieved in her own mind by associating herself, through a mistaken notion of love, with someone who appears to have much in common with the peers featured in the magazines she reads. In this respect, *Stamboul Train* presents popular culture, as reflected in women's magazines and, for that matter, in newspapers that trade in lies and exaggerations, as an imposed culture that impoverishes and subdues the public.

These metonymic representations of popular culture – women's magazines and newspapers – are both tied to different constructions of feminine culture. Coral Musker, an early version in Greene's fiction of the waif who later appears as Rose in *Brighton Rock*, Helen in *The Heart of the Matter*, and Phuong in *The Quiet American*, to name three, is only partly aware of the extent to which the culture industry constructs and scripts every aspect of her life and identity. She recognizes a reality that is not part of the popular novelist's realm (47) but does not see how she is made and controlled by the ideological forces of the women's magazines. Significantly as well, she is an actress performing in the musical review *Dunn's Babies*, a title that defines her as a baby – helpless, small, incapable, and an object of male desire possessed by an older man, Dunn.

Mabel Warren is also tied to popular culture through her ability to give the public what it desires in her newspaper columns. Constructed as a thoroughly unpleasant character, Mabel Warren is seen as drunken, obnoxious, insensitive, and predatory (35). She is a lesbian, too. Unwilling to respect male authority in the persons of Czinner, Savory, and her editor, she is a symbol of everything that disgusts Greene about both women and popular culture. And while the question of Greene's misogyny is not within the purview of this study, the link between the feminine and popular culture in *Stamboul Train* reflects and is consistent with a strain of thinking also found in, among other places, Henry James's "The Future of the Novel," which relates popular writing and the decline of literary standards to women authors and a growing number of women readers.[5] Implicitly, this line of thought valorizes a literary canon that is largely oriented towards male experience and written by men. "Serious" literature, in brief, is primarily intended for men of intellect. Quin Savory's work is clearly not of this order, since his popularity, particularly with women readers (104), marks him as other than a "serious" writer.

This perceived link between the feminine and the popular might be another reason for Greene's decision to choose the thriller rather than another form, such as the historical romance with which he had experimented in *The Man Within* and *Rumour at Nightfall*, as the medium for his attempts to align serious purpose with entertainment. Like the adventure stories he admired so much as a boy, the thriller is predominantly a male genre, written and read by men and embodying codes of masculinity similar to the adventure story's. Rather than radically challenge and restructure these codes or question the link between the feminine and popular culture, Greene could explore these things only obliquely, as he does in *Brighton Rock* for example.[6] In any case, few readers have found Greene's representations of women sympathetic to them.

In the matter of popular fiction, however, *Stamboul Train* displays a certain ambivalence that is reflected both in the character of Savory and in Greene's decision to produce a deliberately popular book. As a popular writer who comments both on his craft and on modern literature, Savory anchors discussions about literature in *Stamboul Train*. The hugely successful author of *The Great Gay Round*, he is Greene's portrait, modelled on J.B. Priestley, of the bestselling author ruined by his own success. In many ways, he is a figure of fun in the novel for his pretensions as a novelist and for his self-righteous attachment to his past as an apprentice in a shop: Mabel Warren says that he "drops his aitches when he can remember to" (36). Because of his success, Savory has gained wealth, fame, and, he believes, social mobility. Yet in this last he is mistaken, for he is dismissed by those of the upper class as a "counter-jumper" (212). Also adding to the irony is that he rides second-class. The interview he has with Mabel Warren exposes the disparity between his personality as a novelist and as a man. In one guise, he sagely declares that "Joyce, Lawrence, [and] all that" will pass, while "Shakespeare, Chaucer, Charles Reade, that sort of thing" will live (61)[7]; in the other, "he [is] a man overworked, harassed by a personality not his own, by curiosities and lusts [he pursues Janet Pardoe], a man on the edge of a nervous breakdown" (62) – a description that makes him a rather pathetic figure.

Certainly, in much of what Savory says to Warren, particularly about other writers and his own hopes for literature, there is an element of absurdity, especially in light of subsequent events in the novel: "One 'opes, one 'opes … to bring back cheerfulness and 'ealth to modern fiction. There's been too much of this introspection, too much gloom. After all, the world is a fine adventurous place" (62). Yet Savory also displays a genuine sense of his craft:

he wondered what terms he could use to describe the night. It is all a question of choice and arrangement; I must show not all that I see but a few selected sharp points of vision. I must not mention the shadows across the snow, for their colour and shape are indefinite, but I may pick out the scarlet signal lamp shining against the white ground, the flame of the waiting-room fire in the country station, the bead of light on a barge beating back against the current ....[8]

...

One thing the films had taught the eye, Savory thought, the beauty of the landscape in motion, how a church tower moved behind and above the trees, how it dipped and soared with the uneven human stride, the loveliness of a chimney rising towards a cloud and striking behind the further cowls. That sense of movement must be conveyed in prose, and the urgency of the need struck him … (103–4)

Savory, however, fails to respond to this urgency since Janet Pardoe's reappearance again arouses in him "the prick of desire" (104) and pride in his esteemed reputation (105); and so he sacrifices his art for the pleasures his success has brought him.[9]

Savory, therefore, is ruined as an artist by his popularity, yet his desire to convey a sense of movement in prose similar to that achieved by the cinema and his belief that the novelist must be a "spy" (61) both find correspondences in Greene's own thinking. In A Sort of Life, Greene, revealing more about himself than was perhaps realized at the time, echoes Savory in declaring that "every novelist has something in common with a spy" (103).[10] Similarly, in The Other Man Greene says, "When I describe a scene, I capture it with the eye of the cine-camera rather than the photographer's eye – which leaves it frozen. In this precise domain I think the cinema has influenced me" (132).[11] While these comments were made long after the publication of Stamboul Train, the novel can still be seen to reflect Greene's own ambition to capture a sense of movement in prose, particularly if one looks at part 3, section 2, where Greene presents a montage of bits of conversation being heard up and down the dining-car.[12] During an abrupt silence in the train the narrator records the inner thoughts of the characters. When this sequence is completed, the fragments of conversation are again presented. The section ends with the driver increasing the speed of the train, figuratively the image of the narrative's increasing pace (Sharrock 48). The whole scene is an attempt to find the equivalent of film in writing and suggests one way of bringing a sense of movement to prose.

The ambivalence in the characterization of Savory, coupled with the fact that *Stamboul Train* – a deliberate attempt to be popular – contains elements of the thriller, suggests that, while Greene may have denigrated certain aspects of popular culture, the structures of popular fiction could be valuable so long as they did not become, as they do for Savory, a trap for the writer. (Savory's next novel, *Going Abroad*, despite its exotic settings, will again be "an adventure in the Cockney spirit" [60].) Although Grahame Smith sees Greene playing with self-parody in his creation of Savory (28), one detects in Savory a certain amount of genuine anxiety on Greene's part. Indeed, Greene later described *Stamboul Train* as "laden" with the "anxieties of the time," (*SL* 151), some of which were surely related to his concern for his future as a novelist. Savory is Greene's warning to himself that popular success for the writer may be crippling.

By the time of *England Made Me*, many of Greene's misgivings about popular forms of art and popular writing had started to subside. In *England Made Me* there is no figure comparable to Savory; none the less, the novel continues Greene's examination of questions related to canon formation, the function of art, and the relationship between "anti-popular" modernist art and monopoly capitalism, which is supported by violence and crime (figured in the actions of Fred Hall) and indirectly tied through Greene's imagery to militarism.

Greene attacks, in *England Made Me*, the assumption that art – especially modernist art – is for only an élite class. We see this idea most clearly in Krogh's patronage of the arts, which has at its root the belief that social status and aesthetic taste are related; that is, members of the upper class are assumed to prefer works of art that address their own tastes and values, and so they come to yield cultural and economic power. Hence, Krogh's factory reflects the latest in architectural design, and the statue in the fountain in the central courtyard is "by the best modern sculptor in Sweden" (82); similarly, Krogh regularly attends the opera. Because his presumed appreciation for the products of high culture masks his peasant birth, art is a means of enhancing his social prestige.

But the price of this prestige is high, for we quickly find out that Krogh knows that he is "pander[ing] to a fashion he [does] not understand" (34); and, in not understanding, he is uncomfortable in "the cube of glass and steel" (34) that is his Bauhaus-inspired office building. He is also made uneasy by "the brutal shape" (35) of the statue in the fountain. The relationship between economic power and cultural power is thus shown to be bankrupt. Believing that he has no instinct to tell him whether something is good art or bad art (34), Krogh relies on the critical opinions of experts who dictate what he is supposed to like: "He had employed men whom he had been told were the best architects, sculptors, interior decorators. He looked from the curved tuiya wood desk to the glass walls, from the clock without numerals to the statuette between the windows of a pregnant woman. He understood nothing. These things gave him no pleasure" (36); instead, this "shrewd modernity" (182) leaves him in a state of "Arctic isolation" (35). Similarly, he replies to Anthony's suggestion that the two of them leave the opera by saying, " 'This is Art. Great Art.' ... 'I read about it somewhere' " (93). But at the opera, he is "always in a small wilderness of his own contriving" (36).

For Krogh, it is more important to be perceived as a representative of the cultural élite than actually to be one; in his mind, the value of the products of high culture exists solely in the status that they bring him. So he defends the statue to the doorman at Krogh's, despite being unable to remember the artist's name: " 'Understand this' ... 'That statue is by Sweden's greatest sculptor. It's not the business of a door-keeper to understand it; it's his business to tell visitors that it's the work of, of – get the name from my secretary, but don't let me ever hear you suggesting to visitors that the group's difficult to understand. It's a work of art' ... 'If it wasn't a work of art, it wouldn't have been commissioned by Krogh's' " (37–8). The irony here is unmistakable: modernist art is produced by an élite for an élite; it is not meant to be understood by the public at large, though the public is supposed to recognize some kind of inherent value in the art. Even the door-keeper later boasts of the statue to Young Andersson; like Krogh, the door-keeper also measures the value of the art in economic terms (154). Ultimately, what the text suggests is that there is no intrinsic value in a work of art separate from the function the work performs for a particular audience. As Krogh says, "There's no such thing ... as actual value" (131).

At the same time, however, Greene expands his critique of modernist art through Krogh's changing response to the statue. Anthony, though well born, is strongly identified with elements of a popular culture that may be in need of renewal: he reads *Film Fun* and Edgar

Wallace's *Four Just Men* (60) – a book Greene greatly admired (*CE* 172) – and he is a crack shot at carnival booths. He presents Krogh with a populist response to art that seems to free Krogh from his own cultural inhibitions so that he can enjoy the popular and, coincidentally, accept himself for who he is.

Anthony sees the statue as "highbrow" and can freely admit his dislike of it (82). Trusting to "a natural taste," he dismisses the opinions of the "best judges" as ideologically biased – "they all have an axe to grind" – and urges Krogh to "ask the common people" if the statue is any good (82). Because of Anthony, Krogh is able to admit his distaste for the statue and the opera (94) and to discover an enjoyment in popular culture. Krogh is both elated at adventurously leaving the opera to go to Tivoli (98) and relieved by his experience there: the next day he considers that he "never felt so rested" (133). And so, in the world of *England Made Me* the products of popular culture are presented as functionally of greater value than those of high culture because they take into account the will of the people.

Also a part of Greene's condemnation of modernist art in the novel is his perception of a relationship between it and a right-wing capitalist ideology that denies the past. Kate considers the nationalist past – of England before the war, for instance – no longer viable in the internationalist present and deliberately attempts to cut herself off from her origins (she lives in Stockholm) to embrace uncomfortably (in the figure of Krogh) a vision of the future that is both modern and international: " 'We haven't got a future away from here. This is the future.' … 'We're national. We're national,' Kate said, 'from the soles of our feet. But nationality's finished. Krogh doesn't think in terms of frontiers' " (135). In this regard, she is like Krogh, who has also deliberately, though uneasily, cut himself off from his past. Krogh thinks that "to live [is] to leave behind; to be as free as a shipwrecked man who has lost everything" (133). Yet Anthony's presence recalls for both Kate and Krogh the past they are seeking to escape; both temporarily discover a sense of who they are because they confront their origins through Anthony. In the case of Kate, this discovery is illustrated by her desire to have Anthony with her and by the feeling of wholeness she gains through his presence: "It was the nearest she could get to completeness, having him here in the same room" (135). In the case of Krogh, Anthony is the catalyst that enables him to remember his early life and the beginnings of his industrial empire when he was a bridge worker in Chicago. Krogh not only remembers the names of his old friends while sitting with Anthony at the opera, but, on the way to Saltsjöbaden with Anthony driving, Krogh visits a new bridge that his company is building and, in a figurative sense, looks into his past to see himself – one of the workers is named Erik (157) – as a young man before he had become conditioned by his career (156–8).

Since both Kate and Krogh recover parts of themselves through Anthony (a figure identified with the English past), there seems to be some truth to Maria Couto's observation that Greene expresses in *England Made Me* "a lingering feeling of affection for a culture whose confidence and security rested in large measure on assumptions of the imperialist idea" (97). Couto argues that the ideals of the world of the fathers are "neither betrayed nor abandoned even when they are most earnestly being questioned" in *England Made Me* (95). Support for this suggestion can easily be found in Kate's reflections that "there had been a straightness about the poor national past which the international present did without. It hadn't been very grand, but in their [Kate's and Anthony's] class at any rate there had been gentleness and kindness once" (136). Nevertheless, I believe that the novel, for the most part, denies Couto's argument by emphasizing the destruction of spirit that accompanied the passing on of the old values. The mention of Anthony's many beatings by his father (63–4), which are the cause of Anthony's double-standard in matters of sexuality (25), and the reference to Minty as one who has been "slowly broken in by parents, by schoolmasters, by strangers in the street" (72) clearly illustrate this point, while also underscoring the title's implication that the past is responsible for the present situation of cruelty and "inhumanity" (139). Through Anthony, who is said to be "too innocent to live" (186), Greene demonstrates the inability of pre-war values to survive in the modern world. Repeatedly Anthony is tied to the decaying liberal-humanism, handed down from his father, of Edwardian England. As an ironic allusion to Rupert Brooke's 1914 sonnet "The Soldier" suggests, wherever Anthony is "that is forever England" (74).[13] Anthony carries his "dusty" nationalism (11, 136) into the world of the 1930s where it cannot survive because its values have been thoroughly discredited. The result is that he and others like him such as Minty lack "the resources to hold their place" (180); they are, as Kate reflects, "done ... broke ... belong[ing] to the past" (135). Like the England of the 1930s and perhaps like Greene himself, Anthony is caught between two worlds; he wants to believe in something – "in the old country, in the king, in 'shoot the bloody Bolsheviks,' in the comradeship of the trenches" – but he is too old to do so (180). What is left for Anthony is a vague sense that there are "things he would not do" (11, 180), but he has little else to replace the old beliefs.

Yet, if Anthony's nationalism is untenable in the modern world, Krogh's internationalism of economic imperialism is equally unattractive for Greene since its materialism crushes spirituality and dehumanizes individuals and relationships. Under this capitalist regime every aspect of life becomes subordinate to economic interests: workers are made into little more than machines servicing machines (148), and the most personal of relationships become affairs of business not love, as Kate and Krogh's proposed marriage illustrates. Similarly, Kate thinks that nothing, save Anthony with whom she identifies herself, is more "real" than figures (134), while Krogh finds human relationships difficult – because unpredictable (49) – and consequently prefers to be alone (34).

What is significant about this situation for the critique of modernist art that the book develops is that art itself manifests the dehumanizing effects of the prevailing capitalist ethos. It, too, is said to be "internationalized" (89), and those who accept it – like Kate, who is explicitly called "highbrow" by Anthony (82) – are those who seek to replace the "gentleness and kindness" of the past with "the present, this crooked day, this inhumanity" (139). Hence, when Krogh renounces his past, the statue takes on new meaning for him.

I've been thinking too much about the past. He had always despised people who thought about the past. To live was to leave behind; to be as free as a shipwrecked man who has lost everything ...

Passing the window to reach the door, he was caught again by the fountain. But this time, suddenly, he saw it, the great handled block of green stone, with delight. It wasn't the past, it wasn't something finished to the nipple, to the dimple, to the flexed knee, it was something in the present tense, something working its way out of the stone. His delight was momentary, but it enabled him to forget the fountain. He thought: Next week America, and then we can go ahead, no depression can hurt us then and he thought with pity: They call it fraud, this clarity, this long intricate equation of which at last I can see the solution. He was possessed all the way up the glass lift shaft to the silent room next to the roof with a pure inhuman joy. (133–4)

The significance of this new understanding is emphasized a few pages later when, after he explains the fraud perpetrated by Hall in Amsterdam, Krogh tells Kate that he now likes the fountain (140). The fraud, which is necessary to the survival of Krogh's empire, marks a crucial moment in the history of his company since this is the first time that the law has been transgressed (140). Since it is also the moment when Krogh comes to appreciate the statue and experience "inhuman joy," Greene draws attention to a relationship between modernist, "anti-popular" art and a capitalist ideology that is supported by and accepting of criminal action, the "solution" to any problem.

This relationship is further illustrated in the figure of Hall, a brutal and vicious follower of Krogh who relishes the opportunity for violence. Like Grünlich in *Stamboul Train*, Hall is a proto-fascist anxious for power. It is he who carries out the stock fraud, beats the naïve and trusting Andersson, and eventually kills Anthony; significantly, the narrative also ties him to the statue: "There was something admirable, pathetic, vicious in his [Hall's] love [for Krogh]: he had completely surrendered himself. He was as much Krogh's as the block of stone in the courtyard, the marked ash-tray, the mono-grammed carpet ... and Krogh's for that reason was his. It was marked with his cheapness, his particular brand of caution, his irresponsible ferocity; it was Hall-marked" (190). The final pun does not mitigate the fact that Krogh's empire and, by extension, monopoly capitalism itself have within them an underlying cruelty and viciousness that Greene sees as part of highbrow culture and a step away from fascism.[14] As "the self-appointed defender of the great glass buildings, the works at Nyköping, the log-mills in the north" (191), Hall is the defender of capitalism's empires and of modernist art and architecture. In this way, Greene places modernism in a complex equation with big business and a fascistic acceptance of crime and brutality. The cultural élite to whom modernist art addresses itself is, after all, the same élite who wield economic and political power.

Within *England Made Me*, high cultural assumptions are also questioned in relation to the judgments of literary critics. In having Hammarsten describe *Pericles* – certainly one of Shakespeare's lesser known plays and a collaborative effort at that – as Shakespeare's greatest work, Greene, while underscoring the theme of incest in the novel, again seems to be parodying the kind of evaluative criticism practised by the Leavises, L.C. Knights, and other Scrutineers.[15] Similarly, by telling us that Davidge reads "obscurer classics" which "if they had ever lived were by now dead and buried" (96), the narrative ironically questions the common critical assumption that a classic will "live" forever. Indeed, the authors Davidge reads – J.G. Lockhart, R.H. Horne, Alexander Smith (all nineteenth-century poets and essayists) – were, even in 1935, well on their way to being forgotten.[16] What is more, in that Davidge's reading is "conditioned ... by what he could buy from the sixpenny boxes at the second-hand booksellers" (97), critical judgments are shown to have no bearing on a particular text's readership; yet, in contrast to Krogh, who cannot separate aesthetic pleasure from economic desire, Davidge takes genuine pleasure in the authors he reads. Whatever their reputations and however cheap their books, these authors offer Davidge an aesthetic pleasure not recognized by the artists and critics of the cultural élite. In this respect Greene recognizes, first, the extent to which particular texts or works of art have their value determined not by any inherent qualities of "excellence" – whatever the criteria a cultural clerisy may use to define this attribute – but by their users, and, secondly, the importance of enjoyment in the experience of art.

Yet, despite the force of the novel's condemnation of "serious," meaning modernist, art, there continue to be in *England Made Me*, as in *Stamboul Train*, traces of Greene's ambivalence about modernism and popular culture. Whereas in *Stamboul Train* Savory is at once both the insincere writer of popular fiction spoiled by his success and the mouthpiece for a number of Greene's own ambitions as a writer, *England Made Me*, though it attacks modernist experimentation, displays Greene's own attempts to make use of the innovations of modernist experimental writers such as Joyce and Woolf by employing long passages of interior monologue. Equally telling in the novel is the identification of Anthony with both an outmoded liberal-humanism and a pre-war popular culture, typified by Rupert Brooke's "The Soldier" and Wallace's *Four Just Men*, that is rich in the ideology of imperialism. Greene's uncertainty about the place of popular art is most apparent when we realize that the influence of Anthony, which seems beneficent insofar as it frees Krogh from his cultural inhibitions so that he can be himself, also stimulates Krogh's own will to power and, paradoxically, his sudden appreciation of a dehumanized art form. I do not think we can deny that the values Anthony represents are viewed nostalgically in *England Made Me*, but it is equally apparent in the novel that most of what he stands for no longer applies in the world of the 1930s.

Stamboul Train and *England Made Me* reveal the emergence in Greene's writing of two interrelated concerns that were eventually to lead to his unabashed use of the thriller and the "entertainment" label. The first is a political consciousness inspired by the circumstances of the 1930s. The second is the gradual rejection of an aesthetics based on culturally élitist critical assumptions and a corresponding acceptance of popular forms of art and literature as necessary and valuable for the dissemination of an alternative to the dominant ideology. Given the nature of the social, political, and economic crises of the period, social change had to occur; for Greene, as for many on the left, the agent for this change had to be the people. It hardly mattered that the public Greene addressed might not be sophisticated enough to grasp the subtleties of his narrative technique; what was important was that his intended readers show a healthy scepticism towards the structures of authority that defined their socio-economic and cultural status. By turning to the thriller, Greene sought to make the need for social re-alignment apparent to those who might otherwise not see the desperation of the situation.

3 Aspects of Detective Fiction

For many of Greene's critics, all his novels are thrillers[1] but those called "entertainments" are most explicitly associated with the genre. As any student of detective fiction quickly realizes, however, generic terminology is a vexed issue and what constitutes a "thriller," or "shocker" to use a synonymous British term,[2] is hardly a matter of agreement among analysts of crime or detective fiction. Mary McCarthy, for instance, gives historical priority to the thriller as a literary type when she suggests that Greene discarded the detective-story plot for the "more old-fashioned machine" of the thriller (228). Tzvetan Todorov, on the other hand, uses "thriller" to describe a genre that emerged in the United States prior to and during the Second World War (*Poetics* 47). This kind of diversity in the term's use is quite common, but for the purposes of this analysis "thriller" is used as a broad term applying to all of the various types of detective fiction, except the classical detective story, from spy story to adventure story.[3] This is the way in which most critics of Greene's work use the term, and it is by and large the way the term was used in the 1930s.

Although T.S. Eliot proposed three categories for detective fiction (detectives, thrillers, and "curdlers") (Eliot, Review 175), W.H. Auden's 1938 essay "The Guilty Vicarage" (147) and Greene's film criticism (*PD* 89) distinguished only two: classical detective stories and thrillers. (Auden preferred the former and Greene the latter although both men were attracted to detective fiction for similar reasons.) For Auden, the classical detective story is like a modern morality play in that it ritualistically presents the discovery and expulsion of guilt from an "Eden-like" setting through the agency of an individual – the detective – "who is ... in a state of grace."[4] The result is the restoration of a "state of grace" to the "Great Good Place." Auden goes on to suggest that "the typical reader of detective stories is ... a person who suffers from a sense of sin" and that "to have a sense of sin means to feel guilty" (157). The classical detective story offers the reader an escapist "fantasy of being restored to the Garden of Eden, to a state of innocence, where he may know love as love and not as law" (158). The thriller, on the other hand, presents "the ethical and characteristic conflict between good and evil" in terms of "Us and Them" (147); it "gratif[ies] in fantasy the violent or murderous wishes they [readers] dare not, or are ashamed to, translate into action" (157).

Greene shared Auden's metaphysical and religious reading of the classical detective story and quickly echoed Auden's essay, which appeared in the May 1938 issue of *Harper's Magazine*, in a 17 June 1938 review of *L'Alibi* and *A Slight Case of Murder*: "Murder, if you are going to take it seriously at all, is a religious subject; the interest of a detective-story is the pursuit of exact truth, and if we are at times impatient with the fingerprints, the time-tables and the butler's evasions, it is because the writer, like some early theologians, is getting bogged in academic detail" (*PD* 192). Yet, as these remarks suggest, Greene's views differ from Auden's in a number of ways. For instance, Greene sees classical detective stories, which he elsewhere describes as "modern fairy tales" (*CE* 161), as too often mired in detail. Their public of "the perpetually immature" (*WE* 73) consists of tired intellectuals and crossword-puzzlers (*PD* 48) who, refusing to allow authors to deal realistically with sexual passion (one of the most likely motives for murder among those who were not members of the so-called criminal classes [*WE* 73]), make their sole concern the logical puzzle presented in such texts. Here, death is only a "cypher" of which readers and film audiences have grown tired (*PD* 11). As Greene notes, the actual detection, because it involves an intellectual exercise undertaken by the detective, is usually the weakest part of any detective film (*PD* 48), and what action there is in a detective story involves little more than talk (266). Correspondingly, the pace of a detective story is considerably slower than that of the thriller. Hence, Greene finds the film versions of Charlie Chan or of Sherlock Holmes stories wanting.[5] For him, the detectives of classical detective stories are seldom convincing because their upper-class backgrounds would, he feels, prevent them from being effective in the criminal milieu. He prefers Perry Mason, because "he belongs to the same class

as his criminals," to Lord Peter Wimsey or to William Powell's portrayal of Nick Charles in *The Thin Man* movies (*PD* 49). In addition, he
complains that the classical detective story fails to give the "vivid
sense of life" that is found in some of David Frome's novels, in the
early work of Dorothy Sayers, and in all of Dashiell Hammett's
fiction (*PD* 48). In *Ways of Escape*, he expands his attack on classical
detective stories, particularly those written by Dorothy Sayers: they
were "with all their carefully documented references to Bradshaw's
timetable or to the technique of campanology or to the geography –
complete with plan – of a country house … lacking in realism. There
were too many suspects and the criminal never belonged to what
used to be called the criminal class" (73). No one would dispute that
Greene's best work with the thriller is far removed from the classical
detective story as practised by Sayers, Christie, or S.S. Van Dine (W.H.
Wright).

By insisting on a "sense of life" or a standard of realism in detective
fiction (though Greene, like Chandler, knows "realism" to be an
aspect of style), Greene rejects the ritualized world of the classical
detective story that Auden prefers. Instead, he champions the thriller
as a response to the classical detective story, which Raymond Chandler, reflecting on the emergence of the hard-boiled detective novel in
the United States was to describe as "too contrived and too little
aware of what goes on in the world" ("Simple Art" 12). Discussing
popular cinema, Greene wrote: "We are driven back to the 'blood,'
the thriller. There never was a school of popular English bloods. We
have been damned from the start by middle-class virtues, by gentlemen cracksmen and stolen plans and Mr Wu's. We have to go farther
back than this, dive below the polite level, to something nearer the
common life" (*Reflections* 65–6). These remarks reveal a preference for
the "blood" or the thriller as the form best able to reflect the political,
ethical, and historical realities of the modern world. And, in the eyes
of Greene, Auden, and others in the 1930s, the "fantastic realities" of
the modern world are the stuff of thrillers.[6] As Auden wrote, "The
situation of our time/Surrounds us like a baffling crime" (*New Year
Letter* 233–4), while Greene's Arthur Rowe in *The Ministry of Fear*
dreams "thrillers are like life … The world has been remade by
William Le Queux" (65).[7] For many critics, Rowe's remarks alone justify Greene's use of the thriller form, though the suggestion that
thrillers are like life is troubling and hardly powerful enough in itself
to explain his interest in the form.[8]

Greene's dislike of the classical detective story did not, however,
prevent him from making his own attempts at the genre, and in doing
so he sought to get beyond the form's conventionalities. The first of

these attempts, made before the publication of *The Man Within*, was called *The Empty Chair*.[9] In this unfinished novel, a priest discovers that a young girl is responsible for the murder of her governess, but he refuses to betray the child (*SL* 132). While Greene claimed to admire the story's plot, the piece was never completed nor has it been published.

A second, more substantial attempt was the short story "Murder for the Wrong Reason," which first appeared in *The Graphic* in October 1929. Despite its form and its early date, the story looks ahead to Greene's later thrillers. This is the closest he comes to following the formulas of the classical detective story, yet even here we find him striving to make something different of a form that has already ossified into rigid codes and rules of detection. Subtitled "An Unusual Thriller in Three Installments" in *The Graphic*, the story is a variation of the locked-room type, pioneered by Edgar Allan Poe in "The Murders in the Rue Morgue," in which the murder victim is found in a sealed room with no apparent escape route for the killer. With suicide dismissed as a possible explanation, the puzzle becomes twofold: who did it? and how was it done? In Greene's story neither of these questions is particularly puzzling for the attentive reader, who will guess the murderer's identity almost immediately; but what is puzzling is, as the title hints, the murderer's motive for the crime.

In "Murder for the Wrong Reason" Detective-Inspector Mason of Scotland Yard discovers Hubert Collinson murdered. After calling for the constable walking the beat outside Collinson's house, Mason begins the task of investigating the murder with the constable's help. As in Doyle's "Charles Augustus Milverton," E.C. Bentley's *Trent's Last Case*, Christie's *Murder on the Orient Express*, and a host of other tales, the victim "deserved all that he got" (113). In fact, Mason had come to Collinson's in order to execute a search warrant as part of an investigation into Collinson's activities as a blackmailer and philanderer. As the story develops, Mason and the constable begin their investigation with Mason coaching the slow-witted constable along profitable lines of inquiry that finally conclude with Mason confessing to the murder.

That the detective should prove to be the murderer was not, even in 1929, all that "unusual"; although it violates one of Ronald Knox's rules for the detective story, the situation, like Christie's trick in *The Murder of Roger Ackroyd*, is merely a variation on the classical detective story's convention of the least likely suspect being the guilty person. The story is unusual, however, in that Mason's interrogation of two suspects in the case (Arthur Callum and Rachel Mann), which occurs in the last part of the first instalment (October 5) and takes up the bulk of the second instalment (October 12), proves to be no more than imagined "private inquiries" (115 and 131) taking place in Mason's own mind. Collinson, it seems, at one time had an affair with Rachel Mann, who sought to advance her theatrical career through her liaison with the entrepreneurial Collinson. Mason, in his youth a poor medical student whose real name was Arthur Callum, loved Rachel Mann and, in anger at her affair with Collinson and jealous of Collinson's wealth, not only threatened Collinson's life but also killed Rachel Mann sometime after she refused his proposal of marriage. (That Mason as Callum killed Rachel Mann is by no means clearly conveyed, though the story's final sentence strongly implies that she was murdered.) Thus, Arthur Callum, described as "a scientist gone wrong" (128) (a theme that, as will be seen, is common in detective fiction), becomes Mason and embarks on a new life as a policeman. Collinson, we are to infer, knew of Callum's crime and, later, of Callum's identity as Mason and sought to use this information to blackmail the detective. This seems to be the selfish motive behind Collinson's murder, and, in the terms of the story, it is the "the wrong reason." The right reason would have been Collinson's affair with Rachel, which not only ruined her in Callum's eyes but also aroused his jealous passion. (Another side to the question of right and wrong reasons is suggested by Greene's comments in *Ways of Escape*, to which I earlier referred.) In the story, however, he respects the wishes of his "perpetually immature" audience by making avarice Mason's motive for killing Collinson and not passions inflamed by sexual rivalry. At the story's close, Mason credits the constable with the discovery of the murderer's identity and confesses to his disbelieving colleagues. The final sentence reveals the last piece in the puzzle by telling us that Rachel Mann has been dead for ten years.

"Murder for the Wrong Reason" bears all the marks of its author's youth. Norman Sherry thinks it one of the worst stories Greene ever wrote (339), and its opacity and confusion render this judgment credible. Particularly clumsy is the handling of Mason's "private inquiries." There are many clues that alert us to the imaginary nature of these encounters with figures from Mason's past, but to make the point only three need be listed: the narrator remarks in the story's second paragraph that "[a] long, torturous dream is said to last but a few seconds of time as we record it" (110); there are frequent references to Lazarus; and neither Callum nor Mann speaks to Mason during his interrogation of them. Yet the summations that precede the second and third instalments and much of the dialogue between Mason and the constable in the first instalment lead us to assume that Mason does, in fact, visit another apartment nearby. This is precisely the story's trick, but the revelation at the end of part 2 that Mason's discussions with Callum and Mann are only his imaginings in the few seconds during which he examines an old and faded letter of Callum's to Collinson seems, in its abruptness, a trite and clichéd device. As well, the information conveyed in this section of the story and in Mason's own explanation at the story's end is obscurely presented at best. In this we see something of the faults of the young Greene's style that Swinnerton complained of in his review of *Rumour at Nightfall*.

None the less, "Murder for the Wrong Reason" is interesting in light of Greene's later handling of the crime story. Certainly, he incorporates here many of the standard motifs that are part of the classical detective story: the murder victim is deserving of his fate; the detective is accompanied by a less intelligent partner (references to Holmes and to Doyle's stories accentuate this pairing); the investigation is thought of as a "game" by Mason (132, 133); and the point is made that the situation in the story differs from comparable situations in detective fiction. Indeed, in this last respect, the narrative openly declares itself to be fiction, for when Mason reprimands the constable for reading detective stories it is because the constable thinks of Collinson's murder as his chance to impress superiors and possibly gain a promotion. Mason dismisses this fantasy by noting that the constable has "[a] very small chance" (113), and he implies that such a hope could be realized only in fiction. Later, however, Mason accepts the constable's desire and, in commending the constable at the story's end, actively works to bring about a situation that he had earlier said was impossible in real life.

Other aspects of the story are particularly characteristic of Greene's later work. As is usual in classical detective stories, Collinson's murder takes place outside the frame of the narrative's discourse and is investigated by Mason from the story's outset; but, because the murderer Mason seeks is himself, his investigation is, in fact, a self-investigation. The work of detection, therefore, occurs within his own mind and involves the exploration of his past: significantly, his reverie occurs while he reads one of his own letters, signed Arthur Callum, to Collinson. The story of Oedipus is the paradigm for this kind of search for self-knowledge, though Mason is no Oedipus since all of the details of the crime are known to Mason from the narrative's beginning. It follows a certain logic, then, that clues pointing to Mason as the killer appear quite early in the text: the narrator refers to a long dream lasting only a few seconds and to a strange melancholy that comes over Mason (111); as well, the description of Mason as he examines the body is equivocal (his glance "seem[s] perfunctory and without pity" [110] and his smile is "almost a malignant grin" [112]). These descriptions suggest not only the narrator's uncertainty but also the possibility that the detective, while playing the role of the professional investigator, finds a private satisfaction at Collinson's death.

As the story progresses, Mason, who is both detective and detected, strives to transfer the duties of detection to the constable, an action that, if successful, would greatly ease the conflict within himself because it would allow him to live freely without the constrictions of his public persona. But, as the constable lacks the ability to take on the role of the detective alone, Mason, tired of a life of deceit, is obliged to lead the bewildered man through the case. Like Andrews in *The Man Within*, the Assistant Commissioner in *It's a Battlefield*, and Rowe in *The Ministry of Fear*, Mason is a prototype of the divided man at war with himself and pursued by himself – by the "Eumenides of conscience," as McCarthy would have it (220) – who appears in so much of Greene's work. In this sense, he prefigures guilty investigators in the later thrillers such as Raven and Rowe.

A final point that might be made about "Murder for the Wrong Reason" is that Mason's self-investigation illustrates, even at this early stage in Greene's career, Greene's interest in the origins of character and of action. Equally significant is that Mason's search takes place in an imagined realm comparable to a dream world. His reverie shows him and us something of the origins of both the crime and his identity as Mason; the discovery of the criminal involves the discovery of the detective's personal identity.

Among Greene's early efforts with the detective story, "Murder for the Wrong Reason" presents itself as a story of reading. It could hardly do otherwise given its form. Yet it would not be fair to see in this story the same kind of ideological or socio-political critique that is present in *Stamboul Train* and Greene's later novels. While the idea of the detective as murderer is rich in its political connotations (evoking ideas of the "enemy within" and corruption among society's guardians), Greene does not exploit these possibilities here, so the story remains a classical detective story tied to another age. Its final instalment appeared in the 19 October 1929 issue of *The Graphic*, less than two weeks before the Wall Street crash that signalled the beginning of the Depression and, if not on the calender at least in the popular imagination, the 1930s.

Despite the essentially apolitical nature of "Murder for the Wrong Reason," detective fiction offered Greene a ready-made, enormously popular formula that could challenge established political, cultural, and critical assumptions, since the plot of the detective story figures the process of reading. As Ross Macdonald says, the detective's "actions are largely directed to putting together the stories of other people's lives and discovering their significance" (185). The detective "reads" the story of the crime in the clues that he or she finds. But the murderer attempts to keep this story hidden from the detective by creating a fiction, an alibi, which will cover the story of the crime. That is, the murderer is the author of a palimpsest in which the story of the crime as it really happened lies beneath the story of the crime that claims to be the truth of what happened. The detective is forced to interpret one text, the alibi, in such a way that he or she is able to uncover the hidden story that is the true account of the events, for showing through the fictional account of the crime are indications of the truth. The detective story ends with the detective producing a new narrative, which is the explanation and interpretation of the criminal's fiction. In this way, "detective fiction, particularly of the classical formula ... thematizes narrativity itself as a problem, a procedure, and an achievement" (Hühn 451), and so the detective story is "the narrative of narratives, its classical structure a laying-bare of the structure of all narrative" (Brooks 25).[10] Hence, the classical detective story can be read as a metaphor for the reading process, with the detective's investigation – his or her reading of the story of the crime – likened to the reader's experience of this or of any other text.

The classical detective story exemplifies the primary structure of detective fiction in perhaps its purest sense. Most typically the crime is committed either just prior to or soon after the narrative's beginning. The narrative then recounts the efforts of a detective or other investigator to retrace the criminal's path in order to expose the origins of the crime that instigated the narrative. Fundamentally, this structure contains two stories: the story of the investigation, which is the "open" story present to the reader, moves forward in time in the narrative; and the story of the crime, which is hidden from the reader, exists *in absentia* and is constructed backwards from the scene of the crime to its source (*Poetics*, 44; Porter 29; Brooks 24–5).[11]

In the thriller, however, although it remains the investigator's task to uncover the origins of the crime for those around him or her, the story of the crime is not hidden from the reader (which is not to say that there are no hidden aspects in these stories). Instead, it is foregrounded and vitalized while the story of the investigation is largely suppressed. This structure removes the question of "whodunit?" from the reader's mind, but renders the metaphor of reading more complicated in that both the story of the crime and the story of the investigation change in response to the presence of the other: the investigator still seeks to read the story of the crime but, correspond-ingly, the criminal seeks to read the story of the investigation in order to prevent his or her own story from being read. Both the investiga-tor and the criminal plot their actions in response to each other, and, in this sense, each constructs an interpretation of the other's plot. The reader thus sees in the thriller a dialectical process of textual interpretation and reinterpretation that can theoretically continue without end. But, as will be shown, this same dialectic is also at work in the detective story.

Toward the end of his life Greene remarked that "in the twenties and thirties I was much interested in the detective story" (*Last Word* viii). During this "golden age" of detective fiction, the genre devel-oped along several lines, all of which led from a classical model pio-neered by Edgar Allan Poe and then modified and extended by a number of authors including Arthur Conan Doyle, E.C. Bentley, G.K. Chesterton, Agatha Christie, and Dorothy Sayers. Greene's rework-ing of the thriller in the 1930s is meaningful only in light of how these and other writers such as John Buchan and Edgar Wallace de-veloped the genre of detective fiction, since Greene's thrillers re-spond to their work. In order to see how Greene's fiction deviates from the norms of the classical detective story and the conventions of the thriller in the period, we need to consider the nature of the forms to which Greene was reacting, as well as the epistemological and ideological assumptions underlying the classical detective story and the conventional thriller: we have to ask ourselves how, exactly, detective fiction is a "narrative of narratives." Greene's work devel-ops out of a well-established tradition, yet he exploits qualities inherent in the genre to subvert traditional assumptions.

READING AND THE DETECTIVE STORY

In the purest form, the two stories that make up the classical detective story have no point in common; that is, the "hidden" or repressed story of the crime ends before the second "open" story of the investi-gation begins (Todorov, *Poetics* 44). Also, action in the story of the investigation is limited, since the characters within it "do not act, they learn" (44): as a rule nothing can happen to them, and so the detective is immune to physical harm or judicial persecution. Yet, as Todorov notes, this visible story has a peculiar status in that it is usually told by a friend of the detective (such as Holmes's Dr Watson, Poirot's Hastings, or, in Poe's stories, Dupin's unnamed companion) who ex-plicitly acknowledges, as in Doyle's "The Five Orange Pips" or "The Red-Headed League," that he is writing a book. The second, "open" narrative, then, explains how the story itself came to be written. The first or "hidden" narrative, on the other hand, never confesses its literary nature: it is taken as being of the "real" and so tells "what really happened" (45), while the second story explains "how the reader (or the narrator) has come to know about it" (45).

This second story explicitly concerns itself with two related questions: how does one read a text? and how is a text produced? The detective, in moving towards the full disclosure of the story of the crime, is confronted by a number of different texts which he or she must read and interpret. These texts are the clues, the traces of the crime left at the scene, the statements of witnesses, including the statement of one who will eventually be identified as the criminal, and sometimes, to make the metaphor of detection as reading explicit, a written text which may or may not be in code (as in "The Dancing Men" or *The Thirty-Nine Steps*) and which the investigator must read. By reading or interpreting these texts, the detective constructs a narrative of events which, in the classical detective story, is given the value of truth. Although this value is questionable, convention dictates that, at the end of the story, the detective provide an authoritative reading of events, which is the one true interpretation of the texts he or she reads: the detective's narrative, then, replaces all previous narratives in the text, which are exposed as fictions.

Central to the detective's reading is an ability to see the fissures in the texts he or she confronts, particularly in the murderer's account of his or her own actions. What the murderer seeks to do is to construct the perfect alibi. Such a text, which Roland Barthes might call a "readerly" (*lisible*) text, attempts not only to cover all traces of its author's actual activities but also to direct the detective's reading along a single line of inquiry, which will ensure that suspicion is shifted from the criminal-author to another suspect. This "readerly" text "is controlled by the principle of non-contradiction ... [stresses] at every opportunity the *compatible* nature of circumstances, [and attaches] narrated events together with a kind of logical 'paste' " (*s/z* 156; Barthes's emphasis). The readerly provides the illusion that everything in the text is both determined by and the subject of denotative reading. Its governing precept "is to *fill in* the chains of causality ... in an ultimate progression" towards closure (181–2). Particularly suggestive in a study of detective fiction is Barthes's description of the readerly as having "the careful and suspicious mien of an individual afraid of being caught in some flagrant contradiction ... always on the lookout and always ... preparing [his or her] defense against the enemy that may force [him or her] to acknowledge the scandal of some illogicality" (*s/z* 156).

The murderer's fiction, his or her alibi, tries to account for every one of its author's activities in the period before and after the commission of the crime. Yet the detective's careful analysis of this fiction, when coupled with his or her examination of other clues and the statements of witnesses, reveals that the "readerly" text of the criminal is not the coherently seamless and univocal account its author would like it to be, for both language and narrative are always subject to "writerly" (*scriptible*) properties, specifically connotation and the play of intertwining textual codes, that prevent a purely denotative or univocal reading from emerging.

The writerly traits in a text force the reader to become an active producer of the text rather than its passive consumer (*s/z* 4). For Barthes, the writerly text is ideally "absolutely plural" in its meaning; it is "a galaxy of signifiers," without a beginning or an end, and there is no authoritative way into this text: although specific "systems of meaning can take over this absolutely plural text ... their number is never closed" because of "the infinity of language" (*s/z* 5–6). In the end, a purely writerly text is as impossible as a purely readerly text; and just as any attempt to construct a readerly text will fail in the unavoidable inclusion of writerly qualities, so will any attempt to produce a writerly text fail in the unavoidable inclusion of readerly qualities that are inherent in narrative structure, grammar, and logic.

In a conventional detective story, the murderer hopes that his or her text will be read in only one way, which will yield a univocal or denotative meaning that will attest to his or her innocence. The detective encountering this readerly text seeks those spots which are the indications of a plurality of meaning. Hence, the detective discovers the writerly qualities of the murderer's fiction in order to become the producer of another text at the end of the narrative. Things such as the traces left at the scene of the crime or contradictions between differing accounts of the night of the murder are the clues that reveal the unavoidable presence of the writerly within the texts the detective reads.

The pertinence of the readerly/writerly paradigm to works of detective fiction is easily demonstrated. As Hercule Poirot remarks in *The Murder of Roger Ackroyd* (1926), cases of the sort described in the novel all resemble each other in that "everyone concerned in them has something to hide" (*Ackroyd* 84). In this novel, Poirot confronts a number of readerly texts supplied by those with "something to hide" that are all aimed at lulling their readers, Poirot and us, into "idleness" (*s/z* 4). The witnesses Poirot questions assume that he believes in the representational function of writing and in its power to construct and convey logico-temporal sequences, but Poirot, alert to the hidden writerly qualities present in any text, refuses to be a mere consumer of their testimonies. Instead, he focuses on those areas in their texts where he sees indications of an attempt to cover over something. Like Dupin, Holmes, or John Buchan's Richard Hannay, Poirot is constantly aware of the symbolic nature of language within narrative and, consequently, is attentive to equivocations, double meanings, and the possibility of a repressed content in any narrative. He recognizes that the texts he encounters are deceptive in that they both reveal and conceal meaning; he knows that even Sheppard, chronicler of his case, is suppressing something.

Christie's novel holds a special place in the history of detective fiction because its innovation consists of concealing the identity of the murderer behind the "I" of the first-person narrator, Sheppard. Usually, "in the novel, the 'I' is … a spectator, and … it is the 'he' who is the actor" (Barthes, *Writing* 34–5). The use of "I" as "eye" is a "typical novelistic convention" (35), and we expect the "I" of Christie's narrative to function conventionally so as to give us a passively observed account of Poirot's investigation. Christie's departure from this convention caused some critics, Ronald Knox and S.S. Van Dine among them, to see the novel as a fraud and a violation of the literary codes governing the genre,[12] yet this violation allowed Christie to fulfil another convention of the detective story, that of the criminal as the least likely suspect.

Just as the first-person narration helps conceal the murderer's identity from the reader, so does Dr Sheppard's social position help shield him from suspicion. As "a doctor [he is] the very man to be trusted with the individual's bodily secrets and a hope of continuing life, [and he is] the emerging figure of wise authority in an increasingly secular society" (Knight 113). For these reasons, a doctor has long been a favourite villain in mystery fiction. Holmes, we recall, in "The Adventure of the Speckled Band", remarks to his own Dr Watson, "When a doctor does go wrong he is the first of criminals. He has nerve and he has knowledge" (270). Sheppard betrays the trust the people of King's Abbot place in his profession as easily as Christie betrays the trust of her readers. Just as he hides behind the title of "Doctor," so does the murderer hide behind the pronoun "I." Indeed, Christie's use of the "I" as the actor has potent ideological consequences. The extreme reaction of critics such as Knox and Van Dine expresses a sense of "genuine alarm rather than literary disapproval" because "she cast doubt on the very conventions of narrative fiction. It was a brilliant structural device, enacting the fear the respectable bourgeois held that disorder within society, threats against the self, might be caused from within the charmed circle, and by someone thought trustworthy" (Knight 112). Christie's innovation shows us how, in detective fiction, language deceives and conceals at both the level of the word and at the levels of structure and narration.

Sheppard's version of events attempts not only to suggest that Ackroyd's death took place well after Sheppard's departure from Ackroyd's home, but also to cast suspicion on a number of other characters (Parker, Miss Russell, Ralph Paton, Geoffrey Raymond, Ursula Bourne, and Charles Kent) so as to deflect attention from himself as the murderer. What makes this particular Christie novel interesting in a discussion of how detective fiction metaphorically represents the activity of reading is that Sheppard's text constitutes the text of the novel: what we read is what Sheppard writes in his journal. That is, he records the narrative of Poirot's investigation while suppressing the narrative of events leading up to Ackroyd's death. Although any classical detective story contains a layering of narratives, *The Murder of Roger Ackroyd* is distinctive in that this layered structure is embedded in Sheppard's own text. The reader, then, is placed in a role analogous to Poirot's, since both the reader and Poirot confront the same text, as is explicitly figured in chapter 23 where Poirot also becomes a reader of the text.

When Poirot recalls the assistance he often received from Hastings's records, Sheppard reveals his own account of the Ackroyd case, which is complete to this point. Sheppard's manuscript, we are told, comprises the first twenty chapters of Christie's novel (228). Poirot reads Sheppard's journal and so imitates the activity of the novel's reader. Reading and detection merge in this story (as they do in others, including *The Thirty-Nine Steps* and "Murder for the Wrong Reason" insofar as Mason's reverie occurs as he reads the old letter) so as to become identical activities. Poirot's response to Sheppard's narrative is an attentive reader's response to Christie, for Poirot sees Sheppard's text not as the determined, univocal reportage Sheppard intends but as the connotative, plural text no author can entirely avoid.

Although Poirot may already suspect Sheppard, the manuscript reveals an important, somewhat Holmesian, clue:

> "I [Poirot] congratulate you – on your modesty!"
> "Oh," I [Sheppard] said, rather taken aback.
> "And on your reticence," he added.
> I said "Oh!" again.
> "Not so did Hastings write," continued my friend. "On every page, many, many times was the word 'I.' What *he* thought – what *he* did. But you – you have kept your personality in the background ... A very meticulous and accurate account," he said kindly. "You have recorded all the facts

faithfully and exactly – though you have shown yourself becoming reticent as to your own share in them."

"And it has helped you?"

"Yes. I may say that it has helped me considerably." (228–9)[13]

Although he notes the suppression of the narrator-author, Poirot discovers nothing in Sheppard's text through any special or "inside" knowledge. In fact, Poirot assures us of the journal's accuracy, although he does add one qualification: "It was strictly truthful as far as it went – but it did not go very far" (240). Poirot arrives at the knowledge of Sheppard's guilt because he sees indications of an absent, and therefore repressed, content within the narrative. In Sheppard's account, this repressed content is literally signalled by Sheppard's reticence, but, as Barthes observes, reticence is the emblem of the "dilatory area" that exists between the formulation and the resolution of an enigma in a narrative. It is the emblem of all that stands in the text between the presentation of the initial mystery (the crime) and its solution (s/z 75). Sheppard's journal, like Christie's novel, explicitly illustrates the dynamics of narrative. The journal that was to have been an account of one of Poirot's failures (253) becomes an incriminating piece of evidence, which allows Poirot to construct his own version of what happened.

In *The Murder of Roger Ackroyd*, Poirot, a figure for the reader, also takes over the production of Sheppard's text from the moment he begins to read. Certainly, Sheppard remains the novel's narrator to its end, but he has no opportunity to continue his manuscript except for the one that Poirot gives him. For the remainder of the novel, Poirot directs Sheppard both physically (Poirot suggests "an overdose of sleeping draught" [252] for Sheppard) and textually ("I should suggest that you finish that very interesting manuscript of yours – but abandoning your former reticence" [252]). After Sheppard observes that "there was not much which escaped Hercule Poirot" (211) at the end of chapter 20, the novel's last seven chapters do demonstrate less "reticence" on Sheppard's part as the investigation comes to focus on him. Many of the enigmas that the text had posed, such as the question of Ursula Bourne's relationship with Ralph Paton, are resolved in these final chapters and with their resolution comes the end of reticence. Sheppard increasingly finds that he cannot control his destiny ("It was a very uncomfortable minute for *me*" [238]; "I was too abashed to argue" [240]; "He [Poirot] suddenly became dangerous" [241]) or his discourse ("'Let us get back to the culpable conduct of Dr. Sheppard,'" Poirot directs [239]). In the final chapter, rife with over seventy first-person references in slightly more than two pages of text, all affectations of reticence disappear as Sheppard himself exposes the seams within his text: "I am rather pleased with myself as a writer. What could be neater, for instance, than the following: '*The letters were brought in at twenty minutes to nine. It was just on ten minutes to nine when I left him, the letter still unread. I hesitated with my hand on the door handle, looking back and wondering if there was anything I had left undone*' ... what a judicious use of words: '*I did what little had to be done!*' " (254–5; Sheppard's italics).

Once Poirot has discovered them, the sites of repression within the narrative are explicitly marked. Poirot brings about the end of narrative reticence and the end of repression, the condition that had sustained the life of the narrative. In this respect, he is responsible for ending both Sheppard's manuscript and, when it ends, Sheppard himself: the process of reading is completed. Poirot's reading demonstrates that no textual sequence created out of language can be subject only to a single, denotative meaning determined by its author; Sheppard's secrets are found out by the detective.

What prevents the construction of an univocal or solely denotative text is the presence of intersecting textual codes, or "voices," within the text. Over time, language, as it is used within the literary work, becomes increasingly connotative, recalling previous usages, and increasingly symbolic, and so it defies attempts to limit its interpretation. A code is the product of literary tradition and of our (and the writer's) individual experience with that tradition: it is, in Barthes's words, "a perspective of quotations, a mirage of structures" which have "always been *already* read, seen, done, experienced" (*s/z* 20; Barthes's emphasis). Or, as Jean-Paul Sartre puts it, "For the reader, all is to do and all is already done" (32). A text is intelligible to us because it reminds us of something already known, and so we, too, are in some sense "already ... a plurality of other texts ... which are infinite or, more precisely, lost (whose origin is lost)" (*s/z* 10). We bring to the text materials that are reworked and reflected back to us; as John Buchan makes explicit in *The Thirty-Nine Steps*, "The whole story was in the notes – with gaps ... which he [Scudder] would have filled up from his memory" (45). In short, reading is an "uncanny" experience, in Freud's sense of the term, in that the seemingly unfamiliar is made familiar to us by the play of codes.

Given this conception of the text, the experience of reading one work is clearly dependent on previous experience with other texts; familiarity with one detective story leads the reader to have certain expectations of another detective story. Yet, while the text is before us, our reading of it must be indeterminate, since our understanding of what we read is continually altered as we read; as Sartre writes,

"Reading is composed of a host of hypotheses, of dreams followed by awakenings, of hopes and deceptions" (28). For instance, Conan Doyle's story "The Norwood Builder" initially keeps with the conventions of detective fiction by presenting at its outset, through a quoted newspaper account (literally a text), the facts concerning the murder of Jonas Oldacre. As readers familiar with the genre, we expect a murder either before or soon after the beginning of a detective story, and so we readily accept the report of Oldacre's death. Despite McFarlane's protestations of innocence, we have no reason to suspect the report's truth, though we may and probably do believe in McFarlane's innocence. The central question of the classical detective story is raised: whodunit? But, when it is revealed at the end of the story that Oldacre is not dead and that no murder of any kind has been committed, we are forced to reassess our interpretation of the earlier sequence, which had been read in error. In this way, "The Norwood Builder" exemplifies the sort of thing that goes on as we read any narrative: all narrative demands that we constantly reorient our perceptions of the text as we read. Each statement we encounter in a text arouses in us certain expectations of what is to come while also changing our perception of what has gone before (Iser 278). Reading is a process rooted in flux, as the text continually defies our attempts to fix its meaning while we are reading.

Barthes identifies the process of reading a text in light of one's previous experience of other texts as proaireticism, whose "only logic is that of the 'already-done' or 'already-read'" (s/z 19). Of the five codes he describes in s/z, the proairetic and the hermeneutic are the two that are particularly relevant to a discussion of detective fiction, since they are foregrounded by the genre.[14] The first of these, the proairetic code (or the empiric voice), discerns and locates actions in an irreversible metonymic sequence that is determined by our experience with both texts and the world (s/z 19). For instance, if one is to enter or leave a room, one must first open the door: the sequence cannot be reversed. Similarly, barring unusual circumstances, we do not expect a murder victim to reappear in a novel, and so when such an event seems to occur, as in "The Norwood Builder" or Greene's *The Third Man*, we are startled by the gap between what should have happened and what did happen.

The second of Barthes's relevant codes, the hermeneutic code (or voice of truth), "governs all intrigues modelled on the detective novel" (*Grain* 75). It controls the processes whereby the reader's desire is provoked and includes "all the units whose function it is to articulate in various ways a question, its response, and the variety of chance events which can either formulate the question or delay its answer; or even, constitute an enigma and lead to its solution" (*s/z* 17). Crucial in the hermeneutic code's operation is the ability "to maintain the enigma in the initial void of its answer" (75). That is, we expect and desire the solution to a problem, but for the narrative to continue this solution must be postponed or delayed. This space of postponement is the "dilatory area whose emblem might be named 'reticence' " (*s/z* 75) and which operated in Christie's *The Murder of Roger Ackroyd*. While the narrative moves towards its end, the resolution of the enigma, it also seeks to prevent this occurrence through a variety of "dilatory morphemes" (209) – thematization, proposal, formulation, promise of an answer, snare, equivocation, jamming, suspended answer, and disclosure – which simultaneously move the narrative forward and contribute to the discourse's reticence by retarding the process of resolution. The narrative's "reticence" (also indicated in the presence of such things as false clues or subplots) preserves the life of the discourse by refusing to allow the discourse to reveal all at once. "Reticence … ensure[s] the interests of reading, that is, its own survival" (*s/z* 141).[15]

In detective novels the hermeneutic code is highly developed because everything described or mentioned in the text has the status of a potential clue. On a mimetic level, something may or may not represent reality; that is, it may or may not participate in creating the "effect of the real." But, on a hermeneutic level, it is always either a clue or a false clue contributing to the solution of the enigma or else delaying the solution by diverting the attention of the detective and/or the reader. Two points follow from this conception of narrative as "occult," as revealing and concealing details, promising and deferring meaning. The first is that all narrative *suspends* meaning and so some sort of suspense is always felt by the reader; and the second is that all narrative involves deception. In a detective novel we see how narrative is used by the criminal to deceive the detective while the novel itself presents the reader with false clues aimed at preventing his or her discovery of the origin of the text's central mystery; yet, structurally, the detective novel is no different from any other narrative because narrative always withholds and gives information.[16]

Digressive or delaying components become central in the best examples of detective fiction because, like all novels we admire and take pleasure from, they are enjoyed for reasons other than the desire to find out "what will have happened." In this respect, "the most effective or, at the least, the most challenging texts may be those that are most delayed" (Brooks 102). From the moment of the crime a tension is present in the text which the narrative strives to eliminate through the detective, whose investigation figures the reader's desire for the story's conclusion. The obstacles the investigator encounters delay the narrative and are attempts by the discourse to preserve its existence through narrative "reticence." One effect of this process is to increase narrative suspense, which keeps the narrative sequence open for the reader but also threatens the reader with an incomplete sequence and so produces both anxiety and pleasure.

Suspense, which Barthes sees as fulfilling "the very idea of language" ("Introduction" 130), occurs at all levels of narrative discourse from the postponement of the narrative's end to the hesitation between alternative meanings in a single word (as is represented in *A Study in Scarlet* [1887] by the two meanings suggested for "RACHE" – the police read it as a partial inscription of the name "Rachel" [Doyle 31] while Holmes reads it as the German word for "revenge" [32]). A skilled author can load even the simplest of narrative descriptions with elements aimed at preserving the status of the enigma and so of narrative suspense. For instance, in Greene's *The Ministry of Fear* the enigmas Arthur Rowe and the reader encounter are clearly marked either with explicitly presented questions ("Who had given her [Mrs Bellairs] instructions? … why had she chosen him to win the cake?" [17]) or else with diction that raises questions in the reader's mind. Thus, Poole is frequently referred to as "the stranger" in his first meeting with Rowe (22–8). Similarly, pronouns such as "we" and "they" are used freely without mention of specific antecedents (25, 27, 99) to draw an adversarial relationship in the narrative while at the same time contributing to the atmosphere of uncertainty that pervades the book and conceals from Rowe and the reader the enemy's identity.

Also augmenting the narrative's suspense is a strategy of delay based on the text's episodic practice of placing key information at the end of clearly marked structural units such as sections, chapters, or books. The surprise of the new information raises new enigmas which are usually partially answered within the next few pages, although the answers provided raise only further enigmas. This is particularly evident at the end of book 1, where we encounter ellipses after reading that Rowe "opened the lid of the suitcase." The next chapter begins with Richard Digby, and so what happens in the intervening time remains suspended (105). This technique is also used at many other structural junctures in the narrative. For example, at the end of section 1, chapter 2, in book 1, Rennit, a private detective, and the reader learn that Rowe is a murderer (35). In the next section, Rowe recalls parts of his trial and explains that he killed his wife in what the papers said was an act of mercy (37); yet, while the initial enigmas presented at the end of the chapter's first section are answered – whom did Rowe kill? why did he do it? – a new one takes their place: "'Mercy for her or mercy to me. They didn't say. And I don't know myself'" (37). This problem resonates throughout the narrative and is never clearly resolved for the reader or for Rowe. Even when twenty years have been erased from his memory, the knowledge of his wife's death, though repressed by the "Freudian censor" (110), remains an "enemy" memory (196). The frequent and obvious presentation of enigma and suspense in *The Ministry of Fear*, particularly when the enigmas are posed as questions by the text, highlights the operations of the hermeneutic code while creating the dilatory space wherein the narrative can perpetuate itself.

DETECTIVE FICTION AND REPETITION

Returning to Todorov's analysis of the classical detective story, we find that the hidden story of the crime is "the story of an absence: its most accurate characteristic is that it cannot be immediately present in the book" (46). This "absence" is the narrative's repressed content that is both revealed and concealed by the clues which are left for the reader and, within the story of the investigation, the detective to discern. The manner by which this repressed content is brought to light in the detective story is analogous to similar processes that are always at work in the construction of any narrative or of its interpretation, and crucial to these processes is the role of repetition.

Peter Brooks, taking Doyle's "The Musgrave Ritual" as his example, finds that "the work of detection in this story makes particularly clear a condition of all classic detective fiction, that the detective repeat, go over again, the ground that has been covered by his predecessor the criminal" (24). In "The Musgrave Ritual" both Brunton and Holmes interpret a particular text, the Musgrave family's rite of passage, as coded instructions meant to guide an initiate to a secret location where crown jewels are hidden. Brunton, seeking to find these jewels, traces the route described in the ritual. Holmes, seeking to solve the mystery, retraces this route in the same manner as Brunton by plotting the points of the ritual in turn. This basic activity of reinscribing an already existing text suggests that the detective story itself is a story of repetition, of reading a text and then writing another. The detective, in fact, rewrites the murderer's story to produce a new account that is also an interpretation of the first account.

Structurally, Todorov tells us, this process figures, in the terms of the Russian Formalists, the reworking of the *fabula* (story) by the *sjuzhet* (discourse), which is also an interpretation of the *fabula* (*Poetics* 45). The criminal's hidden story stands as the *fabula* of the text and the detective's inquiry stands as its *sjuzhet* while the interaction of these two structures gives rise to the plot of the narrative (*Poetics* 45; Brooks 25). Since the detective story makes the reworking of a *fabula* by a *sjuzhet* explicit, it presents us with a paradigm for all narrative texts because every narrative claims to be a repetition of what has already happened; narrative is always retrospective (Brooks 25).[17] In the detective story, this necessary retrospectivity is embodied by characters, such as Watson or Hastings, who record experiences after they have occurred and so know the story's ending even before they begin to write; yet the same can be said of any narrator and any narrative, for, as Frank Kermode argues, its beginning always implies its end (*Sense* 148). And this means that "all narrative posits, if not a Sovereign Judge, at least a Sherlock Holmes capable of going back over the ground, and thereby realizing the meaning of the cipher left by a life. Narrative thus seems ever to imagine in advance the act of its transmission, the moment of reading and understanding that ... always comes after the writing, in a posthumous moment" (Brooks 34). The confounding of beginnings and endings is an integral part of the detective story's structure, since the initial crime, standing at the beginning of the story as the impetus for the narrative (an act of "deviance" that upsets a quiescent state), also stands at the end of the story; its disclosure is the objective of both the detective and the narrative (Porter 29). The discourse gradually releases the repressed story of the crime into the main story of the investigation so as to make it visible to the reader, and, when the repressed content of the tale is fully brought to light, the discourse concludes. For instance, in "Murder for the Wrong Reason," the process that began with Arthur Callum's figurative death and Mason's birth ends with the repetition of the act of murder that is Collinson's death. This death signals the figurative death of Mason both as an adopted persona and as a representative of law, and the corresponding resurrection of Callum in Mason's confession of his true identity as Callum. (The engraving of Lazarus rising from the dead that decorates Callum's apartment foreshadows this return.) The disruption that occasioned the narrative – Collinson's murder – is therefore quieted by Mason's death in both the figurative and, we are to assume, the literal sense.

The principle that the story of the inquiry consists of the *sjuzhet* while the story of the crime consists of the *fabula* of any narrative structure implies a hierarchy based on priority in the detective story; that is, first there occurs the crime and then its detection. This pattern of reinscription, however, is problematic. The detective story, like all narrative, expresses a kind of double logic: the crime precedes its detection and *fabula* precedes *sjuzhet* (because the *sjuzhet* is a retelling of the *fabula*), but, at the same time, the hidden story of the crime is revealed only because of the story of detection (the *sjuzhet* supplies us with our only indication of the *fabula*). According to this latter view, the story of the detection precedes the story of the crime – the priority of *fabula* to *sjuzhet* is inverted (Culler, "Story and Discourse" 183, 186). The story of the detection and the story of the crime are, as in Hillis Miller's analogy of Ariadne's thread tracing the labyrinth, "each the origin of which the other is a copy, or the copy which makes the other, already there, an origin" ("Ariadne's Thread" 67–8). Or, as with the thread and the labyrinth, the one is the other and, at the same time, a repetition of the other (70).

This problematic is often thematically figured in detective fiction in the relationship between the detective and the criminal. Holmes expresses open admiration for his arch-foe, Moriarty (Doyle 471), and occasionally, as in "The Abbey Grange" or "Charles Augustus Milverton," is himself outside the law.[18] More obviously, in both Greene's thrillers and hard-boiled detective fiction, figures such as Raven or the Continental Op and Sam Spade are frequently presented as being little better than those they pursue.[19] Dupin, too, has his double in the Minister D___ of Poe's "The Purloined Letter," but here the confounding of the two stories of crime and its detection is also manifested in the doubleness of the story's structure. The first half of "The Purloined Letter" consists of the Prefect G___ of the Sûreté telling Dupin and his companion-narrator how an important and somewhat compromising letter was stolen from the Queen while she stood helplessly by. In the story's second half, Dupin tells the prefect and the narrator how the letter was retrieved by a duplication of the original crime.[20] In this case, the mystery's solution depends upon a re-enactment or repetition of the crime or, in the Aristolian terms Porter uses, of the scene of suffering, which precedes the actual recognition scene wherein the detective presents his solution (Porter 38). Not only does "The Purloined Letter" bear out this pattern of re-enactment, but so do *The Moonstone* (1868), *The Hound of the Baskervilles* (1902), and *The Big Sleep* (1939). In each, the act of detection repeats the criminal act and so the story of detection is also the story of the crime. The detective's "murder" of the criminal, whether in the figurative or in the literal sense, is a final repetition that purges the community and the narrative of deviant forces to establish a new equilibrium signalled by the silence of the discourse.

In the thriller, where the stories of crime and detection are intertwined, the relationship of the original to the repetition is more complex. If we look at *Brighton Rock*, for instance, Ida Arnold explicitly takes as the starting-point of her pursuit of Pinkie Brown the place from which Hale disappeared (81) and then works to reconstruct the crime, an approach that, as even Pinkie realizes (86), is the standard investigative process. In a general sense, she traces over the previously laid path of Pinkie and his gang – an activity that is consistent with the structural dynamics of the classical detective-story plot – and so she figures the actions of the *sjuzhet* (the discourse) upon the material of the *fabula* (the story). As well, her retracing represents the act of writing that produces narrative as a *re*writing of a prior narrative which is repressed in the later narrative – the narrative of the investigation – but its presence is revealed in the clues, the tangible signs marking the return of a repressed content. In *Brighton Rock*, the two narratives of Ida and Pinkie, of investigation and crime (or of detective story and tragedy in R.W.B. Lewis's formulation), are each the repressed content of the other: each reveals its presence in intermittent clues that surface into the mainstream of the other narrative. Whichever way we choose to regard *Brighton Rock* depends on our point of view; as Todorov observes, the twin concepts of *fabula* and *sjuzhet* are essentially two different ways of looking at the same thing (46).

What happens in the novel is that Ida's pursuit of Pinkie intensifies his efforts to avoid capture. As she proceeds in her reading of events she uncovers indications of Pinkie's story marked in the narrative's details, which in more orthodox detective fiction are formalized as clues: things such as Hale's dislike of Bass beer (a point revealed early in the novel [10] and given importance later on) and his confession that he was "going to die" (18) arouse Ida's "instincts" so that she senses that "there [is] something odd" about his death (31). Details that come out after his death, such as the fact that he used a false name (31), had bruises on his arms (79), and left a restaurant without eating despite telling Ida he was hungry (33), confirm her suspicions while, at the same time, revealing details of Pinkie's story.

As the novel continues, it becomes clear that Ida's investigation of Hale's death forces Pinkie's actions. Since the official investigators agree that Hale died of natural causes, they have closed the case (78–80) and so it is only Ida whom Pinkie has to fear. Just as it is the reader who imaginatively realizes the narrative content of the text, so does Ida's search originate, explain, and validate all of Pinkie's actions from his courtship of Rose to his murder of Spicer to his attempt to arrange Rose's suicide. To be sure, Pinkie fears that the police may ask questions about the man who left the card at Snow's, but, as we realize, the police do not and will not reopen their inquiry. In their place, however, is Ida.

The story of the investigation determines the story of the crime; yet, conversely, it is Pinkie's story that gives rise to the detective narrative. The two lines of action in the novel are entangled in each other, with each standing as the origin of the other: Ida's investigation uncovers the contents of Pinkie's story, but the narrative that describes Pinkie's activities also becomes the means by which Ida's story is revealed to the reader. Indeed, the question of origin is complicated further by the fact that the disturbance that excites the narrative of *Brighton Rock* into being – the murder of Hale – is considered an act of revenge: the initial action in *Brighton Rock* is taken only in response to an earlier action – the murder of Kite – whose story, though sporadically erupting into Pinkie's story (63, 218–19), lies in another narrative[21]; as the text explicitly remarks, "The whole origin of the thing was lost" (217). As a model of narrative mechanics, then, *Brighton Rock* illustrates two things – the ability of narrative to perpetuate itself by inscribing within itself at least two separate narrative strands that generate and then feed on each other, and the reader's role in the construction of narrative.

Greene's handling of the detective story's structure demonstrates the indeterminate nature of the *fabula/sjuzhet* distinction. As *Brighton Rock* stands, the story of the detection is interrupted by the story of the criminal, which reveals details of the crime[22]; the two stories are presented in roughly alternating chapters occurring more or less along a shared time-line, although each persistently underlies the other. The reader gains knowledge of the circumstances of Hale's death from two sources, the chapters dealing with Ida and those dealing with Pinkie. As the novel continues, the two stories of the investigation and the crime become blurred as each begins to include the other. One illustration of how this works can be seen by looking at part 4, section 1 (99–120), where Pinkie and Spicer are at the racetrack. Although the story-line in the foreground tells of Pinkie's betrayal of Spicer to Colleoni's men, we receive glimpses of the other narrative line involving Ida. Spicer tells Pinkie about a woman who "backed Black Boy for a pony" (103). We then find out that Black Boy won the race, and again Spicer mentions the woman who now has won so much money (104); the narrative goes on to report that Pinkie "heard a laugh, a female laugh," which is attributed to the woman who won on Black Boy (104–5). The woman, of course, is Ida, who bets on a tip Hale gave her before he disappeared and, more important, wins the money she needs to enable her to continue her investigation.

Repetition is the means whereby the detective solves the mystery, but the detective's retracing of the criminal's preinscribed plot illustrates the narrative's own reliance on previously inscribed texts. Both the detective's solution and the narrative of that solution are created out of the "tissue of quotations" that is the "already-read" or "already-written" (figured in the detective novel as the criminal's narrative). Even the story of the crime that is exposed in the course of a detective story has other narratives behind it, and these in turn have other narratives behind them. For instance, in "Murder for the Wrong Reason," we find that the origin of the narrative of Mason's investigation lies in an earlier narrative that, though suppressed by the present narrative, emerges sporadically in briefly mentioned clues, such as those already listed, and returns in a fuller sense in the reverie or waking-dream of Mason. In this way, the story textually figures and demonstrates the paradigm of any narrative within a textual network. As a classical detective story it takes its place within the generic context established by the work of Poe and Doyle, among others. Their stories are precursors of Greene's story, and, though repressed by Greene's narrative in order that it may preserve its integrity as a unique text, they return in Greene's text to varying degrees. Hence, the situation of the locked room and references to the chimney and the drain-pipe as possible methods of escape recall Poe's "Murders in the Rue Morgue." Similarly, Doyle's texts surface in the narrative both overtly ("'Has the origin ever occurred to you, constable … of Sherlock Holmes's cleverness? It's simply that the author knows the answer and works backwards'" [132]) and covertly ("A long band of yellow light from a street lamp outside fell between them [Rachel Mann and Mason], and the band was constantly speckled and its appearance altered by the invisible gusts of rain which beat irregularly against the glass of the lamp" [127–8]). Such revelations not only indicate the textual network of which "Murder for the Wrong Reason" is a part but also point to the text's immediate precursors, although in an absolute sense the story's origins remain mysterious.

Similarly, in "The Musgrave Ritual," the recession into deeper levels of narrative is clearly marked, since the (re)construction of the story of Brunton's and Rachael Howell's disappearances exposes a deeper level of narrative that lies in English history. In uncovering one mystery, Holmes uncovers another, which he designates as the last meaning for the ritual beyond that of being a rite of passage in the Musgrave family. He discovers that the mystery opens onto the story of the Stuarts, who had hid their gold and jewels at the Musgrave estate, Hurlstone, and left the ritual as coded instructions for their recovery. And so, into the story of Holmes's investigation comes not only Brunton's story but also a larger story of regicide and usurpation which has other narratives behind it, narratives that constitute the whole of English history (Brooks 26). The story allegorizes the idea that the recovery of one narrative leads to the simultaneous recovery of further narratives through patterns of embedding that are infinitely regressive.

In this fashion the story also expands forward in time by imaging its retellings. Holmes's final explanation of the old coins, told to Reginald Musgrave, is not the last word on the case, since Holmes tells the story to Watson to explain how "a crumpled piece of paper, an old-fashioned brass key, a peg of wood with a ball of string attached to it, and three rusty old discs of metal ... are history" (387). These items are the clues to a mystery for both Watson, who asks Holmes to solve it for him, and the reader, who has Watson's narrative of Holmes's narrative as the solution before him or her. "The Musgrave Ritual," therefore, like other classical detective stories, locates the reader in a chain of narratives which both recedes into the past and continues endlessly into the future with each retelling and each interpretation.[23]

As with all narrative texts, the detective's final solution is a retelling, or a repetition, of an already existing text. Doyle seems to acknowledge this truth by telling us in *A Study in Scarlet* that Holmes's knowledge of "sensational literature" is immense (22). Holmes is familiar with Vidocq's memoirs, Poe's Dupin stories, and Gaboriau's stories of Lecoq, but he finds shortcomings in each.[24] (In this way, Doyle establishes a space for Holmes within an already defined genre.) Similarly, we are told not only that Holmes believes that "there is nothing new under the sun. It has all been done before" (29), but also that he urges both Gregson and Lestrade to read accounts of previous cases to help them solve the ones they are working on (29). For Holmes, as Doyle conceives him, the "already-read" is the ground out of which he develops and articulates his solution.

It is also apparent that the relationship between the criminal's interpretation of events and the detective's interpretation is one of interdependency and not one of substitution. In this respect, too, the detective novel is like any other novel in that narration and interpretation oscillate between and blur into each other (Kermode, *Art* 135).[25] The detective's narrative, his disclosure (exposure) of the murderer's actions, is both an interpretation and a retelling, with significant differences, of the murderer's narrative. Both tellings rely on each other for their existence and both contribute equally to the overall effect of the detective novel, wherein the reader takes pleasure in the ingenuity involved in the presentation of the enigma and the solution.[26] The detective's narrative is created out of the criminal's narrative; that is, it refers back to a prior interpretation of events which is analysed, elucidated, and then interpreted in turn. Conversely, the discourse of the criminal seeks to suppress evidence of guilt and so must already anticipate the detective's suspicions and, thus, his or her later account of events.

The two narratives, the criminal's explanation and the detective's explanation, offer different but complementary readings of the same set of events, of the same text. Indeed, the detective novel may be thought of as a dialogue, analogous to the detective's interrogation of witnesses (including the criminal), between two interpretations of the same text. Furthermore, since the detective is an inscribed figure for the reader, these interrogations also enact the dialogue between text and reader; that is, the reader's perception and interpretation of the text undergo continual change in response to the text. In a sense, neither party in these exchanges can have the last and definitive word because, as Barthes comments, "there is no 'primary,' 'natural,' 'national,' 'mother' critical language" (s/z 120). The meaning of a text can lie nowhere but in the totality of its readings, not in any single reading.

Yet this plurality of meaning does not diminish the solution's importance in a detective story. Since the hermeneutic code – the voice of truth – unavoidably delays the solution to an enigma, "expectation [or suspense] ... becomes the basic condition for truth" because "truth ... is what is *at the end* of expectation ... [The design of the hermeneutic narrative] implies a return to order, for expectation is a disorder" (s/z 76). The solution, then, is the fulfilment of the hermeneutic code while narrative, the dilatory space between the proposal and the resolution of the enigma, is conceived of as a "disorder." In this regard, all narrative becomes "a movement between two equilibriums which are similar but not identical" (*Fantastic* 163); and so, as Todorov suggests, narrative begins in an act of transgression, which disturbs an existing state of quiescence, and proceeds through plot to a new equilibrium. In the classical detective story, or in a thriller such as *The Thirty-Nine Steps*, the initial transgression is the murder which disrupts the existing social order and inspires the story of the investigation, which in turn aims to uncover the story of the crime so as to restore social order. Plot, therefore, is "a condition of deviance and abnormality" (Brooks 139); yet, as Brooks elaborates, "deviance is the very condition for life to be 'narratable': the state of normality is devoid of interest, energy, and the possibility for narration. In between a beginning prior to plot and an end beyond plot, the middle – the plotted text – has been in a state of *error*: wandering and misinterpretation" (139). The detective story is the figurative record of this "wandering" and "error," since it tells the story of the detective's pursuit both of the criminal and of the truth.

Traditionally, the end of a detective novel fulfils readers' expectations by having the detective unmask the criminal and then explain the process whereby the criminal's identity was discovered. In this way, the text's central enigma is solved and order is conferred on the seemingly contingent structure of the narrative – false clues are distinguished from actual clues and what had been hidden or suppressed is brought into the light. As with any narrative, this sort of ordering can be done only from the perspective of the end,[27] which in the detective novel is the site of convergence between the final term of the proairetic code (the solution) and the final term of the hermeneutic code (disclosure or decipherment) (Porter 86), and between the story of the crime and the story of the investigation (the logico-temporal gap between the two is closed) (Porter 29). With disclosure comes the end of the criminal's "reticence," and so "the discourse can do nothing more than fall silent" (s/z 188) because the narrative has reached a second equilibrium, which is both the same as and different from the equilibrium that existed prior to the act of "deviance" that began the narrative. The social order is restored without the murderer (a cancer on the body politic) and without the victim (generally deserving of his fate and so no real loss to the society).

None the less, the classical detective story masks what William Stowe calls a "semiotic trap" ("Semiotics" 375). In *The Murder of Roger Ackroyd*, Poirot is right about how Ackroyd died. (Indeed, like many detectives in the classical detective story, he is never wrong.) His account of events stands at the end of the text as the true interpretation of the many texts he has read; and his explanation, presented in the novel's two penultimate chapters (aptly entitled "The Whole Truth" and "And Nothing But the Truth"), is the meaning, from the point of view of the novel's reader, of everything that has gone before in the narrative. As something similar occurs in most classical detective stories, they are frequently considered models of readerly texts (Porter 83), since their narratives come as close as possible to being entirely "singular" in their meaning and goals. Yet this aspect of the traditional detective story exposes a contradiction within the logical structure of the form, namely that detective fiction "insists ... on denying the strangeness it first evokes" (Porter 247).

At the end of the narrative, the detective, having deconstructed one readerly text, seems to erect another in its place and so a narrative that shows us how a readerly text breaks down because of its inherent qualities turns back to the readerly text in the concluding explanation by the detective. Not only does this explanation declare itself to be seamless and coherent, but the reader acquiesces to these claims of coherence because of a desire for closure that is stimulated by the workings of the hermeneutic code: the detective's remarks are given the status of truth.

SOLVING THE CASE

From its beginnings, detective fiction has promoted the myth of the necessary chain – of the readerly text, in fact – whereby the solution is discovered through a step-by-step logico-temporal reconstruction. As Sergeant Cuff's reprimand of Superintendent Seegrave in Wilkie Collins's *The Moonstone* aptly illustrates, any sign, no matter how insignificant, points towards an intelligible end: "'I made a private inquiry last week, Mr. Superintendent,' he [Cuff] said. 'At one end of the inquiry there was a murder and at the other end there was a spot of ink on a tablecloth that nobody could account for. In all my experience along the dirtiest ways of this dirty little world, I have never met with such a thing as a trifle yet ...'" (136). In the classical detective novel every incident finds its place in the detective's final explanation. Because that explanation is also governed by readerly qualities, however, it is no different in kind from the criminal's narrative (his or her alibi) that it replaces: one system of interpretation is seemingly substituted for another. It is possible to argue, then, that to privilege the detective's narrative and assign it the value of truth is to practise a self-deception; for, in the contest between the two narratives, "what applies to the first must apply to the second. The undoing of the first by the second also undoes the second. The second destroys itself in the act whereby it fragments the first" (Miller, *Fiction* 107). Writers of classical detective stories were not unaware of this problem, and individual texts, such as Poe's "The Mystery of Marie Roget" (1842), Doyle's "A Scandal in Bohemia," "The Missing Three-Quarter," or "The Dancing Men" (to name but three), and E.C. Bentley's *Trent's Last Case* (1913), which was intended as "an exposure of detective stories" (Symons, *Bloody* 88), easily demonstrate the weaknesses of the semiotic trap and undercut the authority of the detective's final explanation.

Equally problematic is the means by which the detective arrives at his or her conclusions. In brief, to recognize the necessary role of hypothesis in the detective's interpretation of events is to expose one of the great misconceptions that surrounds the method of detection in the classical detective story. Although Doyle called an early chapter in each of the first two Holmes books "The Science of Deduction," Holmes does not practise deduction; rather, his method combines induction and hypothesis. In "The Adventure of the Six Napoleons" Holmes terms his process of thinking "inductive reasoning" (594) while elsewhere he describes "the basis of [his] art" as a "mixture of imagination and reality" ("Thor Bridge" 1070). The same is true of Dupin, Poirot, and most other detectives of the classical school – each employs a synthetic form of inference based on a mixture of induction and hypothesis or theorizing, which support each other. But, however valuable the hypothetical inference is, it is a weaker method of reasoning than either deduction or induction because "it often inclines our judgment so slightly toward its conclusion that we cannot say that we believe the latter to be true; we only surmise that it may be so" (Pierce 130).[28] This mode of reasoning introduces an element of uncertainty into any conclusion (such as those of the classical detective): the hypothesis is a "fiction" (Pierce 240) used to assist in the production of another fiction.

We are confronted with a situation where the detective, in order to offer his or her final interpretation of events (a fiction amassed from diverse elements of other fictions), must construct an interim fiction (a hypothesis or theory) en route to his or her final interpretation. And more significantly, this interim fiction influences the contents of the fiction presented in the scene of disclosure, since it serves to direct the inquiry along lines that it has already prescribed.[29] The final statement of the mystery's solution is again a repetition in that it repeats the interim fiction with difference. In this respect, the final discoveries of the detective are, in fact, rediscoveries, since the interim fiction, the hypothesis, has anticipated these discoveries, although it has not expressed them in the form in which they are finally presented.[30]

The relationship between the interim fiction of the detective and his or her final disclosure is analogous to that of the "already-read" and a reader's understanding of a text. The detective, by a combination of imagination and past experience, which includes the "already-read," constructs his or her hypothesis to serve as a tentative plot wherein clues are given significance by reference to a concordant structure supplied by the hypothesis. In other words, the fiction of the hypothesis attempts to structure the repressed content of the detective novel (the story of the crime) along points (clues) that mark the return of the repressed within the open narrative of the inquiry. The clue in the detective story is made to stand as the signifier of a hidden signified that has to be uncovered. Yet the hypothesis or what Pierce also calls the abductive fiction, which is a necessary step in the recovery of this hidden signified, does not itself enclose the hidden signified. Instead, it posits a second mediating set of signifiers (the hypothetical fiction) whose immediate signifieds are the clues, which are in themselves signifiers of something else that is the hidden content. The clue, then, is given a double-sided nature in that it is both the signified to which the signifying units of the hypothesis point and the signifier of a deeper, repressed signified which is the story of the crime. Ultimately, the sought-after base of the signified is lost in layers of signification. The clue, like the Derridian trace, is constituted by the double force of legibility (it can be understood within the interim fiction) and illegibility (it stands as evidence of an enigma, of an absence that is the repressed narrative). Standing without origin or at least with an origin lost in the recesses of repetition, the trace, or in detective fiction the clue, becomes the space where writing exists.[31] The clue's presence determines the production of both the hypothesis and the final text of the detective.

The notion that the detective's final interpretation of events is authoritative crumbles in light of both the fictional nature of the hypothesis and post-structuralist conceptions of the text. Any version of events, whether the criminal's or the detective's, is but one text within a vast intertextual network. The detective's final interpretation does not usurp the position of previous interpretations (the criminal's or otherwise) but is one among many existing in the play of differences. The detective's version may be presented last but, as Cameron McCabe (Ernst Bornemann) realized in his novel *The Face on the Cutting-Room Floor* (1937), "the possibilities for alternative endings to *any* detective story are *infinite*" (McCabe 236; McCabe's emphasis).

The narrative processes of a detective novel compel its reader to determine how things fit together, but, like the detective within the text, the reader receives no assurance from the text that his or her ordering will be the correct one. Similarly, he or she cannot be completely sure that the detective's solution is the correct interpretation of events. Within the structure of the hermeneutic code, the final disclosure is the moment when the initial probable becomes the necessary (*s/z* 188) and so the text is hermeneutically sealed. While this finale meets the reader's expectations of closure, the hermeneutic is only one aspect of reading and activates other systems of reading. The central paradox is that for textual and ideological reasons we privilege the detective's solution, but we also recognize, as writers of detective fiction have recognized, that the detective's authority both as an instrument of law and order and as a reader is fragile.

IDEOLOGY AND DETECTIVE FICTION

The concept of truth in detective fiction is linked to an ideology.[32] The detective's version of events seems natural to us not only because it is possible for the astute reader to construct a version of events that can match the detective's version (implying that truth is tied to the possibility of consensus) but also because it conforms to and reasserts the dominant cultural and political ideology which we are enticed to share (Stowe, "Popular" 656). The criminal's narrative of events, on the other hand, differs from both the reader's and the detective's narratives, and this difference defines the criminal as unnatural because he or she has broken the law of the natural. Hence, his or her punishment (or more often his or her elimination) becomes an ideological necessity in order for the ideology to survive in the face of the criminal's revolt.

The detective story, like any text, springs from an ideological conception of the world. By conceiving of ideology as the whole matrix of ideas, values, assumptions, images, and feelings which define individual behaviour within society, we can see that the classical detective story reflects a conservative value system whose goals are to legitimatize the power of the ruling class and to preserve the established social order. There is, says Ross Macdonald, "an air of blithe satisfaction with a social system based on privilege" permeating the thought and language of Conan Doyle's work and of the classical detective story generally (181). The classical detective story adopts a strong liberal-humanist position that reassures readers of justice within society, of the personal nature of criminality and guilt, and of reason's ability to penetrate mystery. The assumption is that "we live in an intelligible and generally benevolent universe, that crime is the aberration, peace and tranquillity the norm, and that the proper occupation of man is the bringing of order to chaos" (P.D. James 639).

Tied to these social concerns are individualist epistemological assumptions that reinforce the detective's authority. The classical detective story, like the readerly text in general, declares that the world and texts are intelligible and governed by principles of sequence and causality. All signs can be read as references to other signs which, though they may refer to still other signs, reveal truth. As is the case with Collins's Sergeant Cuff, the smallest of clues allows the detective to know the truth and so his universe is explainable. Thus, in terms of reading, a text is thought to have one true meaning, which the correct interpretation will reveal.

This attitude was basic to nineteenth-century bourgeois story-telling, which relied on a consensual definition of truth: "Bourgeois aesthetics had traditionally presumed a passive audience ... of literate recipients sharing homogeneous backgrounds, values, and attitudes" (Berman 96). Given this presumption, the possibility of a text having multiple meanings was severely weakened and, in the detective story, ultimately overshadowed by belief in a univocal text.

Yet as the homogeneity of the reading public broke down over the course of the nineteenth century, the individualist belief in the possibility of discerning the true meaning of any text or event was thrown into question. The detective story, which developed concomitantly with the fragmentation of the reading public and the decline of hermeneutic authority, emerged to buttress individualist epistemological assumptions and preserve established authority. Holmes, as John Carey points out with a nod towards Auden, acted in the late nineteenth century as "a comforting version of the intellectual for mass-consumption – specifically for the middle- and lower-middle-class readers of the *Strand* magazine ... his function being to disperse the fears of overwhelming anonymity that the urban mass brought ... The appeal ... and reassurance [Holmes' skill] brings to readers are ... residually religious, akin to the singling out of the individual soul, redeemed from the mass, that Christianity promises" (8–9). Ideologically, in Doyle's stories and others of the period, the authority of the detective's final account reflected the established order's desire to preserve its position in a time of social and political change.

The classical detective story, then, expresses a bourgeois ideology that reduces all mysteries and complications to readily solvable problems. From this point of view, not only do the gentrified settings of the classical detective novel locate the narratives in a paradisal upper-class world inhabited by "obscurer peers," but the detective's success preserves the structure of this world and provides a middle-class readership with the illusion of the inevitability and permanence of bourgeois society (Mandel 29). None the less, the form also reflects the insecurities and fears of a social hierarchy that underwent tremendous strain in the forty years before the end of the First World War, a period in which the aristocracy and its values lost much of their political power. The development of an aesthetic approach to crime in the nineteenth century (expressed early on in Thomas De Quincey's essay "Murder Considered as One of the Fine Arts" [1827]), represented one of the ways the social order sought to protect itself from a true knowledge of society as a whole. "An increasingly serious moral and social problem [was made] into an entertaining pastime ... something potentially dangerous and disturbing was transformed into something completely under control" (Cawelti, *Adventure* 105).

In this fashion, most classical detective stories metaphorically render detection a form of play wherein the rules of sportsmanship and fairness prevail. When these rules are broken the detective is more disgusted by the breach of decorum than by the crime. Poirot is outraged to find a murder in Christie's *The ABC Murders* (1936) to be "not an English crime – not above-board – not *sporting*" (178) because the murderer is not playing by the rules. Frequently, too, the reader is encouraged either explicitly, as in the Ellery Queen novels, or implicitly to join in the game of detection. Not surprisingly, the detective novel makes games and game-playing important aspects of plot and structure. The plot of Christie's *Cards on the Table* (1936) depends on a game of bridge, which Poirot reconstructs with the aid of the game's score-sheets (conveniently reprinted at the front of the book so as to provide the reader with the same evidence that Poirot has), while in Bentley's *Trent's Last Case* Trent, the detective, and Murch, the police inspector, explicitly conceive of detection as a game they play against each other according to the "rules and limits" of "detective sportsmanship" (44). The contest between the detective and the official police is standard in the genre; it appears in Poe's work, wherein Dupin and the Prefect G___ of the Sûreté are seen to compete, and in Doyle's, where Holmes frequently delights in out-detecting Lestrade: again, crime is reduced and controlled, through the formulation of strict literary conventions, to a puzzle, a game with two players. Yet the very fact that the private detective should emerge to augment the powers of an inadequate and often incompetent police force suggests the failure of bourgeois structures and institutions to contain the disruptive forces threatening the social order. As well, the presentation of crime as an individual problem and not a systemic one masks the possibility that crime may have its roots within the established social order. Although there is often an implicit awareness in the classical detective story that crime is an ubiquitous phenomenon not confined to any single social class (the murderer is frequently a member of the privileged circle), the criminal is made the scapegoat for society's ills: the assumption remains that his or her discovery and elimination will solve the problem of crime.

Along with the scapegoating of the criminal comes the elevation of the detective. Seen against the background of an incompetent police force, the detective appears as a gifted genius capable of discovering what no one else has been able to discover. He or she is able to find order in the universe and make what had been opaque and mysterious, clear and cogent.[33] From his or her reading of the criminal's text, the detective constructs a master narrative that accounts for all discrepancies and all contradictions, and, in doing so, he or she becomes a figure of power and the emblem of bourgeois faith in the individual's ability to control and dominate his or her environment (Knight 43).

The reader's admiration for the power of the detective also reflects a strong desire for order, and so the detective becomes an "extralegal superman who is called in to accomplish by extraordinary measures what is impossible within the traditional organization of society" (Aydelotte 93). In William O. Aydelotte's view, the detective is, in fact, a dictator standing above the law who controls both the lives of the other characters and the world of the story through his or her superior powers of surveillance and intellect. The genre itself, in other words, embodies the structure of totalitarianism. Aydelotte goes on to speculate, almost in anticipation of Foucault, that "the detective story marks a kind of transition from liberal to authoritarian society: it arises in and reflects some of the values of the one, but is also a sign which may point toward the other" (94).[34]

The same might be said of the early thrillers of Buchan, Wallace, or Oppenheim, which explicitly portray liberal or socialist points of view as naïvely ignorant of the world of *realpolitik* and of the real dangers surrounding England (see, for example, Buchan 53). Marked by a strong sense of xenophobia ("It was not that they [Germans] looked different; they *were* different" [Buchan 135]), these texts urge the total surveillance of both foreign and domestic environments since danger, as *The Four Just Men* also demonstrates, can come from any where at any time. Implicitly, they argue for the transformation of the social milieu into a panoptic schema that can subdue disparate elements within the society and strengthen existing social forces (Foucault 208). The good citizen, like Richard Hannay, is both eternally vigilant and completely willing to place himself at risk in the service of the state, whose righteousness is without question.

The view that the classical detective story and the thriller reflect a totalitarian structure may be extreme, but it is not without validity. In the 1930s writers such as Greene, who wished to make popular writing something other than propaganda for the established order, found the structures of authority in the existing detective-story and thriller formats unacceptable. Indeed, in the interwar period, the classical detective's authority and the view of reading implicit in the classical detective story were challenged from at least two directions. The first challenge came from hard-boiled detective fiction, which emerged primarily in the United States in the 1920s, and the second came from a renewal of the British thriller undertaken by writers such as Eric Ambler and, of course, Graham Greene. These authors developed what Michael Denning describes as an "anti-fascist aesthetic" manifested by an ironic approach to the genre, a reversal of earlier codings of heroes and villains, and a realistic approach to violence which discredited the antiseptic treatment accorded it in earlier thrillers and detective novels (65–6).

In the post-war period writers could not assume shared "homogeneous backgrounds, values, and attitudes" within the reading public, and the experience of the First World War ensured that they could not accept a single authoritative reading of events. The result was the emergence of new, more sceptical theories of reading such as were exemplified in Dashiell Hammett's or Raymond Chandler's work, which stands in sharp contrast to the classical detective story typified by the stories of Poe, Doyle, and Christie among others.[35] Whereas the classical detective story presupposes the certainty of a correct reading, hard-boiled detective stories "are caught up in the uncertainties of the activity of interpretation itself, for which a final and valid result may be imagined but can never be confidently predicted" (Most 350). As Stephen Marcus explains in a discussion of Hammett's work, the problem of interpretation is never resolved in this kind of fiction. Hammett's detective

soon discovers ... that the "reality" that anyone involved will swear to is ... itself a construction, a fabrication, a fiction, a faked and alternate reality – and that it has been gotten together before he ever arrived on the scene. [His work] ... is to deconstruct or reconstruct out of it a true fiction, that is, an account of what "really" happened ... [But] the story, account, or chain of events that the [detective] winds up with as "reality" is no more plausible and no less ambiguous than the stories that he meets with at the outset and later. (201–2)

In Hammett's fiction the work of the detective is clearly a fiction-making activity, and the detective knows it. For example, in *The Dain Curse* (1929) the Continental Op concludes a lengthy interpretation of Joseph Haldorn's activities by affirming that none of it happened. Speaking to Fitzstephan (who is the murderer though the Op is not aware of this at the time), he says, "I hope you're not trying to keep all this nonsense straight in your mind. You know damned well all this didn't happen" (103). More to the point, Fitzstephan accuses the Op of never being satisfied "until you've got two buts and an if attached to everything" (63).

Raymond Chandler, who admired Hammett's work immensely, expressed a similar attitude towards interpretive authority in *The Big Sleep* when, at the end, the detective, Marlowe, does not turn in the murderer, Carmen Sternwood. Instead, Marlowe suggests that she be taken away, and he offers to hide both her role in Rusty Regan's death and her whereabouts from the police. Also at the end of the novel, Eddie Mars, a racketeer and the centre of a network of crime and municipal corruption, emerges unscathed.[36] Unlike the classical detective novel, *The Big Sleep* concludes by rejecting the fiction of a world so ordered that the elimination of a single individual (the murderer) is all that is needed to restore the social order. The discovery of the truth behind the crime does no good whatsoever, for guilt cannot be localized in a corrupt society. The novel ends not with the detective's triumph but with his realization of his own impotence.[37] Marlowe cannot bring Mars to justice and, instead, makes himself a party to the crime by lying to General Sternwood – an act of deception that protects the network of corruption Marlowe has uncovered. Neither Hammett nor Chandler is able to accept a simple and determinate reading of society and, by extension, of narrative in general. For them, any ending is only a temporary respite in a continuing struggle against forces of disruption and corruption that forever evade attempts to have patterns of order imposed upon them.

The second challenge to the classical detective story is exemplified by Greene's thrillers, which, as the next chapter shows in greater detail, share the hard-boiled writers' ethos and, beginning with *It's a Battlefield*, offer their own challenges to the conventional structures of authority and ideology that the classical detective story and the pre-war thriller embody. As in Hammett's and Chandler's fiction, there is no certainty in these books. As Calloway remarks in *The Third Man*, "There are too many 'ifs' in my style of writing, for it is my profession to balance possibilities, human possibilities, and the drive of destiny can never find a place in my files" (56).

4 Approaches to the Thriller in Greene's Early Work: *Rumour at Nightfall* and *It's a Battlefield*

In the years prior to the publication of *A Gun for Sale*, Greene's fiction shows him not only reconsidering the role of popular culture and popular literary forms but also experimenting with different sub-genres for the novel, though the basic pattern of pursuit that was to dominate all of his novels through to *The Ministry of Fear* remains by and large a constant. In *Rumour at Nightfall*, one of the two novels not subsequently reprinted, Greene explored, as he had in *The Man Within*, the historical romance. None the less, the story's plot of a journalist, Francis Chase (the surname is significant), searching for an outlaw known only as Caveda links it to the narrative structure of the classical detective story. Here, as in more conventional detective stories, including "Murder for the Wrong Reason," the investigator and the investigated are presented as doubles of each other. That is, Chase, who desires to interview the rebel leader Caveda for his London paper, is twice mistaken for Caveda by other characters in the book: once by his friend Michael Crane and once by an old woman who was Caveda's nurse-maid. (As well, Caveda's gloves are said to fit Chase perfectly.) This pattern is complicated, however, by the fact that Michael Crane, seen as a mirror image of Chase, is also linked to Caveda. Crane is shot by troops who mistake him for Caveda and, at the novel's end, Eulelia Monti – one-time lover of Caveda and now the betrothed of Crane – drops Caveda's picture on the face of the dead Crane so that Caveda's face is set upon Crane's body. To compound the doubling even further Caveda, the enigmatic leader whom everyone seeks, never appears as a character: he is entirely absent from the narrative. Even descriptions of him are given in the most general of terms. He is said to be good looking, well dressed, charming, and brave, and to have large hands and small feet. In this respect, *Rumour at Nightfall*, like the classical detective story, has at its core an absence around which the other characters can only circle. Furthermore, the characters seek to fill this central void by telling stories about Caveda and by guessing at his motives. In this sense, the novel is a narrative that builds itself around other narratives, none of which can be privileged or authenticated as true. That narrative construction mirrors itself in the character's ponderous speeches, which never seem to reveal the kernels of their meaning. Here, too, there seems a central absence which can be filled only with language but never with the heart of the matter, as it were.

Chase's search for Caveda becomes a search for meaning, since it is Caveda to whom all the novel's characters respond; everyone's actions are aimed at discovering or fulfilling the plans of Caveda. (Even Crane and Monti, who plan to marry each other, must deal with the threat of Caveda.) Thus, Caveda is the signifying value that determines all else in the novel; yet, insofar as he is absent, this determining value is shown to be illusory, which is to say fictional. As a reader, however, Chase does not take this view.

In terms of the structure of detective fiction derived from the classical detective story, *Rumour at Nightfall* differs from the paradigm described in the previous chapter by not making the absent narrative (of Caveda) a presence in the primary narrative of the investigation. The reason for this is the nature of the investigator himself. Chase, though he is seeking Caveda, does not attempt to read Caveda's story in his investigation. Instead, he is looking for Caveda so that Caveda can tell him the story. For Chase, the various clues he comes across, such as Monti's picture, the letter, or the gloves (all found in a captured mail-bag), do not signify the presence of a hidden narrative; rather, they point to a centre, Caveda, that will provide an authoritative explanation for all the questions posed by the narrative. The picture of Monti is illustrative: as a visual representation of a real person it points to that person. That is, the story behind the picture of Eulelia Monti is Eulelia Monti herself; no further interpretation can be admitted despite the fact that Monti, too, occupies an interim position beyond a centre: Chase believes that finding the woman in the picture is the way to finding Caveda. He does not read these clues (the picture, the gloves, or the letter), as Holmes would, for knowledge of Caveda because, unlike the sleuth of detective fiction, Chase is not attuned to the possibility of there being more than one reading of things. He sees Caveda as the author of a univocal text and is indifferent to the indications of plurality in Caveda's story that he comes across (for example, the idea that Caveda is a double of either Crane or himself, or the suggestive fact that the names Crane, Caveda, and Chase all share the same initial[1]). He does not seek the hidden story of Caveda; instead, he seeks the story Caveda would tell with his own lips. As a reader, Chase is naïvely credulous in assuming a single authentic story behind the stories that people tell of Caveda. Yet, insofar as Caveda never appears, *Rumour at Nightfall* denies Chase's theory of reading because no authentic story emerges; only the fictions about Caveda remain.

Chase's limitations as a reader are one of the things that separate *Rumour at Nightfall* from more orthodox forms of detective fiction. Because Caveda does not appear, there is nothing in *Rumour at Nightfall* that can take the place of the detective story's concluding explanation, which brings the absent narrative of the crime fully into the tale of the investigation. To be sure, as we have noted, this final explanation need not be correct or authoritative: detective fiction also opens onto the prospect of infinitely recessive or continuing narrative. But in *Rumour at Nightfall* the whole question of Caveda, while remaining enigmatic, drops away from the narrative as Chase no longer seems concerned with it. We are told that the "town is Caveda's" (298), but at the novel's end it is the dead Crane who will be the absent presence that unites Chase and Monti. Their subsequent tale will be dedicated to keeping alive the memory of their dead friend. In this sense, Crane replaces Caveda – a movement already signalled by the presentation of Crane as Caveda's double. This replacement might allow one to argue that the narrative's central absence does emerge figuratively as a presence in the primary narrative (the story of Chase's investigation); yet, insofar as Caveda is still assumed to exist (his forces control the town), the enigma surrounding him persists at the narrative's edge. Although Chase gives up his investigation, nothing discourages him from his particular view of reading, despite the novel's denial of it.

Certainly, *Rumour at Nightfall* touches on aspects of reading and of narrative that are the province of detective fiction, but as the novel develops these ideas there is a corresponding measure of confusion – particularly in the triangle of Chase, Crane, and Caveda – that suggests Greene is not really at home here. Some of this confusion is no doubt due to the fact that Chase is not meant to be a detective in the sense that Holmes, Poirot, or Marlowe is (and so we should not expect more than we can of Chase), but some is also Greene's fault. Indeed, Greene said *Rumour at Nightfall* represented the debilitating influence of Conrad upon him at its worst, for the Conrad of *The*

Arrow of Gold, Greene claimed, had fallen under the influence of the later James (*SL* 111). In the ponderous speeches of its characters and in the absence of the crucial figure who determines the narrative's direction, *Rumour at Nightfall* resembles a text like James's *The Ambassadors*, where Mrs Newsome remains a controlling absence. Equally of concern is that *Rumour at Nightfall* presents a view of narrative and of language which is more amenable to the modernist writers of the late 1910s and early 1920s than to the realists of the 1930s. For Caveda's absence implies that fiction need not, indeed cannot, tie itself to the real world. In this view, fictions exist only to propagate more fictions. While this argument may have some validity as a reading of literary history, it was not, as Greene came to realize, a suitable model for dealing with the socio-political realities of the thirties, which demanded that one see beneath the surface of political rhetoric to the underlying problems of ideology.

That Greene sees Chase's reading as inadequate is demonstrated not only by the structure of *Rumour at Nightfall* but also by statements made in *Stamboul Train*. At one point in the journey described in that novel, about mid-way through the book, Czinner seeks to confess his failings to the Reverend Opie. Opie then begins a discussion of confession that links the religious process to that of psychoanalysis.[2] While he is speaking, Savory interrupts with a literary interpretation of the subject and suggests that as an author he makes a confession to the public: " 'In a way surely *I* am the penitent. In so far as the novel is founded on the author's experience, the novelist is making a confession to the public. This puts the public in the position of the priest and the analyst' " (119). Savory's view is similar to Chase's in that Savory assumes the direct communication of experience through representational language. That is, a text clearly and authentically states its author's intention. Chase, of course, makes the same assumption in seeking to learn Caveda's story only from Caveda.

In *Stamboul Train* this view is challenged in two ways. The first is Opie's reply to Savory, which takes Freudian dream analysis as its paradigm for reading, while the second is allegorized in the novel itself. Opie responds to Savory: "'But your novel is a confession only in so far as a dream is a confession. The Freudian censor intervenes. The Freudian censor,' he had to repeat in a louder voice as the train passed under a bridge" (119). Opie suggests that the content of the confession, of the novel, is encoded in a series of images or symbols which demand they be read for something other than what they appear to be. That is, the text is assumed to have both a manifest and a latent content. In this way, meaning is distanced, filtered through symbols of which the most obvious for the text's reader are the words themselves.

The presumption of a latent content behind manifest appearances, a suitable one given Opie's position as a clergyman, undermines the authority of those appearances as transparent signifiers. Consequently, any system of representation is called into question because the latent content of a particular symbol may, itself, have its own latent content so that meaning becomes deferred since the manifest/latent paradigm can be brought to bear at any stage of the process. For Opie, this process is not infinitely recessive, since faith in a transcendent meaning or value (God) halts the division of meaning into manifest and latent senses. For the novel, however, as Gabriel Josipovici points out, the failure of language to be transparent and the deferral of meaning are allegorized through Czinner's desire to confess. Czinner comes to Opie to confess but instead of doing so he becomes involved in a discussion about confession. The actual confession does not take place. Thus, the attempt to express "the heart of the matter" through language finds itself stifled in language (Josipovici 122–3).[3]

The paradox of language and of writing that Josipovici sees reflected in *Stamboul Train* and elsewhere in Greene's work points to a central problem for the thirties' realist writers, who felt that they had to reflect the visible world's socio-political realities in their work. In that decade, the distinction between manifest and latent contents (to keep momentarily with these terms) of an image or text continued to be respected, but a bedrock of truth was supposed to lie beneath the surface at some point. (Documentaries, reportage, Mass Observation, and the recording of collective experience were some of the strategies by which this truth could be presented.) The consequences of this understanding for Greene's fiction, particularly as he uses the paradigm of the detective story to investigate reading, are numerous, but one is that Greene's investigators do achieve some limited success. In *A Gun for Sale*, for instance, Raven does track and kill Davis and his employer, Sir Marcus, before the police, who are tracking Raven, kill him. Similarly, Ida Arnold in *Brighton Rock* forces Pinkie's death; D. in *The Confidential Agent* prevents coal from being sold to L.; Rowe in *The Ministry of Fear* corners Hilfe; and Martins in *The Third Man* kills Lime. This development in Greene's fiction, in contrast to Chase's failure to find or to continue to pursue Caveda, suggests that there is a reality – a univocal meaning – behind the clues that the investigator reads. The novels, then, assume the existence of the real world. Still, Greene's investigators, unlike the detectives of the classical detective story, achieve their ends almost in spite of their methods. In Greene's work, a text's authoritative, univocal reading cannot be determined given the overwhelming complexity of society, the world, and language. (Hence the emphasis on "the ... appalling ... strangeness of the mercy of God" [BR 246] in *Brighton Rock* and *The Heart of the Matter*.) Rationality or intellect, the traditional power of the classical detective that leads to the correct reading of events, is not enough for Greene's investigators and is frequently undermined by the efficacy of irrational practices (for example, extrasensory impressions lead Raven to rescue Anne from her entombment in the chimney, and Ida uses a ouija board) or coincidence (D., after failing first in his mission to buy coal and then in his attempt to persuade the miners not to go back to work, is surprised to learn that L. has been refused the coal both of them sought). Greene's novels present reading and interpretation as problematic activities, but undeniable connections between the world of the novels and the anterior world of the reader allow the reader to affirm the truth of Greene's presentation despite the complexities, ambiguities, and mysteries that surround his endings. Ultimately, Greene's texts show reading and interpretation to be always indeterminate, and one of the ways they do this is to undermine conventional reading strategies by challenging the traditional, largely conservative, ideology both of the detective story and of the pre-First World War thrillers, such as those by Buchan or Wallace. In this respect, *It's a Battlefield*, considered one of Greene's best novels in the thirties,[4] reflects an uncertainty about the interpretive project that recalls the sensibility of the hard-boiled writers.

That the novel was at least partially conceived as a response to the ethos of the detective story is surely made clear in Greene's statements about the book's conception. In *Ways of Escape*, he records "a piece of rough verse" written in his diary on 21 November 1932:[5]

This the analysis of blood-stain –
　'on woollen beret of a common make';
the experts complain
　that the fingers left no mark

On the park chair
　or the young breast;
microscopic stare
　at uncertain past,

Grass inspected, note-book entry,
　'torn bodice and lace';
Over the body the solitary sentry
　of her certain peace. (27)

Similarly, in *A Sort of Life* Greene quotes from his diary (19 August 1932) a description of the initial idea for *It's a Battlefield*: "A large inclusive picture of a city, the connecting link the conviction of a man for the murder of a policeman. Is it politic to hang him? And the detectives go out through the city listening ... " (152–3). Both of these entries (and a number of others outlining dreams that Greene had in late 1932 and early 1933, mentioned in Sherry's biography [457–8][6]) explicitly link *It's a Battlefield* with the detective novel and, particularly, with the idea of detection as surveillance, which, following the thought of Foucault, acts in the novel as an expression of political power and as a metaphor for both reading and narrative itself.

Greene described *It's a Battlefield* as "a panoramic novel of London" (Sherry 456) that traces the actions of a number of characters throughout the city. The narrator's gaze plays over these characters – none of whom singly dominates the plot in the role of a protagonist. Instead, the city itself comes to dominate the narrative, and within its bounds class differences are sharply contrasted as the narrative moves between the world of the upper classes and the world of the lower classes. The first is characterized by Caroline Bury's literary salon, Surrogate's bourgeois bedroom, and the Berkeley hotel where Beale's private secretary meets with the Assistant Commissioner; and the second is typified by the basement flat Milly and Kay share, the match factory where Kay works, and the prison where Jim Drover awaits his execution. Between these two worlds lies the battlefield of London.

The emphasis *It's a Battlefield* places on the city itself, while displaying the fascination with the urban landscape that is widely reflected in the literature of the modern period, also recalls comments by G.K. Chesterton, who saw the detective story as unique in expressing "some sense of the poetry of modern [which is to say, urban] life" ("Defence of Detective Stories" 158). For Chesterton, author of detective stories featuring Father Brown and of the thriller *The Man Who Was Thursday*, the detective story offers the "realization of the poetry of London" because for the detective the city, indeed the world, is a mysterious, even occult, text that demands interpretation:

there is no stone in the street and no brick in the wall that is not actually a deliberate symbol – a message from some man, as much as if it were a telegram or a post card. The narrowest street possesses, in every crook and twist of its intention, the soul of the man who built it, perhaps long in his grave. Every brick has as human a hieroglyph as if it were a graven brick of Babylon; every slate on the roof is as educational a document as if it were a slate covered with addition and subtraction sums. (159)

Such a vision of the world is certainly that of Sherlock Holmes, whose "Book of Life" asserts that "by a man's finger-nails, by his coat-sleeve, by his boots, by his trouser knees ... [his] calling is plainly revealed" (Doyle 23); and, though doubts about the classical detective's ability to read these signs correctly appear in later detective fiction, this vision of the world as text remains in Greene's thrillers and in most detective fiction.

Chesterton also goes on to remark that detective fiction "tends to remind us that we live in an armed camp, making war with a chaotic world, and that the criminals, the children of chaos, are nothing but traitors within our gates" (161). This conception of the detective story translates itself into the traditional thriller's emphasis on a clear division between opposing forces, between an "us" and a "them," as Auden puts it ("Vicarage" 147). *It's a Battlefield* highlights both of the qualities Chesterton describes: the second through the Assistant Commissioner's conception of the city as a battlefield, and the first through a vision, derived from Greene's precursor texts, Conrad's *The Secret Agent*, and, to a lesser extent, the "Wandering Rocks" section of Joyce's *Ulysses*,[7] of the city as a textual field wherein language circulates.

The sense of the city as text is partly conveyed through the repeated mentioning of street names, particularly as the paths of characters are traced and retraced. Not only does this naming lend a geographic realism to the book's setting, but it also transforms the city's streets into a metaphor for a restrictive and governing social structure since the city and the society are perceived as an interlocking web that is linked to the circles of Dante's hell (22–3). In one sense, the cartography of London is laid over the novel as a container for the narrative, but in another the network of streets becomes the concrete and asphalt image of the invisible "wires" of influence (64) that govern the lives of the book's characters and bind separate and seemingly unrelated elements in the novel's plot. Compatible with this theme is the title's implication, supported by the epigraph from Kinglake's *The Invasion of the Crimea*, of individual and seemingly unrelated battles taking place under the direction of remote and invisible high-ranking commanders whose orders travel along a chain of command.

The city's role as a site where language circulates is also confirmed in the novel by the frequent inclusion of newspaper headlines (some of which deal with real political events at the time of the book's composition), by the repeated allusions to the "Sale. Premises damaged by fire" sign (55, 61, 155), and, perhaps more important, by the recurring mention of "the pram on top of the taxi" (10, 16, 60, 113, 155, 193), a phrase first overheard by the Assistant Commissioner while with the private secretary. Each of these repetitions suggests the circulation of language within the text and functions, like the city itself, as a unifying force in the novel. For example, since the "pram on a taxi" recurs in the thoughts of Conrad Drover (Jim's brother) and the assistant commissioner, the phrase links the two characters. Yet, at the same time, the phrase itself is a fragment of another narrative, which is never told in *It's a Battlefield*. What happens is that a second suppressed narrative intrudes into the discourse of the primary narrative though, unlike the criminal's story in the more conventional detective story, the pram-and-taxi story remains enigmatic. The puzzlingly surreal quality of the image suggests the chaos of the modern city, but, more significantly, it demands interpretation from those who encounter the fragment. For the Assistant Commissioner it is nothing more than a bizarre joke emblematic of the chaos he guards against; but, for Drover, it becomes representative of the mocking provocation of an establishment that is tied to a particular concept of the rule of law and justice (60, 193). Ultimately, the "pram on the taxi" is a narrative fragment, like the stories alluded to by the fire-sale sign or the recurring mention of the Streatham murder case, whose repetition allegorizes the circulation of texts within a textual field wherein individual texts intersect, run parallel, and repeat each other. (Conder, the newspaper man, is perhaps dimly aware of this textual property: "He gave the impression that all human stories were often repeated and that it was his unfortunate fate to listen to every repetition" [103].) And so the city's street-grid represents the linguistic field in which texts are found, that is to say, detected. Similarly, the "battlefield" of the title identifies this space as a site of struggle where a number of narratives, roughly corresponding to the number of characters but also including things such as the story of the pram on the taxi, compete for dominance both within the novel and within interpretations of the novel. In the text, no one narrative emerges as central and so the conflict of narratives continues throughout.

All this is well illustrated by Surrogate's telling of the story of Jim Drover to Caroline Bury: "He told her all he knew, humbly, a little grudgingly, watching the wheels of a fine intellect beginning to turn. He was jealous. Beneath Drover's story, buried only just beneath the succeeding words, "policeman – wife – Hyde Park – appeal," buried so shallowly that between the phrases scraps of old bones showed plain ("It reminds me ... by the way ... you remember"), lay his own tale, the first example he knew of Caroline Bury's passion to help" (88). Here, two narratives struggle for dominance in Surrogate's report, with Surrogate's own story about himself penetrating his telling of Drover's story. The passage illustrates a general quality of narrative in that any narrative has other narratives behind it and within it and so is intertextually related to them. Similarly, any narrative is in some ways a repetition or reinterpretation of previous narratives (Todorov, *Poetics* 244). On another level, if "Surrogate" is taken in the sense of "deputy" or "substitute," we can see in the passage a reference to Greene's own telling of Drover's story and its effects on the characters of *It's a Battlefield*. The implication is that behind the literal story of the novel there are other stories – at least one of which is the story of its telling, inspired by the condition of England in the early 1930s, but another of which is surely Conrad's *The Secret Agent*.[8]

It's a Battlefield, however, is not a detective story in the sense of having a detective who works to uncover the story of the crime in the conventional manner. Rather, it is a novel that begins after the crime has been solved, and, in this respect, differs markedly from both the classical detective story and the thriller. Conventionally, the classical detective story ends with the discovery of the criminal's identity and an accompanying explanation of the crime. The criminal's punishment is generally not made a part of the story; the murderer is occasionally left to commit suicide (as is the case with Dr Sheppard in Agatha Christie's *The Murder of Roger Ackroyd* or Matthew Cayley in A.A. Milne's *The Red House Mystery*), or is handed over to the authorities (as in many of the Sherlock Holmes stories) or, if the workings of justice are to be presented, is summarily dealt with (as in Greene's own short story "Murder for the Wrong Reason"). Neither the reader nor the detective is forced to witness the execution of justice. As Foucault would argue, this development in the history of literature dealing with crime, from the Newgate Calender to Christie's work, indicates a shift in the way society is disciplined as the explicit emphasis on the manner of punishment is replaced by the coercive force of surveillance (Foucault 67–9).

Yet, since the criminal is often presented as a double of the detective, as in the pairings of Holmes and Moriarty in some of Doyle's stories or Dupin and the minister D___ in Poe's "The Purloined Letter," the fact that punishment takes place outside the narrative demonstrates a moral aporia that paradoxically preserves the rigidity of the classical detective story's moral structure. The force of law, of the good, is seen to triumph over the force of disorder, of evil, but the moral ambiguity inherent in the expiation of evil by a process that involves the repetition of the initial crime is suppressed in the interest of preserving the sense of the criminal as "other," despite his or her kinship with the detective and with other members of the society. By placing punishment outside the bounds of the narrative, the illusion of localized guilt and the assumption of moral superiority on the part of other characters and the reader is maintained. Crime, in the classical detective story, is rooted in the individual; it is an aberration and not a response to social conditions or the expression of a shared and innate tendency towards violence.

This kind of literature places enormous trust in the mechanisms of justice, which are assumed to be impervious to the vagaries of the everyday world's political squabbles and individual preferences. But, when this trust disappears, or when these same mechanisms of law and order show themselves to be unworthy of the public trust, a new kind of literature emerges that realigns the matrix of criminal, detective, judge, and jury. In the thrillers of Hammett or Chandler, for example, the instruments of justice are perceived as ineffectual or corrupt and so the detective, as is partly the case with Conrad Drover in *It's a Battlefield*, takes on their functions with limited or, perhaps, no success.[9]

It's a Battlefield both formally and thematically challenges the conservative moral absolutism of the classical detective story by employing techniques similar to those used by the American writers of hard-boiled thrillers. In making "the injustice of men's justice" his main theme (*WE* 28), Greene explicitly focuses on that part which is either treated perfunctorily or ignored altogether in the classical detective story. In terms of genre, the novel leaves the classical detective story behind for the thriller's ambiguous world of corruption and indeterminacy. In *It's a Battlefield*, Jim Drover awaits execution for his murder of a London police officer, but the novel works against the Assistant Commissioner's confident assertion that "we got the man" (11). Circumstances surrounding the crime blur the issue of Drover's guilt and extend culpability to those charged with enforcing the laws and administering justice. Indeed, the whole question of what defines a murderer is brought into the text. Ultimately, blame is shown to rest with the society itself and, more particularly, with the dominant ideology that directs socio-political life.

In *It's a Battlefield* political power is exercised and maintained by means of surveillance, which, as Foucault argues, acts as a technique of coercion by making the visible subject the principle of his or her own subjection (202–3) and by incorporating that person into a panoptic schema whose aim is to strengthen existing social forces (208). Greene shows surveillance occurring at every level of a disciplinary society. Of course, there are the police throughout the city reporting on the expected political reaction to Drover's execution (as Greene describes in his diary), but at least half a dozen other incidents of overt or covert surveillance are also apparent: Conder, a reporter with the *Evening Watch*, tells the detective Patmore of events at a Communist Party meeting in exchange for an exclusive on the Paddington trunk murderer's arrest (a bargain that suggests police control of an always vigilant press); the offices in Scotland Yard and in the insurance company where Conrad Drover works are partitioned with glass; overseers in the prison and the factory observe their inmates; a pair of watchers keep their eyes on Jim Drover in prison; the Assistant Commissioner is unable to keep out of the way of his men; and Conrad Drover stalks the Assistant Commissioner through the city. Each of these incidents stresses the controlling nature of observation in the city, for surveillance is used here, as it is in the world of *The Confidential Agent*, as a means of exercising power over individuals because it inspires fear – a point best seen in Conrad Drover's paranoid belief that he is being watched (172) and in Conder's and Bennett's responses to their mutual suspicion that each is being followed by the other (137–8). The gaze of others establishes totalitarian control, as in Jeremy Bentham's Panopticon, because it constitutes a network of observation that links and subdues disparate elements within the city (Foucault 202–3). The skills of detection possessed by the police and particularly by the Assistant Commissioner are tied to the maintenance of an oppressive "existing order" (19), which is capitalist and authoritarian.

As a character, the Assistant Commissioner is a type derived from both the classical detective and, perhaps more specifically, Conrad's character of the same name in *The Secret Agent*. Greene's Assistant Commissioner possesses a passion for accuracy (13) and Holmesian skill in the reading of minute detail: "But turning over in his mind the woollen beret, noting the texture of the wool, the pattern of the crochet, he understood more than the most sensitive artist, noticed more than the most inquisitive woman" (13). As well, he makes his work the sole focus of his life. (He fears retirement [81] and the pleasures of detection can move him to ecstasy [202].) Yet, because his concentration on detail at the expense of any larger vision is inadequate in the face of the need for social change in the 1930s, the novel questions the detective's authority. Unlike earlier detectives such as Holmes or Poirot, the Assistant Commissioner cannot put everything right at the end of *It's a Battlefield* – indeed, his report on Drover is ignored by the government that commissioned it – because the problems are ones to which he contributes by continuing to work "to preserve the existing order" (19). In this sense, the Assistant Commissioner is implicated in Drover's crime because not only is he the supervisor of a force that attacked demonstrators, including women and children, with clubs (Drover is defending his wife when he stabs the policeman Coney), but also he works for and helps to perpetuate a regime that exploits workers to the point where they demonstrate *en masse*. In this way, he resembles Chandler's Marlowe at the end of *The Big Sleep*; there, Marlowe not only lies to General Sternwood but also fails to bring the criminals to justice.

The duality of the Assistant Commissioner's position is reflected in his own conceptions of himself as a "general" (128) and, alternatively, as "a mercenary soldier" (129) or a "private soldier fighting in a fog" (166) in "a civil war" (165) in which the demonstration is only one struggle. For him the urban landscape is a battlefield: "the front line was only a hundred yards away, where the trams screamed down the Embankment and the buses circled Trafalgar Square ..." (129). Greene continues:

His enemies were not only the brutal and the depraved, but the very men he pitied, the men he wanted to help; if he had done his duty the unemployed man would have been arrested for begging. The buildings seemed to him then to lose a little of their dignity; the peace of Sunday in Pall Mall was like the peace which follows a massacre, a war of elimination; poverty here had been successfully contested, driven back on the one side towards Notting Hill, on the other towards Vauxhall. (165–6)

As Peter Widdowson points out, this kind of martial imagery, typical of Greene's work in the 1930s and 1940s, is at once a metaphor for both the violence of the modern world and the class war within society (Widdowson 154). In this "civil" war, the Assistant Commissioner is charged with the defence of the city against crime, which is explicitly tied to poverty, and, more crucially, against social upheaval: "His work was simply to preserve the existing order" (19), or, as he thinks to himself, "the State ... employs me to keep order, to see that the unemployed beg and do not demand" (163).

This role, however, is not one that the Assistant Commissioner relishes, and so he protects himself by taking refuge in comforting thoughts of doing one's duty (76) and by compartmentalizing his vision of the world in such a way that things such as justice, morality, and politics are conceived of as independent and separate:

It was as well to be conventional when one fought so fierce and so indecisive a war; one's thoughts had to be canalized: Streatham, Paddington, wireless inventions, these principally had held the mind, so one bought a poppy and saved the time which might have been wasted on the dead; one raised a hat and forgot the done-with past; one wore one's school tie and dispensed with introductions; one touched wood and saved the harassing and useless thought: perhaps I am wrong. (170)

Although encouraged by the established order in the person of the private secretary, who twice assures the Assistant Commissioner that he need concern himself only with London's "poorer parts" (13, 14), the Assistant Commissioner's compartmentalized vision fails because it ignores the undeniable connections – represented again by the city's streets – between things. The Assistant Commissioner may think his job has nothing to do with justice, but for Conrad Drover he is the very embodiment of justice (161). Similarly, though the Assistant Commissioner insists on having nothing to do with politics, he is engaged in an explicitly political task – the writing of a report on the expected reaction to Jim Drover's execution. His vision of society is thus shown to be both naïve and narrowly focused, yet its very limitations allow him to function within society.

The problem is that, although he is the defender of the established order, he knows that "the laws were made by property owners in defence of property" (169), and so, personally, he is sympathetic to those who are marginalized or impoverished by these laws (16, 162–3). The result is a separation between his natural feelings of sympathy and his responsibilities to his employer, the state. This division produces a sense of alienation since it forces him to adopt both a public and a private persona; he is compelled to act against his own inclinations to defend a system in which he does not believe: "His business was not justice; his business was only to catch the right man; but in private, in his secret life, he was troubled by the slightest deviation from the strictest justice" (162). In the face of this dilemma he dreams of "an organization which he could serve for higher reasons than pay" (130), but age and weariness have sapped his faith in the possibility of a new social order and his will to help bring it about. Ultimately, by providing protection against the terror of "the demands which might be made on him" (166) and by defending the social order from revolution, his blinkered social vision allows the Assistant Commissioner to continue doing his job. (Of course, this kind of social vision also leads to extremist political ideologies such as fascism or Stalinism, the crimes of the Nazis, and the abdication of personal morality and responsibility.) As with most characters in the book, the Assistant Commissioner's actions are largely directed by self-interest. "The truth is," he tells Caroline Bury, "nobody cares about anything but his own troubles. Everybody's too busy fighting his own little battle to think of ... the next man" (188).

This meeting with Caroline Bury inspires the Assistant Commissioner to condemn himself for his own cowardice in not helping to create a new order. Yet, instead of taking the necessary action of resigning, he slips back into his old habit of mind, forgetting the drama of Drover and the chaplain and Conrad's attempt at murder, to focus his thoughts solely upon the Streatham case. The book ends with the Assistant Commissioner finding his moment of contentment, yet we cannot help wondering at the cost. Unlike other politically un-committed figures in Greene's novels who for whatever reasons are compelled to take some action – Fowler in *The Quiet American*, Brown in *The Comedians*, Plarr in *The Honorary Consul*, and even Chase in *Rumour at Nightfall*, for instance – the Assistant Commissioner cannot regain "faith" (190) and act on his sense of social justice.

Just as the idea of the detective as the representative of a tradition of law, order, and justice is questioned in *It's a Battlefield*, so too is the conception of the murderer as an aberration within an otherwise stable and contented society. In large measure this is done through a consideration of Jim Drover, who is awaiting execution. Early in the novel, Kay confidently thinks, "They'll reprieve him. He isn't a mur-derer" (31), and later Conrad Drover considers the official judgment that one is a murderer meaningless:

... I've seen through that; you can't shame me any longer with a word like murderer; I know what a murderer is – Jim is a murderer. The law told me that, impressed on me through three long days, counsel have made expensive speeches on the point; six shopkeepers, three Civil Servants, two doctors, and a well-known correspondent have discussed it together and come to that con-clusion – Jim is a murderer, a murderer is Jim. Why shouldn't I be a murderer myself? Always, from the time I went to school, I have wanted to be like Jim. It's no good calling me a murderer. I've seen through that. (111)

Still later, he carries these thoughts farther: "A murderer is strength, protection, love" (160). This conception sharply undermines the legal establishment's determination, by and large accepted by the public[10] (who are given their own part to play in the procedure), of a mur-derer as a disease in the body politic. For both Conrad and Kay, Jim is a murderer in name only; he is not, by nature, murderous.

Conder's and the Assistant Commissioner's experiences of other murderers similarly intensify the questions that surround the figure of the murderer within detective fiction. Conder remembers "the man who drowned his wife at Shoreham, flushed and neat in the dock with a tiepin in the shape of a horse's head; the widow of the grocer who drew the Derby winner and who, dead drunk the same night, drove her husband's car into the Thames, a widow with £20,000 of her own; she said, 'I've always been lucky at such things, raffles, I mean, and so on'" (135). While the case of the widow suggests her culpability in her husband's death, the first recalls the paradoxical nature of some murderers that the Assistant Commissioner also finds in Crippen and the Salvationist, who is arrested for the Paddington trunk murder. Although both have committed grisly crimes, Crippen and the Salvationist present themselves as respectable members of society: Crippen, a doctor, is forever neat and the Salvationist calls for the faithful to "Come to Jesus" (81). The inclusion in the narrative of the Salvationist's arrest not only reinforces the metaphor of the battlefield, since the murderer is a member of the Salvation Army, but also subverts the dominant ideology by dramatizing the disparity between the actions of the speaker and the rhetoric of the established order which, in this case, is exemplified by religious teaching. As the analysis of Conrad's remorse after his sexual encounter with Milly shows, this kind of rhetoric is part of the panoptic schema of the disciplinary society in that it intensifies the individual's own conscious self-surveillance: the development of Conrad's sense of remorse demonstrates how he is made the principle of his own subjection:

It had been difficult to believe in the wrong during the commission … but afterwards … he had pasted the proper labels on his memory of it. "A mortal sin." "The bitterest wrong." "A broken commandment." But the labels were not his; he had taken them from others; others had made the rules by which he suffered; it was unfair that they should leave him so alone and yet make the rules which governed him. It was as if a man marooned must still order his life according to the regulations of his ship. (159)

Of course, this is not to imply that Conrad is entirely innocent of wrongdoing (he has, after all slept with Milly and betrayed both Jim and his own sense of honour), yet the remorse he feels is reinforced by the limiting mores of a social order from which he, like Crusoe, is excluded. He had been manipulated into becoming part of the panoptic mechanism.

The contradiction between accepted rhetoric and actual behaviour is similarly exposed in the Assistant Commissioner's reflections on his career among criminals:

He thought of innumerable clerics rising in innumerable pulpits to talk of cleanliness as next to godliness … praising the clean body as an indication of a clean mind. He thought of Crippen shaving carefully every day of his trial, particular about small things. It was these contradictions, the moral maxims which did not apply, that made it impossible for a man to found his life on any higher motive than doing his job. A life spent with criminals would never fail to strip the maxims of priests and teachers from the underlying chaos. (80–1)

As the passage makes clear, the mere fact that the murderer exists undercuts the myth of social and political harmony underpinning the classical detective story, and so the passage reflects a social vision more akin to that of the authors of the hard-boiled school of detective fiction. Greene presents crime and murder as stemming from deep fissures within the structure of society between the wealthy and the powerful, who control the established institutions within the society, and the great mass of people who subscribe to a socio-political ideology that fails to recognize them as equals. The result is that, despite the prevailing establishment's rhetoric, social, political, and economic chaos results from clashes between the powerful elite and the divided majority.

It's a Battlefield, like *The Secret Agent*, exposes the chaos beneath the veneer of civilization, and Conrad's thoughts as he sees the Assistant Commissioner walk down the street aptly characterize the vision of Greene's novel:

He came slowly, justice with a file of papers; he came, respectability with bowler hat and umbrella; he came, assurance, eyes on the pavement, safe in London, safe in the capital city of the Empire, safe at the heart of civilization ("I see no reason to reverse the judge's decision"; the raised truncheon; the forbidden meeting; "after one year we allow them to embrace"; reduced staffs, unemployment; the constant struggle with your fellow man to keep alone upon the raft, to let the other drown; desire; adultery; passion without tenderness or permanence); down the street the upholder of civilization, eyes on the pavement, neat file under his arm. (161)

As the parentheses suggest, at the heart of London exists the brutality and meanness that lie beneath the civilization of empire and the capitalist ideology of imperialism. For Conrad and others who are marginalized by class, gender, or race, safety in London – even civilization itself – is a fiction: " 'Them as knows what London is,' Mrs. Simpson [says], 'would not be surprised to find their nearest and dearest bleeding' " (182). Similarly, the maxims of law and justice within the society are exposed as fictions: "Somewhere, at some time, in a newspaper or a book, Milly had read the words, 'Judgement by your peers.' She had thought it meant judgement by your lords and had been laughed at for thinking so, 'It means judgement by your equals,' but where, she asked now of Mrs. Coney, was a judge who was their equal, a man with three pounds a week, who lived as they lived? And the jury? Tradesmen and gentlemen. It wasn't fair ..." (97)

Given its vision of the central hypocrisy within the society of the 1930s, it is not surprising that *It's a Battlefield* blurs the images of detective and murderer alike while suggesting that true justice may be elusive. In contrast to the classical detective story, not even poetic justice operates in Greene's novel; instead, all forms of human justice are seen as inadequate in *It's a Battlefield* because, as the chaplain says, they are arbitrary and incomprehensible (199). Greene's reshaping of the detective story as a thriller exposed the contradictions and the conservatism at the heart of the period's dominant form of popular writing. With *It's a Battlefield* Greene made his first move towards a popular literature that could suggest moral values. The later Greene thrillers build on the equivocations in the roles of detective and murderer that first emerge in *It's a Battlefield* and in his other early work.

5 Thrillers of the 1930s:
A Gun for Sale, Brighton Rock,
and *The Confidential Agent*

Greene noted in *Ways of Escape* that, since neither *It's a Battlefield* nor *England Made Me* proved to be as popular as he had hoped,[1] he thought it "urgently necessary to repeat ... the success of my first 'thriller,'" yet Greene added that "the decision was not, all the same, entirely a question of money. I have always enjoyed reading melodrama, and I enjoy writing it" (*WE* 54). His turn to a deliberately popular form of writing in 1935–36 was the logical result of the process of interrogation that began with *Stamboul Train*, which in later years he would describe as his first "thriller."

Although *Stamboul Train* was eventually called an "entertainment," whereas *It's a Battlefield* and *England Made Me* were not, Greene's comments elsewhere suggest that in *Ways of Escape* he was looking back on his work with the benefit of hindsight. In the *Paris Review* interview of the early 1950s, he said that *England Made Me* "came about when I began *Stamboul Train*. I had to write a pot-boiler, a modern adventure story, and I suddenly discovered that I liked the form, that the writing came easily, that I was beginning to find my world. In *England Made Me* I let myself go in it for the first time" (Shuttleworth 33). Similarly, in the interview with Allain in 1979–80, he remarked that "the sense of entertainment crops up [in the early work] ... more markedly in *England Made Me*" than in *Stamboul Train* (Allain 128). Certainly, the thriller elements in the later novel match or even supersede those of *Stamboul Train*, but his comments to Allain also throw into question his earlier assertion, made in the introduction for *A Gun for Sale*, that this book was his second thriller while

Stamboul Train was his first. What this equivocation suggests is that the relationship between *A Gun for Sale* and its predecessors is not as well defined as the "entertainment" label given to *Stamboul Train* and *A Gun for Sale* makes it out to be. Indeed, we have already seen how Greene re-evaluated his sense of the popular in years between these two novels. Furthermore, *A Gun for Sale* shares the political and aesthetic attitudes of its three predecessors. As a text that makes full use of the genre of the thriller, it is clearly meant to appeal to a large audience; the "entertainment" label reinforces this appeal and openly challenges the high-brow assumption that "serious" literature cannot be popular.

Greene's reflections in *Ways of Escape* on the origins of his texts prior to and including *The Ministry of Fear* reveal a common intent behind much of his work in the period. *The Ministry of Fear* developed out of an ambition, inspired by his reading of a Michael Innis novel, "to write a thriller … which would be fantastic and funny" (*WE* 74). Similarly, *The Confidential Agent* was born of "a certain vague ambition to create something legendary out of the contemporary thriller" (68), while *Brighton Rock*, though "[begun] in 1937 as a detective story," quickly mutated so that, according to Greene, all that remained of the detective story were the first fifty pages, which he wished he had had the strength to remove (58, 60). Earlier in the decade, *A Gun for Sale* was to have been a popular thriller in the manner of John Buchan, but the world of 1936 was "no longer a Buchan world" (54) and so that book too could not simply recapitulate the Buchan formula. In 1936, "patriotism had lost its appeal, even for a schoolboy, at Passchendaele, and the Empire brought first to mind the Beaverbrook Crusader, while it was difficult, during the years of the Depression, to believe in the high purposes of the City of London and of the British Constitution. The hunger-marchers seemed more real than the politicians" (54). Each of these accounts expressed a desire to revitalize and transform the inherited formulas of popular writing, particularly of the thriller, so as to make these formulas the vehicles of both entertainment and "serious" purpose. In turning away from the classical detective story and in recasting the thriller as it was passed on by Childers, Buchan, and others, Greene challenged the form's implied ideology and brought political, social, and economic concerns – concerns compatible with developments in the 1930s and his own evolving political views – into popular writing.

What Greene illuminates in his 1930s books is the violence and savagery lurking beneath a seeming peace. *It's a Battlefield*, *Journey Without Maps*, and *The Lawless Roads* all contain passages comparable to the following from *The Confidential Agent*:

They bumped slowly on across the Park. The soap-box orators talked in the bitter cold at Marble Arch with their mackintoshes turned up around their Adam's apples, and all down the road the cad cars waited for the right easy girls, and the cheap prostitutes sat hopelessly in the shadows, and the black-mailers kept an eye on the grass where the deeds of darkness were quietly and unsatisfactorily accomplished. This was technically known as a city at peace. A poster said: "Bloomsbury Tragedy Sensation." (136)

When the war came at the end of the decade it did not, for Greene, represent a sudden change; rather, it was the manifestation of tensions that existed within the society of the thirties (McEwen 118). As Greene took pains to describe in 1940,

Violence comes to us more easily because it was so long expected – not only by the political sense but by the moral sense. The world we lived in could not have ended any other way. The curious waste lands one sometimes saw from trains – cratered ground round Wolverhampton under a cindery sky with a few cottages grouped like stones among the rubbish: those acres of aban-doned cars round Slough: the dingy fortune-teller's on the first-floor above the cheap permanent waves in a Brighton back street; they all demanded vio-lence, like the rooms in a dream where one knows that something will pres-ently happen – a door fly open or a window catch give and let the end in.[2]
I think it was a sense of impatience because the violence was delayed … that made many writers of recent years go abroad to try to meet it half-way: some went to Spain and others to China. Less ideological, perhaps less coura-geous, writers chose corners where the violence was more moderate but the hint of it had to be there to satisfy that moral craving for the just and reason-able expression of human nature left without belief. (CE 334)

Hence, the image of the battlefield, which Greene used figuratively to stand for social conflict and class war in his novels of the 1930s, was realized on a more literal level in *The Ministry of Fear*, *The Third Man*, and *The End of the Affair*, which are set during and immediately after the Second World War.[3]

In the novels of the thirties, crime and violence are often shown to be routinely dismissed or denied by an established authority who re-peatedly invokes the idea of London (or England) as the centre of law and order, the heart of civilization, in opposition to contrary claims of a pervasive and underlying menace. For example, the Assistant Com-missioner pacifies Mrs Simpson's fears for his safety by saying, "Come, come … this is London" (*IB* 181); Mather ironically boasts that the assassin of the Czech minister would have been caught within a week were he in England (*GS* 10); the police refuse to give credence to Ida's suspicion of foul play in Hale's death (*BR* 78–81); Forbes dismisses D.'s account of an attempt on his life as a "tall story" (*CA* 94) and then later urges him to give himself up because "this is London" (107); and even Rowe tells Anna Hilfe that they have nothing to worry about because "this isn't Vienna, you know. This is London" (*MF* 103). With *The Ministry of Fear* and *The Third Man*, however, the war brings about a reversal of sorts in that, unlike the detective figures in the pre-war novels – Anne, Ida, and D., who must convince the legitimate authorities of the existence of a hidden menace within a seemingly peaceful society – it is the naïve and amateur investigators of *The Ministry of Fear* and *The Third Man* who must be convinced of the extent of the corruption by the legitimate authorities, Prentice and Calloway, who possess more knowledge of things as they are than do Rowe and Martins. It is as if the war raised the level of criminality to a height of which the ordinary citizen could not conceive. In *The Ministry of Fear* and *The Third Man* the war makes all things possible, including a credulous response to tales of romantic heroism, because reality, from the physical appearance of the world to the moral strictures governing individual and social behaviour, has been so altered as to be unrecognizable – a fact that may account for the increasingly fantastic and fabulous nature of Greene's "entertainments" as time went on.

Thus, we are led back to the often made claim that Greene came to use the thriller because it was the genre best able to reflect the climate of violence and uncertainty in the 1930s and 1940s. That may be so, but it is also true that Greene's thrillers, while continuing to be faithful to the premises of 1930s realism, developed the genre's "literary" tendencies; that is, they became increasingly self-conscious of their status as texts. This aspect of the "entertainments" reaches its apex in *The Ministry of Fear*, where the boundaries between the world and the text collapse: "Thrillers," Rowe dreams, "are like life ... The world has been remade by William Le Queux" (65). *The Third Man* and *Our Man in Havana* consolidate this view by emphasizing the role given to fiction and fiction-making. In *The Third Man* Martins is a writer of "cheap novelettes" (23) while Calloway, as a first-person narrator, indulges in his own literary artistry. In *Our Man in Havana* Wormold, though a vacuum-cleaner salesman by trade, tells Milly that he is becoming an "imaginative writer" (74), and later Beatrice accuses him of talking "like a novelist" (108). In his reports, he creates a fictional world of spies and conspiracy that becomes all too real when his superiors read his fictions as truth. Significantly, from a textual point of view, these reports are communicated through a book-code based on Charles and Mary Lamb's *Tales from Shakespeare*.

Earlier work such as *A Gun for Sale* or *Brighton Rock* used the thriller apparatus to expose and investigate contemporary social problems (James McDonald has even gone so far as to call *Brighton Rock* "a proletarian novel" [199]). These novels are vehicles for social commentary, particularly in the implicit equation they make between the violence and cruelty of their protagonists, Raven and Pinkie, and the background of poverty against which they are presented. As Edwin Muir wrote of Pinkie in a review of *Brighton Rock*, "He is an evil product of an evil environment, a living criticism of society, and on that plane genuine" (76). Muir's remarks could just as easily apply to Raven, who is said to be "made by hatred" (*GS* 66). Indeed, because one of Raven's obsessive boasts is "I'm educated" (15, 46ff.), the social system that shapes him is severely criticized: he, too, is made by England. In *Brighton Rock* there are hints of a repressed desire for goodness and peace in Pinkie that are seen in his emotional reactions to music, his recollections of his days in the church choir and of his desire to be a priest, his faint stirrings of tenderness for Rose and pity for Prewitt, and his sense of an "enormous emotion beat[ing] on him … the pressure of gigantic wings against the glass" as he drives Rose to what he assumes will be her death (242) – all of which indicate that Pinkie's evil arises out of the corruption of his innocence. The crippling effects of his environment destroy a natural tendency to goodness,[4] though, as Roger Sharrock points out, there is less room for implied social criticism when salvation and damnation are brought into play (84). The three "entertainments" that come after *Brighton Rock*, while not abandoning the social critique of the 1930s books, are more obvious in their interrogations the thriller form and focus more intencely on the structures of authority – whether political, literary, or textual – within society.

A Gun for Sale, Brighton Rock, The Confidential Agent, The Ministry of Fear, and *The Third Man* all follow to varying degrees at least one investigator (Raven, Ida, D., Rowe, and Martins) who functions in part as a detective attempting to discover, to read, the hidden story behind the accepted interpretation of events. But while the detective of the classical detective story is often a privileged figure capable of placing an authoritative interpretation upon events – and so admired as a superman standing above and beyond the law – Greene's detectives are deliberately conceived in opposition to what William Aydelotte sees as the genre's incipient fascism (92–4). Indeed, as part of the "antifascist aesthetic" that Michael Denning finds in the "serious thrillers" of the 1930s (66), Greene's detectives demonstrate a distrust of the single authoritative point of view. His detectives are incapable of the kind of confident assertions made by Dupin, Holmes, or Poirot, for instance. Instead, Greene's thrillers foreground the interpretive limitations of any fictional detective and so of any reader. Greene's pursuers have "only a partial understanding of the nature of the crime they are investigating ... Their concern is with human justice, with the Hebraic law of vengeance, with the maintenance of social order" (Stratford, "Master" 73). Yet, as *It's a Battlefield* suggests, Greene has little confidence in the machinations of human justice, and the goal of maintaining the existing order is dubious at best.

Greene's investigators have their authority undermined in a number of ways. As representatives of law and/or justice, Raven, Ida, and Rowe are ironic figures in their respective texts: Raven and Rowe are both murderers themselves, although their crimes are vastly different in circumstance; and Ida is a fun-loving, amoral pleasure-seeker pursuing Pinkie less because she desires to expose his crimes and see justice done than because she wants excitement, fun, and "a bit of life" (45). D. represents a slightly different case from Raven, Ida, Rowe, and Martins in that, although he seeks Else's killers, he is not principally investigating a murder; rather, he attempts to read the truth about his mission in the numerous fictions, the layers of deceit and mistrust, that he encounters.

Also undermining the interpretive authority of Greene's investigators is that the function of detection in the novels is split among or at least shared with other characters. Raven in *A Gun for Sale* may be working to find Davis and Davis's boss, Sir Marcus, but he is not trying to discover the truth behind the murder of the Czech minister of war which opens the novel. The facts of that crime are only incidentally uncovered by him with Anne's help. Raven works merely to avenge himself upon Davis and Sir Marcus for their betrayal of him by paying him with stolen money. Similarly, Mather of Scotland Yard tracks Raven not as a murderer but as a suspect in a bank theft. As Mather shortsightedly says of the murder of the old minister, " 'It's got nothing to do with us' " (10). Only Anne Crowder attaches any importance to solving the crime, and so she too becomes an investigator of sorts, bringing to three (four if one counts Mather's stuttering partner Saunders) the number of detective figures in the book.

The situation is different in *Brighton Rock*, but again the detective's success depends on outside forces. Ida is not only assisted in her investigation by Phil Corkery, but her powers of detection are tied to her belief in the occult – particularly her ability to read the language of the ouija board – and to the workings of chance when Black Boy's victory in a horse-race enables her to win the money she needs to continue her investigation. In *The Ministry of Fear* and *The Third Man*, more orthodox detectives, Prentice and Calloway, assist the principle investigators, Rowe and Martins, and so the prospect of a single authoritative interpretation of events is again thrown into question. Indeed, in *The Third Man*, the interpretation of events established at the narrative's outset is Calloway's, and Martins sets out to make Calloway "the biggest bloody fool in Vienna" (27) by discovering what really happened to Harry Lime. As *The Third Man* plays itself out, Martins succeeds in making Calloway seem foolish, since Calloway, the legitimate investigator, is wrong about Lime's death. This situation is not unusual in the detective story, where amateurs frequently demonstrate the failure of the police; however, when we remember that Martins is also mistaken about Lime's death and that Calloway as the novel's first-person narrator is in part a figure for the writer, a theory of reading that credits the authoritative interpretation of events to the detective/author immediately becomes problematic.

Of the books Greene wrote between 1936 and 1950, *A Gun for Sale* and *Brighton Rock* are structurally closest to the classical detective story (both novels, for instance, contain a murder early in the narrative), though neither follows the form as closely as does "Murder for the Wrong Reason." Indeed, if we are to make a distinction, *Brighton Rock* follows the paradigm of the classical detective story more than *A Gun for Sale*, which patterns itself after John Buchan's stories. *The Confidential Agent* and *The Ministry of Fear* are structured differently from *A Gun for Sale* and *Brighton Rock*, but the later novels heighten the genre's self-consciousness, and so Greene's investigation of reading strategies is more overt there than it is in *A Gun for Sale* and *Brighton Rock*. By the time of *The Third Man*, both the detective's authority and the epistemology of the form had been thoroughly undermined by Greene's earlier books, which reflect an indeterminate world wholly subject to interpretation.

A Gun for Sale, *Brighton Rock*, *The Confidential Agent*, and *The Ministry of Fear* reveal Greene's fullest explorations of detective fiction and extend his conception of the thriller to its limits. This is particularly true of *The Ministry of Fear*. After this novel, the thriller and elements derived from it continue to resonate in Greene's œuvre, but none of the books that follow *The Ministry of Fear* significantly advances his sense of the genre. Even *The Third Man* remains a text that repeats strategies already developed by Greene in the late 1930s and early 1940s. Yet, insofar as *The Third Man* was by Greene's own account "never intended to be more than the raw material for a picture" (10),[5] the story marks the logical extension of his efforts to reach a mass audience through a popular medium, for the filmed version is undoubtedly a significant contribution to British cinema. Perhaps it is not surprising, then, that the first and most prolific phase of Greene's career ended with the publication of *The Ministry of Fear*; after more than a decade of publishing at the astonishing pace of a book almost every year, Greene would not produce another until *The Heart of the Matter* five years later.

A GUN FOR SALE

In *Ways of Escape* Greene described *A Gun for Sale* as a necessary updating of the Buchan thriller, but "the hunted man of *A Gun for Sale* ... was Raven not Hannay; a man out to revenge himself for all the dirty tricks of life, not to save his country" (54). Sir Marcus, on the other hand, was "a more plausible villain for those days [the mid-1930s] than the man in Buchan's *The Thirty-Nine Steps* who could 'hood his eyes like a hawk'" (55). *The Thirty-Nine Steps* was a crucial text for Greene because it established the pattern for all the adventure writers who wrote after its publication. "John Buchan was the first to realize the enormous dramatic value of adventure in familiar sur-roundings happening to unadventurous men, members of Parliament, and members of the Athenaeum, lawyers and barristers, business men and minor peers: murder in 'the atmosphere of breeding and stability'" (*CE* 167). None the less, Buchan's failings became apparent to Greene in the 1930s. In "The Last Buchan," he condemned the in-tellectual content of Buchan's work for emphasizing the values of empire and the ideology of capitalism. The "vast importance Buchan attributed to success, the materialism ... " repelled Greene in 1941 (*CE* 168). Similarly, the "enormous importance" Buchan placed on in-dividuals could no longer be justified in light of events in the 1930s and early 1940s: "It is not, after all, the great men – the bankers and the divisional commanders and the Ambassadors – who have been holding our world together this winter [1940–41], and if we survive, it is by 'the wandering, wavering grace of humble men' in Bow and Coventry, Bristol and Birmingham" (169). Greene praised the Buchan thriller for showing "the death that may come to any of us ... by the railings of the Park or the doorway of the mews" (169) and for reveal-ing "'how thin is the protection of civilization'" [169]), but he also criticized it on ideological grounds. For *A Gun for Sale* and his two subsequent "entertainments" (*The Confidential Agent* and *The Ministry of Fear*), Greene adopted the Buchan pattern of flight and pursuit but rejected his precursor's social and political vision. As Maria Couto succinctly observes,

The subversion of the content of the traditional adventure form reaches its apotheosis in *A Gun for Sale* with the themes of heroic action, violence, the exploited, courage and hope explored at various levels. The empire of capitalism is exposed with a hero who is ugly and deformed. His only sense of purpose is provoked by a deep and sullen rage rather than by heroism; his courage is despair. The description of Sir Marcus lifts him out of nationality and race to make him the embodiment of the forces of exploitation ... (55)

Perhaps because of the "entertainment" label, *A Gun for Sale* at one time was largely dismissed by critics as "a kind of secular rehearsal for *Brighton Rock*" meant to help finance the later "more serious" book (Lodge, "G.G." 95; McEwen 114), but it has recently been more typically praised as "one of the best and most significant novels of the 1930s and a far more nearly perfect work of art than *Brighton Rock*" ("GG: Man Within" 11). Samuel Hynes calls it "a war-novel before the event" and finds it the "best single example of the way in which the real present incorporated the apocalyptic future, while remaining real" (*Auden* 232). And, certainly, there is little doubt that, although the novel's action involves war's prevention, by its end war is seen as inevitable. For Raven, of course, there is always a war (47, 129), but the point is taken further with Anne's thoughts in the book's final pages: "*She* couldn't stop a war. Men were fighting beasts, they needed war ... how they love it ... it occurred to her ... that perhaps even if she had been able to save the country from a war, it wouldn't have been worth saving" (182–3). War is the "just and poetic" (*CE* 336) judgment upon the old order.

In *A Gun for Sale* Raven assassinates the Czech minister of war, is paid for the job in stolen notes, and, when he discovers that the police are after him because of the stolen money, sets out to find Davis and Davis's boss to get proper payment and revenge himself upon those who betrayed him. Raven, therefore, is both murderer and, in a sense, detective, although the consequences of and the truth behind the murder he commits are of interest to him only after Anne points out several parallels between the minister and himself.

For the reader, the explanation for the murder does not come until more than half-way through the novel. Yet Sir Marcus's guilt is hinted at earlier by scattered clues, such as the chief reporter's advice to buy armament shares (23), the disclosure of Davis's connection with Midland Steel (58), and Davis's cryptic remark, "he won't forgive me again," made before he tries to kill Anne (64). As the head of Midland Steel, Sir Marcus sees war as the answer to his company's financial problems because it will increase the company's business and the value of its shares. Midland Steel, we are told, is badly hurt by the Depression; it employs only a fifth of the workers it once had, and its layoffs are "ruining the town" (59). As well, Davis later confesses that the company is on its "last legs" and in desperate need of money (165). To resuscitate this ailing industry, Raven is hired to kill the Czech minister, whose murder, like the archduke's assassination at Sarajevo in 1914, will ignite a series of events leading to war.[6]

Sir Marcus, like Krogh in *England Made Me* and Colleoni in *Brighton Rock*, is esteemed as a successful businessman by the general public and by the established legal authorities (109). As with Krogh and Colleoni, however, outward respectability masks the fact that Sir Marcus supports his success with criminal activity; like the others, he kills with clean hands.[7] When confronted by Raven, Sir Marcus exhibits an indifference indicative of what Hannah Arendt later called "the banality of evil"; he is "apparently unmoved" by the description Raven gives of his twin killing: "Old age had killed the imagination. The deaths he [Sir Marcus] had ordered were no more real to him than the deaths he read about in the newspapers" (165). Earlier, we are told that he is "a man almost without pleasures; his most vivid emotion was venom, his main object defence: defence of his fortune, of the pale flicker of vitality he gained each year in the Cannes sun, of his life" (108). In his physical decrepitude, Sir Marcus is an image of modern capitalism in its decline (McEwen 116), and, like Krogh, he is an internationalist whose origins are lost in obscurity.

Everyone knew a lot about Sir Marcus. The trouble was, all that they knew was contradictory. There were people who, because of his Christian name, believed that he was Greek; others were quite as certain that he had been born in a ghetto. His business associates said that he was of an old English family; his nose was no evidence either way; you found plenty of noses like that in Cornwall and the west country. His name did not appear in *Who's Who*, and an enterprising journalist who once tried to write his life found extraordinary gaps in registers; it wasn't possible to follow any rumour to its source. There was even a gap in the legal records of Marseilles where one rumour said that Sir Marcus as a youth had been charged with theft from a visitor to a bawdy house. Now he sat ... one of the richest men in Europe ... No one even knew his age ... (109)

Like Krogh's, Sir Marcus's internationalism denies loyalty to anything or anyone beyond the maintenance of fortune and of self, and, ironically, to this end Sir Marcus appeals to others' patriotism in his attempt to have the police kill Raven, whom he calls a "traitor" (111). Like the thirties' capitalism he allegorically represents, Sir Marcus depends on violence and exploitation for his preservation while he conceals his ends by appeals to the higher values of king and country. He uses Raven and then sees him as "waste" (110) to be discarded. In this context, Raven's violence, like Fred Hall's in *England Made Me*, becomes an extension of a larger public violence; consequently, Raven's guilt in the murder of the Czech minister is diminished and his pursuit of Sir Marcus and Davis becomes, as Anne realizes, if not the pursuit of law (which is represented in Mather's pursuit), at least the pursuit of justice.

Cold-blooded killer that he is, Raven has at least one ethical imperative, which is that members of his own class not betray each other: "This was evil: that people of the same class should prey on each other" (91). (Raven is consequently outraged at finding himself betrayed by Dr Yogel and his nurse [29].) It is the betrayal of class and not some sense of duty owed to humanity or to the state that drives him to uncover Sir Marcus and Davis. Shortly after Anne has told him of the Czech minister's background (122), Raven confesses to the assassination and adds, " 'I didn't know the old fellow [the minister] was one of us [that is, of the working class]. I wouldn't have touched him if I'd known he was like that. All this talk of war. It doesn't mean a thing to me" (129). Raven is outraged not because he has been used to start a war (certainly cause enough) but because he has been used against someone of his own class. The minister, Anne says, "wasn't one of the rich. He wouldn't have gone to war. That's why they shot him. You bet there are fellows making money now out of him being dead. And he'd done it all himself too ... His father was a thief and his mother committed –." Raven, recognizing parallels with his own life, completes Anne's sentence, "suicide" (122).

The betrayal of one's own class is also evident in Sir Marcus's desire for the old minister's death, since both Sir Marcus and the minister were in the same orphanage and are of the same class. Sir Marcus's villainy is thus compounded because he too has turned against his own people, both in arranging for the minister's murder and in exploiting Raven. Significantly, Raven is imagistically linked to Sir Marcus, who hides a scar beneath his beard, by his harelip. In that Sir Marcus is able to hide his scar, he is able to deny his past, but Raven's poverty prevents him from doing the same (14). Raven's disfigurement, then, is the outward manifestation of his marginal status within society and the source of great pain for him.

This allegory of class conflict and exploitation under capitalism is completed with the figure of Mather who, as the colourless detective stalking Raven, is the unwitting protector of the institutionalized crime existing beneath the veneer of civilization. Like the Assistant Commissioner of *It's A Battlefield* but without his self-awareness, Mather protects a capitalist establishment built on crime, violence, and militarism. He blindly offers his loyalty to the state and places his commitment to the police force above his personal feelings for Anne: he feels "a small chill of hatred against Anne for putting him in a position where his affection warped his judgement" (80), and he hastily assumes her guilt in her dealings with Raven even before he has spoken with her. The things Mather values and desires – certainty, organization, and routine – all account for his dedication to Scotland Yard: "He was part of an organization. He did not want to be a leader, he did not even wish to give himself up to some God-sent fanatic of a leader [although Anne notes that "he always did what other people did" (24)], he liked to feel that he was one of thousands more or less equal working for a concrete end – not equality of opportunity, not government by the people or by the richest or by the best, but simply to do away with crime which meant uncertainty. He liked to be certain." (38) As a member of the force, Mather is freed of personal responsibility for his actions and his emotions; however, in the climate of the 1930s, Greene perceives this kind of freedom as evidence of an incipient tendency to fascism both in the police and, as the medical students' "rag" under Buddy Ferguson's leadership illustrates, in the British people.

Since he is a detective tracking Raven, Mather fulfils the demands of the detective story promised by the "entertainment" label. With Saunders, he fits the role of the master sleuth accompanied by a less able companion, a paradigmatic relationship often found in detective stories – Dupin and his unnamed companion, Holmes and Watson, and Poirot and Hastings are three similar couples. Mather also shares with the classical detective a commitment to the pursuit of an exact truth, which for him means a strict factual accuracy: "He always noted facts, he didn't trust his brain for more than theories, guesses" (78). Similarly, in equating crime with uncertainty, Mather harkens back to the view of detection and of reading seen in Poe's "The Man of the Crowd," where "the type and genius of deep crime" is located in the enigmatic, the unreadable.[8] For Mather, crime and uncertainty, figured as the disruption and transgression of predictable codes of behaviour, are eliminated by turning experience into a readable text which provides order and certainty.

A Gun for Sale, however, demonstrates the limitations of Mather's method of reading experience and, by extension, narrative. With reductive simplicity he declares that the motives behind the Czech minister's murder are "Politics. Patriotism" (10); but the novel goes on to show that for Mather, as is the case for the narrator of Poe's story, experience resists its transformation into readable text. Certainly, as the "entertainment" label seemingly promises, the story of the crime that opens the novel is uncovered through the story of the investigation, and the narrative arrives at a renewed state of quiescence wherein the disruptive forces are eliminated and a new order, following the traditional pattern of romance, emerges: the bad are eliminated (not just Raven but Sir Marcus and Davis as well) and the good are rewarded (Mather gets a promotion and so he and Anne are able to marry). Yet Greene makes clear in *A Gun for Sale* that such a reading is idealistically simple and ideologically naïve.

In part he accomplishes this goal by evoking sympathy for Raven in the reader. Raven's background, his tenderness for a stray kitten (65), his trust in Anne, and his desire to confess his crimes and so remove the burdens of the past all render him a sympathetic victim of environmental forces. As well, the consequent diminution of his guilt is furthered by the contextualizing of his crimes within the larger frame of an economic system that holds Sir Marcus up as a model of success. The unmasking of the traditional assumptions behind the detective story is also accomplished through the presentation of Mather as little more than a parodic caricature of the great detective such as Holmes or Dupin. As Kenneth Alley observes in a discussion of the novel, much of the story's irony emerges from the fact that Mather sees himself as society's protector; although, in reality, he "represents a dead or dying order of things ... he represents an era in which order and a universally accepted moral code had marked the criminal – and even at times the socially inept or untutored – as a force inimical to the group's common good, and the detective's function had been to expose the aberrant's misdeeds for the purpose of restoring harmony to the injured social body" (176). While the comfort Mather gains from being one of many working within a vast organization is not felt by the great classical detectives who usually work independently of or in opposition to the police, Mather does share their assumption that certainty can be established in the reading of experience and of texts. In the world of *A Gun for Sale*, however, this belief leads to a position of political neutrality that plays into the hands of the established order by preserving the dominant ideology; thus, Mather's desire for certainty works against him discovering the full story behind the money Raven is suspected of having stolen.

As Greene presents him, Mather's "logic is not particularly striking, his memory is not exceptional, and his judgment is fallible" (Alley 177). His obsession with accuracy and the narrow vision of his "anchored" mind (*GS* 34, 37) prevent him from seeing beneath the surface of things. He is incapable of conceiving a connection between the assassination of a foreign politician and his own life (" 'It's got nothing to do with us" [10]), despite the fact that the text makes these connections increasingly clear for the reader, whose suspicions of Mather's interpretive authority are consequently aroused.9 As his interrogation of Anne late in the novel illustrates, he labours under considerable imaginative limitations:

Mather said, "There's only one chance you won't be charged with complicity. If you make a statement."

"Is this the third degree?" Anne said.

"Why do you want to shelter him? Why keep your word to him when you don't –?"

"Go on," Anne said. "Be personal. No one can blame you. I don't. But I don't want you to think I'd keep my word to him. He killed the old man. He told me so."

"What old man?"

"The War Minister."

"You've got to think up something better than that," Mather said.

"But it's true. He never stole those notes. They double-crossed him. It was what they'd paid him to do the job."

"He spun you a fancy yarn," Mather said. "But *I* know where those notes came from."

"So do I. I can guess. From someone in this town."

"He told you wrong. They came from United Rail Makers in Victoria Street." (137)

Unable to get beyond the obvious fact that Raven possesses stolen money, Mather cannot penetrate the interpretive depths of the texts he confronts because he is determined to be certain, to make things "fit." *A Gun for Sale* shows us that neither Mather's values of organization, routine, and law nor his conviction that experience can be read with certainty is adequate for the restoration of order in a society whose social, political, and economic values create and encourage the broadest kind of disorder.

Mather's failings are textually linked to the failings of the master detectives of the classical detective story insofar as Mather is presented as a type of the fictional detective. His speech, and that of the other detectives in the novel, is peppered with the clichés of detective fiction. He and the others refer to Anne as a "moll" (76); and he twice remarks on his attraction to the case: "There's something about this case ... I can't leave it alone" (71), and "It's getting to me. There's something about it" (75). As well, Mather regularly responds to colleagues who suggest that there is "nothing" in a report or a location with expressions of Holmesian assurance: "I don't agree with you, sir" (75); "Everybody remembers something" (76); and "There's always something" (78). Greene never lets us forget that Mather is a character in a book, a fiction patterned on other fictions.

Mather's discussion of the case with the superintendent clearly illustrates the point. Soon after the latter notes that "in these stories you read people always remember *something*, but in real life they just say she was wearing something dark or something light" (75), Mather responds, "The books are right. People generally do remember something" (75). Similarly, when the two are reviewing their reconstruction of Raven's movements in Nottwich, they create a fiction in which Anne (though they do not yet realize it is her) is thought of as Raven's girl. Mather conjectures:

"She was coming for a long stay (a woman can get a lot in one suitcase) or else, if she was carrying his case too, he was the dominant one. Believes in treating her rough and making her do all the physical labour. That fits in with Raven's character. As for the girl –"

"In these gangster stories," the superintendent said, "they call her a moll."

"Well, this moll," Mather said, "is one of those girls who like being treated rough. Sort of clinging and avaricious, I picture her. If she had more spirit he'd carry one of the suitcases or else she'd split on him."

"I thought this Raven was about as ugly as they are made."

"That fits too," Mather said. "Perhaps she likes 'em ugly. Perhaps it gives her a thrill." (76)

Aside from the irony of Mather's unknowing speculation about his fiancée (perhaps not entirely mistaken since Mather dominates Anne), what is notable here and in the statements made earlier in the discussion between the two policemen is that Mather openly sides with the conventions of "gangster stories." Instead of using self-conscious comparisons between "real" life and the fictional world of detective novels to give the detective an opportunity to distance himself or herself from the fictional by claiming a privileged status (which, as we saw in "Murder for the Wrong Reason," is the usual practice in detective fiction), Greene, aware that such declarations occurring within a fictional text only double back to confirm the status of the detective as fiction (as text), uses these references to affirm the very fact that his detective is a fictional character existing within a fictional text. That is, Mather explicitly responds as a character in a book would respond: in gangster stories the girlfriends of criminals are called "molls," and so Mather calls the girl accompanying Raven a "moll." Similarly, Mather affirms the validity of practices represented in books: "The books are right" (75). As the narrative proceeds, the text continually indicates its own status as a text because Mather as a character is so one-dimensional as to be almost an abstraction. Greene might very well have called him "the detective" and thus have employed a strategy he uses elsewhere.[10]

Foregrounded here is the formulaic nature of the detective-story plot. In *A Gun for Sale* Greene uses the formula, but the text always points to its own formal structures. The apparatus of the detective story is thus laid bare to the reader with the aim of demystifying fictional conventions. This same reasoning also accounts for the "happy" endings, which are seen by many of Greene's critics as distinctive of the "entertainments" and as serious flaws in these books (Webster 12). Yet the entertainments' endings are not happy ones in any real sense of the word (the point is most obvious in *The Ministry of Fear*), despite the fact that all of them involve the bringing together of two "lovers." In this way, Greene employs what Peter J. Rabinowitz calls "an excessive cadence" ("End" 125) which, like Macheath's rescue at the end of Bertolt Brecht's *The Threepenny Opera*, ironically exposes the artificiality of the conventional ending in detective fiction: the elements of a happy ending are provided in a context that renders them ironic. At the end of *A Gun for Sale*, Anne and Mather arrive home bewildered, if only momentarily, by their success: Mather is not quite sure how or why things worked out so well for him, and Anne is haunted by the thought of Raven.

A Gun for Sale, like so many of Greene's novels in the period (including *The Power and the Glory*), exploits the formulaic pattern of pursuit that Tzvetan Todorov and Peter Brooks both link to the recovery of narrative. As a detective, Mather retraces the path of the criminal, Raven, who, in turn, retraces the path of Davis. In this case, the double pursuit helps contrast, thematically, the pursuit of law with the pursuit of justice, which, as in *It's a Battlefield*, are not identical. But this double pursuit again draws attention to *A Gun for Sale*'s status as a detective story. At about the half-way point in the text, Raven enters a bazaar in order to pick women's purses for money. When he sees an old woman with Anne's purse he follows her home: "She was just in sight, trailing her long old-fashioned skirt round a corner. He walked fast. He didn't notice in his hurry that he in his turn was followed by a man whose clothes he would immediately have recognized, the soft hat and overcoat worn like a uniform. Very soon he began to remember the road they took; he had been this way with the girl. It was like retracing in mind an old experience" (91–2). At the level of the narrative itself, the "old experience" Raven retraces is his walk with Anne out to the new housing estate, but on an intertextual level the "old experience" is the detective's journey to the scene of the crime. More particularly, Raven, pursued by Mather, is heading to a locked room where a woman's body is entombed in the chimney. The situation recalls that of Poe's "The Murders in the Rue Morgue"; Greene's investigators retrace the path taken by Dupin in what is often considered the first detective story. In this way the novel's repressed past – figured as the already-read – resurfaces in the text.

A Gun for Sale, like "Murder for the Wrong Reason," reveals its position within a textual network that acknowledges the narrative's status as repetition with difference. The novel identifies itself as a reinscription of Poe's tale (and of every detective story since) with variations. Because Raven retraces Anne's and Davis's paths and Mather retraces Raven's line, *A Gun for Sale* allegorizes the development of narrative as a process of (re)inscribing earlier narratives.[11] And, again, the narrative, through the allusion to Poe's story, consciously points to its own textuality by likening itself to a previous narrative which stands as the novel's origin – however problematic that concept may be since the very determination of origin relies on a narrative construction.[12] Similarly, the text also looks ahead to its own retellings when Buddy Ferguson's future is briefly alluded to: "All through his life the tale cropped up in print in the most unlikely places: serious histories, symposiums of famous crimes" (148).

A Gun for Sale is both a narrative of narratives and a critical examination that explodes cherished ideas of success within a capitalist economy and of the authority of socially and politically sanctioned readers. Raven's and Mather's pursuits, when taken together, uncover a third narrative line which is the story of Sir Marcus's corruption and the criminality at the heart of thirties' capitalism. Yet neither Raven's nor Mather's tracings fully disclose this aspect of the narrative. Even at the narrative's end, both Raven and Mather remain only partially aware of the extent of their separate investigations. Raven is killed before all can be explained to him, and Mather is perplexed by the whole affair: "I'm to have promotion. I don't know why. It seems to me as if I'd bungled it" (184). Similarly, Saunders reflects that "it hadn't been a satisfying job ... There was a mystery about the whole affair; everything hadn't come out" (174). Even Anne, who is perhaps closest to understanding the implications of Raven's actions, ultimately fails to see the deep truth of things. Too concerned with her own narrowly defined interests (the prospect of war matters only insofar as it will affect her and Mather [55]), she quickly and completely forgets her glimpse into the English heart of darkness when she returns to London (185).

All these characters take little or nothing away from their experience because the ideology they share limits their readings of that experience: Saunders, Mather, and Anne continue to believe in the inviolability of England. It is also apparent at the end of *A Gun for*

Sale that, although Sir Marcus, Davis, and Raven are dead, nothing changes. The people of Nottwich, typified by Ruby and the porter, continue to admire Sir Marcus and Davis and feel sympathy for them (173), while Saunders reflects at a meeting for stutterers that "it almost seemed as if Raven's act had had no consequences: as if to kill was just as much an illusion as to dream. Here was Mr Davis all over again; they were turned out of a mould, and you couldn't break the mould, and suddenly over Mr Montague Phelp's [the speaker's] shoulder Saunders saw the photograph of the Grand Master of the Lodge, above the platform: ... Sir Marcus" (176). Ultimately, Sir Marcus, Davis, and Raven are the inevitable products of forces working within society and of the implicit conflicts within capitalism. Hence, *A Gun for Sale* at once offers the consolation of the happy ending, traditionally the province of the thriller, and withdraws this consolation by suggesting that the enemy cannot so easily be found out and eradicated. In the world of the novel, the social and political corruption that capitalism breeds is found in those figures who are most honoured. In this respect the social and political hierarchy is inverted since it is the economic élite and their protectors, the established legal authorities, who are shown to bear the brunt of guilt.

A Gun for Sale, then, demonstrates both the failure of conventional hierarchies and the limitations of any reading, since none of the text's inscribed authorities are able to do more than partially read the texts they confront. This vision perhaps explains why Greene described the novel as an "entertainment," for in so doing he distanced it from the literature of an élite that was identified with both modernist experimentation and political conservativism. The subheading was a signal of political and literary resistance.

BRIGHTON ROCK

Greene also conceived his next novel, *Brighton Rock*, as a thriller. *A Gun for Sale* had been both a literary and a financial success, and another thriller offered Greene the opportunity both to capitalize on this success and to explose further those issues that he had already dealt with in his earlier novels.

There is something disingenuous about Greene's claim in *Ways of Escape* that the detective story in *Brighton Rock* is confined to the first fifty pages. Even if he had had the strength of mind to do so Greene could not have taken the detective story out of *Brighton Rock*, for its structure is woven into the fabric of the novel and cannot be excised with the surgical removal of a fixed number of pages.

Whatever Greene may say, *Brighton Rock*, though it is many other things, is also a detective story. As a story of reading and interpretation, the novel thematizes reading and so comments on how it is to be read. Within the narrative, scenes of reading abound while the residual structure of the detective story contains these within a larger interpretive frame that is the detective's investigation of a criminal's fiction. These thematic and structural elements raise a number of points about reading in general and, by extension, about how critics have usually approached the novel. Like the stick of candy that gives the book its title and can be broken at any point to reveal the name "Brighton Rock," the novel, no matter where we look in it, always presents the critic with his or her own activity of reading and interpreting.

Central to the novel's presentation of interpretive issues is the character of Ida Arnold, who functions in a role analogous to that of the detective in stories by such writers as Conan Doyle, Christie, and Dorothy Sayers. Ida is the amateur investigator whose self-appointed task is to sift the various clues and the statements of witnesses for information that will help her to construct a true account of Hale's death. She, in fact, reads and interprets others' texts so that she can produce a narrative which is the story of what happened to Hale; and in this way she is also a figure analogous to the reader or critic of *Brighton Rock* who sifts the text for meaning in order to develop his or her own interpretation of the text.

In *Brighton Rock* it is quickly made clear that Hale's death is in some way precipitated by Pinkie's gang, though how they do this remains unclear throughout the novel. As the story opens, Fred Hale, fearing for his life, strikes up an acquaintance with Ida Arnold, a fun-loving pragmatist who repeatedly insists on her knowledge of the difference between right and wrong. After Hale's death, Ida begins her own investigation in order to bring Pinkie to justice and to save Rose the suffering that Pinkie will inflict upon her. As well, Ida sees her quest as a chance to have a bit of fun (37).

Also quickly apparent to the reader acquainted with detective stories is that *Brighton Rock*'s narration treats Ida in quite a different manner from the way more orthodox detective stories treat their great detectives. Characters such as Dupin, Holmes, Poirot, Wimsey, and Miss Marple are part of Ida's lineage, yet, unlike them in their respective narratives, Ida is mocked by the narrative in which she appears: her understanding of the case and of the world she inhabits is clearly shown to be limited by her inability to see beneath the surface of things. Brighton for her is a place of fun and excitement, and life, though she takes it with "deadly seriousness" (36), is always "good"

(19, 72), made up as it is of various physical sensations and corporeal pleasures: "Life was sunlight on brass bedposts, Ruby port, the leap of the heart when the outsider you have backed passes the post and the colours go bobbing up. Life was poor Fred's mouth pressed down on hers in the taxi, vibrating with the engine along the parade" (36). Ida's naïve optimism, which we are told has "something dangerous and remorseless" (36) in it, and her spiritual blindness undercut her authority as an interpreter of events and partially account for the ironic tone that dominates many of the text's descriptions of her:

Ida Arnold was on the right side. She was cheery, she was healthy, she could get a bit lit with the best of them. She liked a good time, her big breasts bore their carnality frankly down the Old Steyne [a Brighton street], but you had only to look at her to know that you could rely on her. She wouldn't tell tales to your wife, she wouldn't remind you next morning of what you wanted to forget, she was honest, she was kindly, she belonged to the great middle law-abiding class, her amusements were their amusements, her superstitions their superstitions (the planchette scratching the French polish on the occasional table, and the salt over the shoulder), she had no more love for anyone than they had. (80)

Like comparable figures elsewhere in Greene's novels (Mather and Raven in *A Gun For Sale* or Rowe in *The Ministry of Fear*), Ida has little in common with fictional detectives such as Holmes or Poirot, who are seldom in error. Because they have powers of interpretation so re-fined as to render even the most opaque texts lucid and easily read, these detectives are granted an authority by the society they serve and by the reader of their stories that elevates them above the norm and above the law. For them, all the universe is intelligible and no mystery is so deep as to defy the power of intellect and reason. In contrast, Ida's belief in "ghosts, ouija boards, [and] tables which rapped" (36) makes her almost a parody of the Holmesian investi-gator. As the above passage makes clear, she is neither rational nor upper-class; instead, the text emphasizes her femininity (something Pinkie is particularly fearful of [92 and elsewhere]) and her ties to popular culture. Ida, we are told, is "of the people" (32), while her room reflects popular taste both in its decor and in the assortment of books displayed: "an Edgar Wallace, a Netta Syrett, from a second-hand stall ... *The Good Companions* ... *Sorrell and Son*" (42).[13] Both by her sex and her "popular heart" (34) Ida is placed outside the do-minant critical community of the inter-war period typified and led by conservative and élitist figures such as I.A. Richards and the Leavises.

None the less, Greene's mocking tone when Ida is described suggests not only that Ida is incapable of loving but also that she lacks a sense of "higher," spiritual, things. (She boasts to Rose that "it's the world we got to deal with" [198], and elsewhere attention is drawn to her "old and vulgarized Grecian name" [16].) This perceived shortcoming, perhaps more than anything else, has dominated readings of the novel because a conflation of interests has enabled critics, most of them male, to attack overtly Ida Arnold's character and her actions while covertly dismissing critical approaches that focus on aspects of the secular, the feminine, or the popular in the novel. Ida is denigrated for her lack of spiritual awareness while Pinkie is elevated to tragic stature as the latest in a line extending from Macbeth and Milton's Satan through the damned heroes and heroines of the Romantics into the present because he professes a belief in a divine order against which he defiantly rebels: "*Credo in unum Satanum*" (165). In Pinkie's "dark theology" (114), the crucial difference is not between right and wrong but between good and evil.[14] Because Rose shares Pinkie's knowledge, she and Pinkie are presented in the text and in critical discussions both as complementary elements and as morally superior to Ida and many of the book's other characters, such as Dallow, Cubitt, Colleoni, and Phil Corkery. The novel makes this point particularly clear in Rose's comments to Pinkie and in exchanges between Ida and Rose:

"Why, won't you lift a finger to stop him killing you?" [Ida asks.]
"He wouldn't do me any harm."
"You're young. You don't know things like I do."
"There's things *you* don't know." ...
"I know one thing you don't. I know the difference between Right and Wrong. They didn't teach you *that* at school."
Rose didn't answer; the woman was quite right; the two words meant nothing to her. Their taste was extinguished by stronger foods – Good and Evil. The woman could tell her nothing she didn't know about these – she knew by tests as clear as mathematics that Pinkie was evil – what did it matter in that case whether he was right or wrong? (199)[15]

On these occasions, the narrative in *Brighton Rock* frequently, though sometime uneasily, contrasts two distinct views of the world – the secular, one is tempted to say pagan, outlook of Ida and others, and the religious perception of Rose and Pinkie. For Greene, the latters' point of view is preferred to Ida's, since a spiritual awareness gives "some significance to living"; as Greene complained in his essay on François Mauriac, the absence of a spiritual context in novels by Woolf or Forster reduces the importance of the human act (*CE* 91).

Similarly, critics[16] grant Pinkie and Rose moral superiority on the basis of T.S. Eliot's remarks in his essay "Baudelaire" (1931), of which Greene thought enough to quote in "Henry James: The Religious Aspect" (1933) (CE 41) and then echo both in "Frederick Rolfe: Edwardian Inferno" (1934) and in the priest's final words to Rose in *Brighten Rock*: "A Catholic is more capable of evil than anyone. I think – perhaps because we believe in Him – we are more in touch with the devil than other people" (246).[17] The "religious sense" (CE 91) that suffuses *Brighten Rock* allows many commentators to interpret Ida as one of the "lukewarm" (*Rev.* 3:16) who is of no consequence in the novel's religious world (Kunkel 102).

To read Pinkie or Ida in this way is to set the book against traditionally canonical authors and their texts, and, for traditionally minded critics, this is easier to do than to look at it through the lens of less canonical popular works or genres, although such an approach, as Neil Nehring's fine article demonstrates, has tremendous potential for expanding our understanding of the text. If one examines the novel from the perspective of other detective stories, a different generic structure emerges: Pinkie may have Macbeth and Milton's Satan as textual antecedents, but his character also has Rico from W.R. Burnett's *Little Caesar* (1929) as a closer precursor, while Ida becomes a central character conceived as both a literary heir to and a reaction against a tradition of extremely rational and esoteric amateur detectives. Like them, she is highly observant – we are told, perhaps ironically, that "she missed nothing" (20) – and, like them, she seeks the truth (37). As well, as is the case with Poirot in Christie's *The Murder of Roger Ackroyd*, her task is explicitly figured as one of reading; however, in her case the texts she reads, "Sukill" and "Fresuicilleye" (44), are literally occult ones provided by the ouija board and not by a naturalized author inscribed in the narrative, such as Dr Sheppard in Christie's novel. Greene may find Ida a flat character who refuses to come alive (WE 61); but, if we read *Brighton Rock* as a detective story and in the context of his other crime novels, Ida must be seen – whatever his view of her – as more than a spiritually ignorant character who is to be mocked. As a detective, she differs only in trifles from Mather, Raven, Rowe, and even Mason in "Murder for the Wrong Reason," and her spiritual blindness serves as one of the means, particular to this novel, of discrediting her authority and of reflecting the difficulty of any one person arriving at a definite, final understanding of events or of texts.

The novel draws attention to this difficulty by suggesting that Pinkie's guilt in criminal matters is mitigated by a background of poverty ("Man is made by the places in which he lives," the text tells us [37]) and by the presence of Colleoni, a self-described "business man" (64), who, though the leader of a vast criminal organization, is also well regarded by the Brighton police and by the Conservative Party, which seeks to persuade him into politics (159). Similarly, although she succeeds in her task of ridding society of the menace of Pinkie, Ida does nothing to alleviate the conditions that produced him; the source of the evil remains, just as Pinkie's voice remains on record and in the reader's mind at the end of the narrative. On one level, then, Ida is like the classical detective because she is the instrument of law and order in *Brighton Rock*; but, on another, the book challenges the ideology of the classical detective story because the elimination of the criminal, as in the hard-boiled novel, fails to purify the body politic, which is plagued on the human plane by systemic corruption and on the spiritual plane by sin.

Also foregrounding the difficulty of arriving at a final understanding of events or of texts is *Brighton Rock*'s handling of the detective story's structure. As elaborated in the earlier discussion of the relationship between *fabula* and *sjuzhet* in the detective story, *Brighton Rock* tangles the two stories of crime and of investigation in such a way that each becomes the origin of the other. Ida's investigation of events, metaphorically represented in her reading of an occult text, both reveals and determines the text she reads, and so *Brighton Rock* illustrates the relationship of readers to texts. Both stand apart from each other, just as *fabula* and *sjuzhet* do in theory, but in the moment of reading, text and reader interact in such a way that the text directs the reader while the reader produces the text. The relationship, like that between Ida and Pinkie, is symbiotic and without origin. For both to exist, reading must always already be present. Where there is no reader, there is no narrative but only the material presence of the book and the person who is its potential reader. The narrative exists only insofar as it is a thing that is being or has been read – even if only by its author, who does not create out of nothing but out of his or her own experience with other narratives. The question of the primacy of reading or writing (narrative production) is insoluble; each relies on the other because the already-read (*déjà-lu*) is always behind any literary production. Hence, reading a text actualizes that text for the reader by inscribing it in his or her consciousness where it previously did not exist. At the same time, the text that is read is determined by the reader, who reads what he or she is, in a sense, programmed to read through his or her experience of the "already-read." This phenomenon is what lies behind the differing judgments on *Brighton Rock*: probable or improbable plot, proletarian novel or moral allegory, detective story or religious drama, light fiction or serious literature, entertainment or tragedy, and so on. However it is seen, the novel is the product of a unique interpretive act. What the narrative shows us is both how these differences are generated and how they coexist within the textual field of the novel.

Perhaps more than in other detective stories, *Brighton Rock* makes the reading process a concern from its first page when we find Hale as Kolley Kibber following a route (itself prescribed by a text) through Brighton in search of someone who has a copy of *The Daily Messenger* in hand and who can repeat a prepared text: "You are Mr. Kolley Kibber. I claim the *Daily Messenger* prize" (5). Language is thus explicitly figured as subject to coding. The text of the novel stresses that the claim must be made "in the proper form of words" (5), and so the possibility of arriving at a correct, univocal reading of a text, of fully understanding the code, is implied. Simultaneously, however, an allusion to Colley Cibber[18] introduces another level of meaning that subverts the overt claim that a text can be read in only one way; and, since the challenge Hale receives ultimately results in his death, the notion of reading for a single meaning, of saying that this novel means this or that it is about that, is presented as inadequate.

This idea is confirmed in the larger investigation of reading enacted in the narrative. As the detective, Ida is the reader of the fictions that Pinkie creates to explain Hale's, Spicer's, and, though the last does not occur, Rose's deaths. In producing these fictions, Pinkie makes use of tangible signs which are intended to mislead their reader. The cards he has Spicer lay along Hale's route are meant to stand as the visible traces of Hale's presence, as Hale's signature. Similarly, in preparing the story of Rose's suicide, Pinkie makes use of a note that Rose herself has written and insists that she "add a piece" to explain her death (231) – as if a few words could adequately explain the complicated relationship between Pinkie and Rose and so justify the suicide of a teenage girl, especially one who considers the act damning. In both instances, and particularly in the latter, Pinkie's fictions are explicitly tied to the production of written texts, and in this way the act of detection that involves the reading of these texts mirrors the activity of the novel's reader and of reading in general.

Like the novel's reader, Ida sifts the stories that emerge from her interrogations of numerous witnesses – Molly, the bartender, the police, Crab, Cubitt, Dallow, and, most important, Rose – for traces of an underlying, suppressed narrative that tells the story of Hale's death. Explicit references to Ida as an interpreter of written texts strengthen the identification between her and the reader of this or any other text. This identification is represented early in the novel in Ida's interpretation of the ouija board's messages (43–4), in her assertion that Tate's mistake of writing "Black Dog" for "Black Boy" means "Care" (70), and in her reading of the police report on Hale's death (79). Yet what the narrative stresses about Ida's particular method of reading is her certainty and her confidence in her own interpretive skills, which, she believes, enable her always to detect *the* meaning of a particular linguistic construction. In the midst of a conversation between Phil Corkery and Ida, we are told that "in every word either of them uttered she detected the one meaning" (145). Similarly, the text implies the importance of the already-read to Ida's own reading by remarking on her past experience as a reader: "She said slowly over to herself: '... Brighton Rock ...' The clue would have seemed hopeless to many women, but Ida Arnold had been trained by the Board. Queerer things than that had spidered out under her fingers and Old Crowe's: with complete confidence her mind began to work" (163). For Ida, as for Mather, texts "must mean something" (44), which is to say, given the importance she attaches to being right, that they must have an unequivocal and determinable sense which closes itself off from ambiguity and plurality. To write "Black Dog" instead of "Black Boy" means "care" and no further explanation is seen by Ida as necessary. Nor is one forthcoming.

What is interesting about Ida's approach to reading in *Brighton Rock* is that the novel repeatedly denies its validity by showing it to be limited and self-reflecting. Sherlock Holmes may be able to assert confidently in *A Study in Scarlet* (1888) that "rache" means "revenge," but fifty years later Ida's equally confident assertions are open to questioning and doubt. Not only is her authority as a detective undercut by her self-righteous sense of justice and her pagan sensibility in the face of Pinkie's and Rose's religious awareness, but her very certainty in matters of interpretation embodies a delusive sense of the world and of language that, as Phil Corkery or Clarence would say, is "terrible" (222, 244): Ida's conclusions are often both error-ridden and misguided. Although she does finally track Pinkie down, her understanding of the circumstances surrounding Hale's death remains vague. Indeed, as the novel progresses Ida explains Hale's death as suicide (44, 75–6), murder (163), and the result of a heart attack brought on by fear (197). Nowhere in the text, however, is an account of Hale's death given, although some critics such as A.A. De Vitis (68) and Sherry (636) suggest otherwise by stating that Hale choked to death on a piece of Brighton rock candy which was pushed down his throat.[19] As Ida realizes, "Brighton Rock" is undoubtedly a clue to the circumstances of Hale's death, but its meaning remains undefined. Similarly, for Greene's readers, "Brighton Rock" is also a seemingly significant piece of information since it is both the novel's title and a recurring phrase in the narrative, although just how it is significant remains enigmatic and open to interpretation.

Ida's understanding of Pinkie and Rose is also inhibited by her lack of a religious sense and her adherence to a middle-class vision of society. Unable to see otherwise, she assumes that her world is the only world; when she looks out the window, she sees only the city she knows (72). She cannot see what is not part of her experience and so is blind to the dark side of Brighton – the poverty, the crime, the early deaths of so many young people.[20] For this reason, she is completely ignorant of the knowledge that comes with the experience of poverty. The point is driven home at the end of her second of three encounters with Rose:

"He doesn't love you [Rose]."
   "I don't care," the childish voice stubbornly murmured.
   "What do you mean, you don't care?"
   "I love *him*."
   "You're acting morbid," Ida said. "If I was your mother I'd give you a good hiding. What'd your father and mother say if they knew?"
   "*They* wouldn't care."
   "And how do you think it will all end?"
   "I don't know."
   "You're young. That's what it is," Ida said, "romantic. I was like you once. You'll grow out of it. All you need is a bit of experience." The Nelson Place eyes stared back at her without understanding: driven to her hole the small animal peered out at the bright and breezy world; in the hole were murder, copulation, extreme poverty, fidelity and the love and fear of God, but the small animal had not the knowledge to deny that only in the glare and open world outside was something which people called experience. (123)

By invoking the authority of Rose's parents, Ida reveals her own particular middle-class conception of family life. What she never realizes, however, is that families in Nelson Place, where Rose grew up, and in Paradise Piece, where Pinkie was raised, are conditioned by their poverty (which is not to say that Pinkie's conduct is ever simply explained in terms of his environment). When, in the novel's penultimate section – a location in the detective narrative that is traditionally the site of the detective's summation which concludes the story – Ida sits back with her friend Clarence and summarizes the case, she asserts that "what [Rose] needs at a time like that is her mother and dad" (243). This assertion characteristically renders the narrator's previous comment, "Ida Arnold had an answer to everything" (243), ironic since we have seen how Rose's parents are brought out of one of their "moods" (141) with no less than the sale of their daughter to Pinkie for fifteen guineas (143). Despite being criticized for being "so terribly certain about things" (222), Ida fails to recognize how her preconceptions colour her interpretation and so does not see that her reading of Rose collapses.

Similarly, Ida's dubious reading of written texts equally undercuts our confidence in her interpretive skills. In explaining the ouija board's "Fresuicilleye," she asserts: " 'It's clear as clear. *Fre* is short for Fred and *Suici* for Suicide and Eye; that's what I always say – an eye for an eye and a tooth for a tooth … See that *Eye*. That as good as tells me what to do" (44). Here, Ida's interpretation of "eye" reflects her own ideology based on a conception of Old Testament justice. In other words, she reads, like any reader, what she is programmed to read: she creates the text, as it were, in her own image. The other parts of her interpretation here are equally questionable in light of subsequent developments; "Fre" may be a cipher for Fred (though this is not Hale's real name), but "suici" for "suicide" is unlikely given the information she uncovers about Hale's death. As well, the two "L's," though suggestive, remain enigmatic since she cannot interpret them at this point in the novel. Towards the end of the book, she rereads the board's text and concludes that "the Board had foreseen it all – Sui, its own word for the scream, the agony, the leap [of Pinkie]" (245). Significantly, the two "L's" remain unaccounted for: Ida's reading is incomplete. Ultimately, she never discovers the method of or the reasons for Hale's death, though as readers we understand that in some way these reasons lie in the fact that Hale is implicated in the murder of Kite. As a detective and as a model of critical authority Ida fails to gain our confidence; consequently, we can only be suspicious of her claims to certainty and her authority as a figure of justice.

None the less, though *Brighton Rock* demonstrates the limitations of any reading, it also insists upon the necessity of reading. Just as Chesterton described every detail within the urban landscape as a sign to be read by the detective in his or her search for truth (159), so is every detail within a detective story of potential significance to the reader's interpretation of the narrative. In *Brighton Rock* the experience of the world is represented in terms of reading; Brighton is explicitly a world of text. Rose's father's face is "marked deeply with the hieroglyphics of pain and patience and suspicion" (142); "the edge of the sea [is] like a line of writing in whitewash: big sprawling letters" (152); and Ida, herself, is likened by the narrative to an enigmatic text that insists it be read: "She stood there like a wall at the end of an alley scrawled with the obscene chalk messages of an enemy" (196). Reading is presented as an unavoidable activity, and, because humanity has a deep-seated desire for intelligibility – for things to make sense – those who claim for themselves the authority to offer explanations (such as the police, Ida, and even Pinkie) are shown to have power over others because it is tacitly acceded to them. In the case of the police, society assigns them the task of determining whether or not a crime has been committed, and they produce their own reading of Hale's death. Their report offers a univocal interpretation of the details of the death that also preserves their power because in their eyes and in the eyes of the society the case is solved. The closing of the case thus maintains an impression of efficiency which, in turn, justifies the authority conferred upon them.

Ida's own "certain" reading of events is shown to be no less powerful, as her investigation is explicitly seen to be the motivating pressure behind Pinkie's actions: Rose thinks Ida is "the explanation" for Pinkie's behaviour (196), and Dallow blames Ida for what happens in the novel: "This [the attempt on Rose's life] is your doing. You made him marry her, you made him …" (236). The source of Ida's power over those such as Rose and, to a lesser extent, Pinkie who are not as sure of their interpretive skills is her belief in her own righteousness. For Pinkie, Rose, Cubitt, Dallow, and Spicer, Ida is frightening because they cannot place her: " 'She scares me,' Rose whispered. 'I don't know what she wants'" (112). The problem is that Pinkie's gang cannot place Ida and Phil Corkery in any context that would provide an interpretive key for a reading of them: " 'Who are you?' Rose implored her. 'Why do you interfere with us? You're not the police' "(196). The question of who Ida is plagues Pinkie (100, 127), Rose (138, 196), and Dallow (232); none is able to read her, and so Ida has power over each of them because she cannot be read correctly and because she believes in her ability to decode the texts they present. In one sense, Ida's power is apparent in the ease with which she is able to gain the confidences of men; in another, her power is clearly seen in her influence on events in the narrative: she pressures Pinkie into killing Spicer and into attempting to kill Rose, she persuades Dallow to help rescue Rose, and she returns Rose to her parents (243).

Similarly, the source of Pinkie's power over Rose is, in part, his confidence in his reading of things and his corresponding belief that one can construct univocal fictions that will be read in only one way. Rose, on the other hand, is uncertain and unable to read the various texts in the world she confronts: "She went cautiously down – seven o'clock – what furious faces – in the hall a ball of paper scuffled under her feet. She smoothed it out and read a pencilled message: 'Lock your door. Have a good time.' She didn't understand it: it might as well have been in code – she assumed it must have something to do with this foreign world where you sinned on a bed and people lost their lives suddenly and strange men hacked at your door and cursed you in the night" (190). To Rose, Pinkie is both knowledgeable and accurate in his readings. In contrast to her own textual ignorance, his skill lies in his ability to manipulate texts and language for his own ends. Hence, he can deceive Rose into believing that he loves her and convince her that suicide is the only way to escape the prospect of their separation.

> He watched her closely while he did his sleight of hand, passing off his idea as hers. "I got the car all ready. We could go out into the country where no one would hear ..." He measured her terror carefully and before she could pass the card back to him, he changed his tone. "That's only if the worst comes to the worst." The phrase intrigued him: he repeated it: the worst – that was the stout woman with her glassy righteous eye coming up the smoky road – to the worst – and that was drunken ruined Mr Prewitt watching from behind the curtains for just one typist. (213)

As Pinkie realizes, the source of his power lies in the phrase itself because it can influence the actions of others, and for this reason he insists on Rose adding a piece to her suicide note because he wants others – Ida and the police – to read his fiction in a certain way; and, in this regard, he shares Ida's conception of reading. Like her, he assumes that a text can be made to direct its reader in a single interpretation.

Yet the power Pinkie and Ida think they have, because it is based on its own fiction of univocal reading, is illusory; despite her claims and his intentions, their sense of reading is shown to be limited and incomplete. Not mindful of his own belief that "it [is] the little things which [trip] you up" (27), Pinkie continues to try to construct "readerly" texts that will close off all but one reading. But, as quickly becomes apparent, "little things" in these texts, such as Spicer's leaving one of Kolley Kibber's cards in Snow's, Spicer's being photographed, Rose's realizing that Spicer was not Kolley Kibber, and a host of other incidents, open Pinkie's fictions to different ways of reading. Consequently, as each of Pinkie's fictions reveals its status as a fiction, he is compelled to create another fiction which will both account for and cover up the weaknesses in the previous fiction. His efforts to conceal the facts of Hale's death lead him to kill Spicer, an action that necessitates efforts to hide the truth about Spicer's death; these efforts, in turn, lead to the fiction of Rose's suicide. The chain of fictions could go on without end – something he despairingly acknowledges: "There wasn't any end to what he had begun" (106). Each murder he commits and each corresponding fiction he constructs are attempts to control the reading of the initial crime because each seeks to be the final "true" account of what happened, though this status is shown to be forever elusive.

In linking power to the construction of readerly texts and authoritative readings and then in exposing the impossibility of this construction, *Brighton Rock* expresses a radical scepticism about any person or institution that claims for itself the ability to discern and present a single meaning or truth. (And it is in this context that the priest's final comments to Rose about no one being able to conceive of "the ... appalling ... strangeness of the mercy of God" [246] have their place, since the authority of church doctrine is also questioned.[21]) This kind of scepticism has far-reaching consequences, because it undermines the basis of any kind of authority, whether political, religious, or critical. The power of these authorities, like the power of Ida and Pinkie, is based on a deluded sense of their own ability to determine what is "true," and so *Brighton Rock* urges a method of reading that can guard against both political and intellectual domination and reveals what Nehring sees as Greene's "anarchist" politics (227).

What is apparent from this discussion of how *Brighton Rock* thematizes reading and of how the novel is usually read is the cost of any interpretation that claims for itself a final authority. Ida is not only a figure for the reader; she is also a figure for the critic of the novel who, like her, sees in the text what he or she expects to see at the expense of dismissing or passing over entirely those aspects of a text that may be most crucial to its structural and linguistic integrity. *Brighton Rock* presents its reader with a vision of a world where any attempt to make sense of something is doomed to failure. In the end there is only the mystery of narrative's power to draw us towards meaning while forever pushing it away from us.

THE CONFIDENTIAL AGENT

The Confidential Agent picks up where *Brighton Rock* left off. Here, too, the world is explicitly figured as a text, and so how one reads is again an issue of vital political importance. From the novel's outset, the world is seen, as it is in *Brighton Rock*, in terms of writing: D.'s memories of England are "rather literary" (9); an organization can have the wrong initial letters (10); a child is "like writing so illegible you didn't even try to decipher it" (11); and we are told that "now there [are] so many varieties of economic materialism, so many initial letters" (56). Similarly, three of the book's characters – D., L., and K. – are identified only by initials, a fact that again underscores the textual nature of this world.[22] When we are told that D. and L. are "separated by different initial letters" (11), our attention is drawn not only to their different names but also to their opposing organizations and ideologies, for these too are represented as texts.

As in *Brighton Rock*, in the world of *The Confidential Agent* one must develop and practise a radically sceptical method of reading; but, as D.'s situation makes clear, such a practice has its own set of difficulties:

> You could trust nobody but yourself, and sometimes you were uncertain whether after all you could trust yourself. *They* didn't trust you, any more than they had trusted the friend with the holy medal; they were right then, and who wâs to say whether they were not right now? You – you were a prejudiced party; the ideology was a complex affair; heresies crept in ... He wasn't certain that it wasn't right for him to be watched. After all, there were aspects of economic materialism which, if he searched his heart he did not accept ... And the watcher – was he watched? He was haunted for a moment by the vision of an endless distrust. In an inner pocket, a bulge over the breast, he carried what were called credentials, but credence no longer meant belief. (10)

D. finds himself caught between different fictions, knowing that any text will always contain the "heresies" that prohibit unquestioning acceptance of a single revealed reading or interpretation. His scepticism carries with it the ideological consequence of any kind of action being impossible as the subject freezes between two poles, uncertain even of the self. For Greene, this situation mirrors his own distrust of dogmatic positions and helps to explain his ambivalent response to the Spanish Civil War, when many of his contemporaries voiced clearly partisan opinions.[23]

As he struggles to find truth among the numerous fictions, the layers of deceit and mistrust he encounters, D. discovers that the only solution is to choose the fiction he wants to believe while acknowledging its status as a fiction open to various interpretations.[24] Ultimately, D. finds that the only authority for any reading of events must lie within himself: "There was no end to the complicated work of half-trust and half-deceit. Suppose the ministry had made a mistake ... suppose, if he handed the papers over, they should sell them to L. He knew he could trust himself. He knew nothing else" (72). In the deceit-filled world of *The Confidential Agent*, where a number of fictions compete for dominance, D. must make his choice and remain bound to it even though he, like Greene, knows that he may be wrong: " 'You choose your side once for all – of course, it may be the wrong side. Only history can tell that' " (60). Yet for all his self-awareness, D. is an amateur unsure of what action to take and incapable, even when outraged, of moving decisively. Only too aware that ideological biases underpin the claims of any text's authority – witness his discussion of the differing versions of *The Song of Roland* (62) – D. cannot promote his own version of the truth: he fails to buy coal, and it is only in spite of his efforts that he prevents its sale to the other side.

Still, if life is not to become "impossible" (32), D. must believe that the truth *can* be discerned, though it may elude his or anyone else's understanding: "It [the problem of choosing] wasn't so much a question of morality as a question of simply existing" (32). The difficulty with this position is that the fiction one chooses determines one's experience of the world. In D.'s case, his choice of a side, of an ideology, brings him into a world of melodramatic conflict where all things are perceived as being involved in that conflict. "He had imagined that the suspicion which was the atmosphere of his own life was due to civil war, but he began to believe that it existed everywhere: it was part of human life ... It was as if the whole world lay in the shadow of abandonment" (64). As the text frequently asserts, D., like Raven, "carried the war within him. Wherever D. was, there was a war ... Danger was a part of him" (9–10); and, given this perspective, a ship reminds him of a "hearse" (9) while its deck is "like a map marked with trenches" (10). As the narrative quickly develops, D.'s "suspicion widen[s] to include the whole world" (37), with the result that he is forced into a position that is almost impossible to maintain:

He hadn't yet had time to absorb the information the child had given him – was the manageress another of his, as it were, collaborators, like K., anxious to see that he followed the narrow and virtuous path, or had she been bribed by L.? Why, in that case, should he have been sent to this hotel by the people at home? His room had been booked; everything had been arranged for him, so that they should never lose contact. But that, of course, might all have been arranged by whoever it was gave information to L. – if anybody had. There was no end to the circles in this hell. (50)

As we will see with Rowe, because D. reads the world as a melodrama or a thriller, the text foregrounds his status as a melodramatic character. Rose calls him "the mystery man" (27) and repeatedly urges him not to be melodramatic because she does not like it (19, 25) and because others such as Lord Benditch, Forbes, Fetting, and Brigstock do not see the world that way (63, 94). On the other hand, D. attributes his own impulses to L. when he speculates that L. may also read melodramas and so may be acting as if he were in a melodrama (53). If this is true, then D. cannot help but play his part in the melodrama conceived by L. Textually, the consequence of D.'s reading of the world is the emergence of explicitly melodramatic moments that the narrative ties to his thoughts:

... this time he couldn't sleep at all – never before had he let those papers [his credentials as an agent] out of his possession. They had been with him all across Europe ... He felt uneasy without them. They were his authority and now he was nothing – just an undesirable alien, lying on a shabby bed in a disreputable hotel. Suppose the girl [Else, to whom D. has given his papers for safe keeping] should boast of his confidence ... suppose she should change her stockings and leave his papers lying about, forgotten ... L., he thought grimly, would never have done a thing like that [give the papers to Else]. In a way the whole future of what was left of his country lay in the stockings of an underpaid child. (55)

Similarly, the moments before his meeting with Benditch exploit the mechanics of narrative suspense:

In three-quarters of an hour, he thought, as a clock told eleven-fifteen, everything would be decided one way or another. They would probably try to take some advantage of the fog ... He came downstairs with his heart knocking; he told himself in vain that nothing could happen in daylight, in London: he was safe ... He turned away, his heart still knocking in its cage, as if it were trying to transmit a message, a warning, in a code he didn't understand ... This was the best policed city in the world ... The fog came up all around him ... He walked quickly, listening hard. ... It couldn't take more than half an hour. Everything would have to be decided soon ... The fog clouded everything; he listened for footsteps and heard only his own feet tapping on stone. The silence was not reassuring ... Somehow, somewhere, they would have to strike. (77–80)

Here, short, simple sentences and repeated references to the fog, which shrouds the safety of daylight, to D's footsteps, to his heart-beat, and to an impending danger combine to create an atmosphere of menace, heighten tension, and foreground the melodrama. For D., the meeting with Benditch is crucial on two accounts: first, D. believes the fate of his country to be at stake; and, secondly, the conclusion of the meeting means the conclusion of his mission, and so represents a possible end for the narrative. But the intrusion of another melodramatic event, the theft of his credentials by the butler, results in the failure of his meeting and the perpetuation of both his melodramatic reading of the world and the narrative's thriller plot;

D., like Rowe, is unable to escape the melodramatic narrative of which he is a part. Self-consciously, he cannot help wondering at the absurdity of his situation:

He was a confidential agent employed in an important coal deal on which the fate of a country might depend; she [Rose] was a young woman, the daughter of a peer whose coal he wanted, and the beloved, apparently, of a Mr Forbes who also controlled several mines and kept a mistress in Shepherd's Market (that was irrelevant); a child had been murdered by the manageress or Mr K. – action, presumably, on behalf of the rebels, although they were employed by his own people. That was the situation: a strategical and political – and criminal – one. (131)

Here, too, the narrative draws attention to its status as a thriller by summarizing and re-presenting important and not-so-important information for the reader. As it is expressed here, D.'s situation prefigures Rowe's in *The Ministry of Fear* when in a dream Rowe describes the world to his mother (*MF* 65); however, *The Ministry of Fear*, more than *The Confidential Agent*, makes it clear that the protagonist's vision is based on his reading of melodramatic texts typified by Charlotte M. Yonge's *The Little Duke*. Yet both D. and Rowe are self-conscious enough to see that they are participating in fantastic adventures without being able to separate themselves from them.

As *The Confidential Agent* develops the link between how one elects to read the world and its apparent reality, stories are shown to be efficacious; that is, we see that fictions determine the reality from which they supposedly stand apart. While this is most apparent in D.'s perception of events as incidents in the melodramatic romance of his own adventure, it is also seen in the effects stories have upon characters in the book. For instance, the text frequently notes that Else's reading of "twopenny trash" shapes her speech (70, 76, 114, 116). Similarly, her diary reveals that she sees her relationship with D. in terms of her experience with these texts (104–5). Again, as is similarly the case with Ida Arnold and Arthur Rowe, Else's reading of events is conditioned by her predisposition which, in turn, is a reflection of her experience of other texts. In this respect, Else illustrates Barthes's notion that the reader is a product of texts who finds in other texts those elements which are already read.

A second illustration of fiction's power is seen in D.'s attempt to force K. to confess his role in Else's murder. After following K. into the elevator of the Entrenationo Centre, D. begins to menace K. by stopping the elevator to tell a detective story he says is written by a man named Goldthorb:

"One man killed another in a lift. Rang the lift down. Walked up the stairs. Rang the lift up and – before witnesses – discovered the body. Of course, luck was on his side. You have to have a fortunate hand for murder."

"You wouldn't dare."

"I was just telling you Goldthorb's story."

Mr K. said weakly, "There's no such man. The name's absurd."

"He wrote in Entrenationo, you see." (124)

As in *The Ministry of Fear*, narrative itself is a weapon. D. uses the Goldthorb story to frighten K., and, despite the fact that it is merely D.'s invention, it has the desired effect: K. reveals the circumstances of Else's murder. What D. cannot know, however, is that the fear he inspires will eventually kill K. Of course, the Goldthorb fiction alone is not responsible for K.'s heart attack; but, insofar as it is a contributing factor, fiction, a detective story in this case, alters the reality outside it.

Although the novel is more than "a book of initials and vague terrors" (Sharrock 77), the circumstances of its composition resulted in its covering much of the ground Greene had already explored in *A Gun for Sale* and *Brighton Rock*. Greene said that he wrote *The Confidential Agent* under the influences of benzedrine and the fear of war in a period of six weeks while working on *The Power and the Glory* (*WE* 67–8) (another book, by the way, that presents us with a sympathetic criminal – the priest – pursued by a representative of the law in the person of the lieutenant), and this explanation has proven itself sufficiently persuasive for most critics in their accounts of the novel's weaknesses. *The Confidential Agent* does investigate some interesting questions, such as the role of intellectuals in the Spanish Civil War and, by extension, the coming war, but, as Greene admits, the book "moved rapidly because I was not struggling with my own technical problems: I was to all intents ghosting a novel by an old writer," who was Greene himself at an earlier point in his development as an author (*WE* 69).

Although *The Confidential Agent* was Greene's last novel published in the 1930s, it certainly was not the last to be shaped by the conditions of that decade. Another work, *The Ministry of Fear*, extended Greene's investigations of the relationship between the text and the world and of the reading experience beyond anything he had done previously or would do in the future.

6 *The Ministry of Fear*

Though *The Ministry of Fear* can be seen as "a summary of Greene's political thrillers in the 1930s" (Spurling 39), it does more than rework familiar material. Pursuing themes first raised in *Brighton Rock* and *The Confidential Agent*, the book develops and explores the implications of a world of texts and of the role of fictions. Perhaps because it was written during the war, *The Ministry of Fear* radically restructures conventional modes of literary realism; it is as though the release of tension that accompanied the explosion of the war's long-awaited violence freed Greene from the textual restraints of his earlier fiction. The "funny and fantastic" thriller that resulted (*WE* 74) moves easily among various levels of textual play while at the same time highlighting the thriller's conventions, with their attendant enigmas, suspense, and danger.

Although one of Greene's favourites (*WE* 78), *The Ministry of Fear*, like most of his books, has had a mixed reception from critics. Many, like Spurling, dismiss the novel as a weak or, at best, uneven rehearsal of earlier concerns; others are more generous and praise it as the finest of the "entertainments" and one of Greene's best novels.[1] Again, much of this praise or condemnation is tied to the novel's perceived status as light or escapist work; yet with *The Ministry of Fear* Greene succeeds in producing what is, and remains, one of his most skilful and complex novels. This is a book that explicitly engages the question of the ideology of popular literature while simultaneously restructuring the popular formula of the thriller. More specifically, as LeRoy Panek suggests, *The Ministry of Fear* "demonstrates that detective novels are impossible" (124), and so the novel justifies its status as a thriller.

There is much that *The Ministry of Fear* shares with Greene's earlier texts. As in *A Gun for Sale* and *Brighton Rock*, its principle investigator, Arthur Rowe, is an equivocal figure whose moral authority as a pursuer of truth and justice is severely undercut by his belief that he is a murderer for having performed the mercy-killing of his wife. Because he is sentenced lightly by the courts and only temporarily confined to an asylum, Rowe is not clearly defined as a murderer by the society at large, although most of his friends have deserted him. Not being considered a murderer, however, does not alleviate his sense of guilt; and, as the novel opens, he is seeking "to mislay the events of twenty years" (13) and return to the time of innocence that had preceded his marriage. This desire draws him to the charity bazaar and so pulls him into the novel's plot; as the text remarks, the fête gives Rowe the feeling that "the familiar pattern of life that afternoon might be altered for ever" (13).

As *The Ministry of Fear* develops, Rowe's feeling is proven to be a harbinger of what is to come. Similarly, his desire to "mislay" twenty years of his life is granted later in the text when an explosion causes the loss of his memory. Within the fantastic world of *The Ministry of Fear*, Rowe's dreams and desires seem to direct the novel's plot: his imagined plots become his reality, which is to say that at one level his own fictions determine the novel's fiction.[2] As this dynamic works itself out, the reality Rowe experiences is shown to be highly questionable because not only is it the product of fictions but it is also explicitly figured as a text, another fiction, which is specifically a thriller since "thrillers," we are told, "are like life" (65).

George Woodcock and other critics may complain that the thriller elements of *The Ministry of Fear* are little more than "theatrical devices" indicative of an undisciplined technique (Woodcock 137), but rather than see these devices as the expression of an "empty virtuosity" (137), it is perhaps better to see them as part of Greene's continued attempt to reshape the genre's conventions. Drawn into the world of the thriller by accident, Rowe is to Richard Hannay what Scotland Yard's Prentice is to Sherlock Holmes.

Book 1 of the novel, entitled "The Unhappy Man," making up slightly less than half of the narrative, includes many of the genre's clichés in what appears to be a straightforward thriller in the Buchan manner about an unimportant man caught in a web of mistrust and conspiracy. Metaphorically, this web is represented by the labyrinth of Mr Travers's hotel. (Indeed, it is indicative of the movement of book 1 that the image of the garden which opened the novel is replaced with the image of the labyrinth at the end of "The Unhappy Man.") Throughout book 1 the enemy is hidden, although clues to his identity abound and are easily detected on a second reading when the text's ironic aspects become clear. Not only do Anna's reactions to her brother suggest his true role, but almost all of Hilfe's and Bellairs' remarks can be read in ways that reveal Hilfe and Bellairs to be Nazi agents: Hilfe, whose name ironically means "help" in German, says that helping Rowe will give him "an opportunity ... to take a more violent line" (48); he confesses that he is "used to dropping spies" (49); and he, accurately it turns out, describes himself as an "enemy alien" (62). Similarly, Bellairs calls Cost "our mystery man" (53) and refers to Hilfe and Cost as "the conspirators" (54). Each of these points hints at a deeper truth than is first realized by either Rowe or the reader.

The narrative also provides us with clues to what is really happening: the tale of Hilfe's escape from Austria is alluded to and then ambiguously passed over: "That's another story" (44); Hilfe, we are told, has "an amusing nihilistic abandon" not shared by his sister (48); and Cost's murder is not reported in the next day's newspapers (69). These and many other clues reveal a hidden narrative, which becomes explicit only much later in the novel, beneath the narrative that is going on in the present. In this way *The Ministry of Fear* follows the structural pattern of most detective fiction.

In the novel's first book Greene loads the text with elements taken from other types of detective fiction and often alludes to particular texts.[3] Nothing is what it seems in the world of *The Ministry of Fear*: the fête Rowe enters at the novel's beginning represents for him a return to the innocence of a paradisal "vicarage garden" (11, 12), but in its heart are menace and mystery – a fact the text later reminds us of when Fullove, a student of eighteenth-century landscape gardening, remarks, "In a good garden you weren't safe anywhere" (92). That danger lies in the vicarage garden recalls both the arguments of Auden's essay "The Guilty Vicarage" and the typical situation of the classical detective story. Similarly, the murder of Cost at the seance is presented as a locked-room mystery, in the manner of Christie or Carr, complete with Dr Forester's cryptic statement, "One of us did it" (59). Indeed, the very fact that the murder takes place at a seance recalls any number of texts, including A.E.W. Mason's *Murder at the Villa Rose* (1910) – a book Greene surely read, written by an author he much admired.

When Rowe falsely believes himself wanted for murder he goes underground both in the figurative sense of hiding and in the literal sense of going into the tube shelter during an air raid. Like Hannay,

Rowe becomes entangled in a secret war which he cannot escape while the larger battle goes on around him. The genre's conventions would demand that he adopt a series of disguises in order to track down the guilty parties and so clear himself of suspicion while saving England from grave danger, but in *The Ministry of Fear* this does not happen in quite so obvious a way. After having alluded to numerous kinds of detective stories, any one of which his novel could follow, Greene opts to explode their conventions and set the narrative on another tack. At the close of book 1, Rowe opens a suitcase full of books that explodes, figuratively signalling the end of this section's straight thriller format.

In a general sense, the second half of *The Ministry of Fear* mirrors the narrative structure of the first half. Book 2, "The Happy Man," begins, like book 1 in a paradisal world now represented by Dr Forester's sanatorium. Yet here too there is danger figured in the presence of the sick-bay. In a variation of the Buchan convention of disguise, Rowe, a blast victim, is now known by the name of Richard Digby (after the name found on an identity card in his pocket), but he has no memory of who he is.

Because Rowe loses his memory, *The Ministry of Fear* develops the idea of the investigation of a murder as an investigation of the self that we first saw Greene use in "Murder for the Wrong Reason." In *The Ministry of Fear*, the pattern is complicated by the fact that Rowe, though he may be a murderer for killing his wife, investigates an expanding series of crimes that are largely unconnected with his wife's death. Beginning his investigation in order to learn the reasons behind Poole's attempt to murder him, Rowe finds himself searching for the supposed murderer of Cost, for a microfilm of secret government documents, and for the leader of a Nazi spy ring operating in Britain. In that Rowe's investigation moves outward from the personal to the national, it conforms to a pattern typically found in the thriller. Like Hannay in Buchan's *The Thirty-Nine Steps*, Rowe spends much of the novel thinking that he must clear himself of a murder he did not commit; the difference between the two is that Rowe's case is ironically complicated by the fact that, while no murder directly tied to the espionage plot has been committed, there is ambiguity surrounding his wife's death.

Rowe now grapples with the mystery of his identity, and central to this struggle is the same question he faced in the book's first half: is he or is he not a murderer? The investigation becomes an inquiry into his past; and, again, numerous clues – Anna calls him "Arthur" (119), he feels dizzy when he considers one may kill for love (132), he feels fear when he sees Poole (127) – offer him the opportunity to read the story of his past, but he is unable to do so. After Forester rashly tells him that he is not Digby but Arthur Rowe, a murderer, Rowe flees the sanatorium with Johns's help – an action that roughly corresponds to his escape from Bellairs' house after Cost's supposed murder. At this point, Rowe goes to the police, where "a stiff consecutive narrative [is made] out of his haphazard sentences" (153). (This action, too, finds its correspondence in the narrative he wrote, but did not send, to the police in the book's first half [71].) With Prentice, Rowe first goes to a tailor's shop, where he sees Cost, and then returns to Mrs Bellairs' house and to Dr Forester's sanatorium: he physically returns to the scenes of his past – just as he had mentally and emotionally returned to such a scene when he visited the charity fête in book 1. Slowly, his memory returns to him "like [pieces] in a jig-saw puzzle" (169); and, in his final confrontation with Hilfe, he learns the story of his wife's death, the telling of which marks the final recuperation of his past and his re-emergence as a "whole man." And so, in *The Ministry of Fear*, the investigation of the self is tied to the investigation of a murder, but the murder of Rowe's wife is not the crime that initiates events in the novel – except insofar as Rowe's desire "to mislay the events of twenty years" (13) is partially the result of his guilt over his wife's death.

As *The Ministry of Fear* deals with it, the whole question of the thriller as the appropriate form for recording the experience of life during the blitz rests on the tautology involved in the paradox of self-inclusion. The war's reality makes the violence and treachery de-scribed in the novel credible, since the reality of the world outside the text is violent and treacherous. Yet Rowe's declaration that "thrillers are like life" (65) presents a self-justifying rationale for the thriller and alerts the reader to parallels between the fictional plot of a thriller and the reality outside the text that is London during the war. Because of the war, *The Ministry of Fear* is able to present the thriller as a reflec-tion of the anterior reality with unusual power. In that this reflection is contained within a thriller that describes the world in terms of a thriller, however, the sense of an anterior reality is lost and in its place is put only another text. As the novel develops, similarities between the outside reality and thrillers allow the text to absorb the reality it describes so that the world the novel presents is seen as a world of texts. Rowe's declaration of equivalence between life and thrillers, made during a moment when "he [is] master of the dream" (65), cancels any sense of *The Ministry of Fear* as a mimetic portrayal of London life during wartime. Ultimately in the novel, reality can be represented only as a text taking its place within a text. After all, as the narrative makes clear, contemporary history is something to be read, not experienced.

It is curious, then, that critics such as A.J.M. Smith, Peter Wolfe, and Maria Couto have praised the novel for its "studiously unmelodramatic, continuously realistic, and minutely observed" portrayal of life during the blitz (Couto 106).[4] Greene himself stressed the novel's realism and its accuracy of detail in *Ways of Escape*. Though he intended *The Ministry of Fear* to be a "funny and fantastic thriller" (74), he later wished that "the espionage element had been less fantastically handled" (78): this work was to be a novel (like the Michael Innis book he read on the way to West Africa in 1941) that would possess a realism the English detective story did not have. Greene complimented himself on how well "the atmosphere of the blitz" was conveyed (*WE* 78); he even went so far as to include, both in his "Introduction" to *The Minister of Fear* for the collected edition of his works and then as part of his remarks about the novel in *Ways of Escape*, a fragment from a journal he kept during 1940–41. While the journal has a certain autobiographical and historical interest in its own right, Greene's decision to include it reflects his desire to convince us of the novel's veracity. (Of course, just how valuable a novelist's journal is as evidence of his fiction's accuracy is certainly a point open to question.)

There are, however, problems with Greene's approach to the novel in *Ways of Escape*. Since *The Ministry of Fear* itself declares reality to be a fiction, specifically a thriller, Greene's strategy in *Ways of Escape* of emphasizing the novel's mimetic aspects denies Rowe's view that life is like a fiction. At the same time, however, Greene's remarks imply that fiction can accurately mirror the world; but, if fiction can accomplish this mirroring and Greene's own novel is a thriller, then his comments about *The Ministry of Fear* must be seen as supporting Rowe's sense of life as a thriller. The result is that we see Greene, as he often does, trying to have things both ways: the novel was to have "realism" while yet being "funny and fantastic." Here, again, we see the impossibility of separating the world of fictions, of text, from a world beyond the text.

This is not to downplay the fact that conditions in London during the war were such that one might believe that commonplace occurrences in thrillers were actually happening – that one's friend or co-worker was a spy, that secret information was being passed out of the country, that high-ranking officials were covertly helping the enemy, or that political blackmail and murder were widespread. In a passage that could sun up Rowe's own experience, Paul Fussell describes the sense of life in wartime: "Even more than today, in wartime everything you might hear and read during the day might be false, planted to be passed on to deceive either you or the enemy. Living in wartime thus resembled living in a play, with nothing real or certain. You literally did not know for sure what was going on, and you had to take on faith the public appearance of things, costly as this might prove for perceptual and intellectual life" (*Wartime* 47). Given this situation, Rowe's bewilderment at being drawn into the violence around him mirrors the experience of people in London in the early 1940s when anyone might seem a potential enemy: Rowe remarks, "That little man with the books was in it too. What a lot of them there are," and Anna replies, "An awful lot. More every day" (101). For Rowe, however, the stigma of his wife's death exacerbates the common wartime experience: "When he came out of what wasn't called a prison, when His Majesty's pleasure had formally and quickly run its course, it had seemed to Rowe that he had emerged into quite a different world – a secret world of assumed names, of knowing nobody, of avoiding faces, of men who leave a bar unobtrusively when other people enter" (47).

In a similar fashion, Rowe's equation of life and thriller is apparently confirmed in the British *Handbook of Irregular Warfare* (1942): "Never give the enemy a chance; the days when we could practice the rules of sportsmanship are over ... Every soldier must be a potential gangster ... Remember you are out to kill" (quoted in *Wartime* 284). Here, government authorities openly acknowledge the end of the values of the Newbolt man; "the rules of sportsmanship," prized by the classical detective such as Poirot, no longer apply in the world or in Greene's novel. In a sense, Rowe's conception of the world as a thriller populated by gangsters receives government acknowledgement of its truth, which again collapses the distinction between fiction and reality.

Yet to think of *The Ministry of Fear* only in terms of its evocation of a specific period is to ignore a large part of Greene's project. This novel places an inordinate emphasis upon the nature of narrative: issues relating to reading and to the thriller as a form are figured in its plot and alluded to in its self-conscious references. The narrative presents the world as an assembly of texts under the rubric of a master text which follows the structure of the thriller. In this respect, Rowe's entry into the fête represents both his and the reader's entry into the world of the text. For Rowe, the songs from the First World War mix with the memory of childhood excursions to similar fêtes to push him into a world of remembered experience that finds a correspondence in his present.

For him, the fête is the place where, figuratively, three roads cross. It calls to him "like innocence" because it is "entangled in childhood" (11). It is a visible sign in the present that contains within it not only an expectation "that the familiar pattern of life that afternoon might be altered for ever" (13) but also the experience of the past: the past coexists with the future within Rowe's memory in the present "as if Providence had led [Rowe] to exactly this point to indicate the difference between then and now" (15). Linking past and present is Charlotte Yonge's *The Little Duke*, a book Rowe buys from one of the stalls in a gesture deliberately designed to repeat the past, since he had bought *The Little Duke* at a similar fête as a child.

The purchase of *The Little Duke* (1854) is a significant moment because it marks Rowe's and the reader's entry into a world of texts: immediately after his purchase Rowe reflects that the people at the bazaar "might be playing a part in an expensive morality for his sole benefit" (15). As a romance of adventure, Yonge's novel represents both the popular literature of the past and Rowe's adolescent dreams of heroism, dreams that as an adult he wishes to recover and live by. Yet *The Ministry of Fear* also thoroughly discredits the ethos of the romantic-adventure tale by contrasting it with the thriller world of war-ravaged London. Not only are such traditional virtues as bravery, courage, loyalty, strength, faith (all illustrated in *The Little Duke*) shown to be lacking in the present, but they are also shown to be impossible to maintain. As Couto observes, "The structure of the novel relates the form and the content of the adventure story to invert it … its romance is hideously transformed" (107). The novel delineates the process whereby the nineteenth-century romantic adventure is replaced in the popular imagination and in Greene's own psyche by the thriller of the 1930s and 1940s.

Just as *The Little Duke* links past and present for Rowe, so does his request of the fortune-teller, "Don't tell me the past. Tell me the future" (16), bind the present to a future course of events that follows the plot of a thriller. Throughout *The Ministry of Fear*, the two popular forms of the adventure story and the thriller are continually held before the reader either thematically, in Rowe's thoughts which explicitly compare the two, or structurally, by means of the epigraphs for each chapter that are taken from *The Little Duke*.[5]

The Ministry of Fear, then, stresses from its outset the role of texts in the narrative itself and in the mind of Rowe. At the fête, he browses over stalls containing "second-hand Penguins for the Forces" and "books too shabby for the bookstall," one of which is *The Little Duke* (14). The scene finds a complement later in the novel when he visits a used bookshop in order to watch the office of the Orthotex detective agency (73–4). Both moments give literal expression to the idea that Rowe inhabits a world of books, or more to the point, texts. (It is perhaps significant that Rowe's visit to a used bookshop alludes to

comparable scenes in Chandler's *The Big Sleep*.) Indeed, Rowe's purchase of *The Little Duke* in the opening pages of the novel also allegorizes his commitment to a form whose ideology, particularly though
not exclusively in the book's second half, powerfully influences his
beliefs and actions:

Rowe repressed for the sake of his companion a sense of exhilaration: he was
happily drunk with danger and action. This was more like the life he had
imagined years ago. He was helping in a great struggle, and when he saw
Anna again he could claim to have played a part against her enemies. He
didn't worry very much about Stone; none of the books of adventure one
read as a boy had an unhappy ending. And none of them was disturbed by a
sense of pity for the beaten side. The ruins [the bombed city of London] from
which they [Rowe and Prentice] emerged were only a heroic back-cloth to his
personal adventure ... (176)

The Ministry of Fear explicitly shows the failure of one kind of popular literature to remain vital in the new world of the 1940s. Those
who remain faithful to it and to its ideology quite literally find the
values of these texts blowing up in their faces: the explosion that
transforms Rowe into Digby comes from a suitcase supposedly filled
with books.

  Certainly, after his loss of memory Rowe accepts the ideology of
the pre-war adventure romance with greater ease since he has mentally returned to his adolescence; he thinks, for instance, of "Path-
finder" and "Indian" (perhaps alluding to James Ferimore Cooper's
Leatherstocking Tales but more generally to a host of adventure stories
for boys) as he embarks on his schoolboy's search for Stone in the
wing of the sick-bay (136). But even before Rowe is robbed of his past,
his character is strongly marked by the ideology of adventure stories.
At the fête, part of Mrs Bellairs's reading describes Rowe as one who
sometimes feels he has "not been allowed a proper scope for [his]
gifts. [He] want[s] to do great deeds, not dream them all day long"
(16). Similarly, Rowe's adolescent desires are suggested by his sense
of "kinship with the detective inspectors, the Big Five, *My Famous
Cases*," by his sense of belonging to a world of old-fashioned murderers (70), and by his belief that his adolescent day-dreams may come
true: "He had in those days imagined himself capable of extraordinary heroisms and endurances ... Everything had seemed possible.
One could laugh at day-dreams, but so long as you had the capacity
to day-dream, there was a chance that you might develop some of the
qualities of which you dreamed" (73). The text goes on to tell us that
"since the death of his wife Rowe had never day-dreamed" (73); yet

subconscious desires continue to have a tremendous influence on his actions.

As a character, therefore, Rowe is imbued with the ideology of popular fiction. His sense of a "primitive idea of justice" (88) derives from the popular literature of his youth, typified by "stories of Captain Scott writing his last letters home. Oates walking into the blizzard ... Damien among the lepers ... a book called the *Book of Golden Deeds* by a woman called Yonge ... *The Little Duke*" (162). And despite the knowledge gained from experience, Rowe continues at some level to believe in the values of this literature: "God is good, the grown-up man or woman knows the answer to every question, there is such a thing as truth, and justice is as measured and faultless as a clock. Our heroes are simple: they are brave, they tell the truth, they are good swordsmen and they are never in the long run really defeated. That is why no later books satisfy us like those which were read to us in childhood – for those promised a world of great simplicity of which we knew the rules ..." (89) That Rowe continually rereads the books of his youth, such as *The Little Duke*, *The Old Curiosity Shop*, and *David Copperfield*, only confirms his repressed desire to be the hero of his own story, of his own romance.[6] With the loss of memory comes the loss of those inhibitions that prevented him from acting in accord with his adolescent desires, and he openly accepts the role of the adventure hero – something that Hilfe did not count on: " 'I thought I could deal with you quite easily until you lost your memory. That didn't work out right. You got so many illusions of grandeur, heroism, self-sacrifice, patriotism ...' " (205).

The novel shows, however, that despite Rowe's success the romantic-adventure hero has no place in the world of the modern thriller. "The Little Duke," with whom Rowe identifies and with whom we identify Rowe (through the epigraphs to the chapters), "is dead and betrayed and forgotten" (89). As the text acknowledges, in the world of the 1930s and 1940s (and the same can be said of the thriller in this period), "we cannot recognize the villain and we suspect the hero and the world is a small cramped place" (89). In this respect, Greene's novel dramatizes his own conflict in having to choose one kind of popular fiction over another which he loved. Two kinds of popular literature are contrasted in *The Ministry of Fear* and one is found wanting. The old adventure story with its values of "sacrifice, courage [and] virtue" (73) is painfully inadequate as a form because it can no longer be accepted as realistic and because its values have led to the destruction of the war: "Courage smashes a cathedral, endurance lets a city starve, pity kills ... we are trapped and betrayed by our virtues" (74); and Rowe, too, knows that "one doesn't necessarily kill because one hates" (132).

As in his earlier fiction, *Stamboul Train* and *England Made Me* for instance, Greene presents the values of the Victorian and Edwardian ages in order to reject them; and, as part and parcel of his approach, he rejects the literary form that promotes those values. An ongoing project in many of Greene's texts, this process is represented in Rowe's experience. In *The Ministry of Fear*'s latter part, Rowe's sense of heroism and adventure slowly alters and with this alteration comes a recognition of how "unreal" the adventure stories of his youth are. We see an indication of this in the description of the night-time journey to Dr Forester's sanatorium:

... their [Prentice's and Rowe's] dimmed headlights just touched the near hedge [lining the roadway] and penetrated no farther into the wide region of night: it was like the coloured fringe along the unexplored spaces of a map. Over there among the unknown tribes a woman was giving birth ... an old man was dying, two people were seeing each other for the first time ... everything in that darkness was of such deep importance that their errand could not equal it – this violent superficial chase, this cardboard adventure hurtling at seventy miles an hour along the edge of the profound natural common experiences of men. Rowe felt a longing to get back into that world: into the world of homes and children and quiet love and the ordinary un-specified fears and anxieties the neighbour shared ... the longing was like the first stirring of maturity when the rare experience suddenly ceases to be desirable. (178–9)

Of course, "this cardboard adventure hurtling ... along the edge of the ... common experiences of men" self-consciously refers to *The Ministry of Fear* itself both as a physical object and as a thriller, which, with its own rapidly moving narrative, is part of a subgenre usually thought of as existing on the margins of literature – here defined as those texts that deal with "the profound natural common experiences of men." The "cardboard adventure" also refers to Rowe's heroic con-ception of himself as a hero and to his growing discomfort with this role and with the youthful adventures he once desired.

Rowe's maturation is most emphatically described soon after he and Prentice arrive at Dr Forester's sanatorium to discover the bodies of Forester, Poole, and Stone: "Looking in through the door, [Rowe] grew up – learned that adventure didn't follow the literary pattern, that there weren't always happy endings, felt the awful stirring of pity that told him something had got to be done, that you couldn't let things stay as they were, with the innocent struggling in fear for breath and dying pointlessly" (180). Rowe's awakening social consciousness expresses Greene's own sense, developed through the 1930s, that his fiction must perform a political task. But Rowe is bewildered (201) by the realization that his investigation is not "an exciting adventure" and that he is not a hero because, with the collapse of his conception of himself as a hero of adventure fiction, he loses his sense of personal identity. The result is that a conflict (perhaps similar to a conflict in Greene himself) between immaturity and maturity – adventure stories and thrillers (187) – takes place that finally pushes Rowe towards the thriller but not beyond fictions because he is unable to conceive of himself in terms other than those of fictional texts.

At the novel's close, Greene inverts the romance ending as Rowe opts to continue to live his life in terms of fiction. In the penultimate paragraph, he and Anna stand, like Adam and Eve at the end of *Paradise Lost*, surveying "the enormous dangerous plain" of the future before them. But unlike Adam and Eve, who embark upon a new beginning with "Providence thir guide" (*PL* 12. 647), Rowe and Anna remain characters in a thriller: "They must watch each other like enemies ... They would never know what it was not to be afraid of being found out" (221). They join "the permanent staff" of a "Ministry of Fear ... as large as life to which all who loved belonged" (220). As the reference to its title suggests, *The Ministry of Fear* itself exemplifies the kind of thriller that, to some extent, replaces and succeeds the romance-adventure story in the popular imagination and certainly in Greene's own mind.

That *The Ministry of Fear* makes popular literature one of its concerns shows in one way how Greene explicitly engages issues concerning textuality and the experience of texts. Because Rowe conceives of himself as the hero of an adventure story, his story can be read as a patriotic story of romantic heroism, but it can also be read as a cautionary tale outlining the dangers of adhering to an antiquated ideology and/or as a critique of the popular literature Greene enjoyed as a boy. In any case, Rowe's character is constructed in a way that explicitly renders him the product of previous texts. From this perspective, Rowe ceases to represent a human creature and, instead, becomes a particular text, metonymically standing for both pre-war adventure fiction and for Greene himself, that exists within a field of texts. Although Greene may be inconsistent in the way these various readings come together, each view of Rowe contributes to the novel's exploration of the nature of literature and of texts.

Part of this inquiry involves the fact that Rowe, like Greene's earlier investigators in *Rumour at Nightfall*, *It's a Battlefield*, *A Gun for Sale*, *Brighton Rock*, and *The Confidential Agent*, is actively engaged in a process of reading. In *The Ministry of Fear*, however, the presentation of the act of detection as an encounter with texts is heightened to a degree not found in the earlier novels because scenes of reading are given an importance beyond that which comparable scenes in the other novels receive. *The Ministry of Fear*, while participating in the investigation of reading that all detective novels partake in, becomes a novel not only about reading texts but about reading *this* text, "this cardboard adventure."

The thriller plot of *The Ministry of Fear* is activated by a specific linguistic moment that, like the formulaic challenge to Kolley Kibber in *Brighton Rock*, foregrounds the idea of texts as coded language. When Rowe says, "Don't tell me the past. Tell me the future" (16), he accidentally hits upon a code which, because of the fortune-teller's error in reading, brings him into the world of adventure stories for which he longs. Like Ali Baba's magic spell of admittance, "Open O Sesame," Rowe's request puts him on the threshold of a bizarre and secret world. Significantly, too, Hilfe, the leading conspirator, repeats this formula at the narrative's end, just prior to his suicide, as a signal of the end of the thriller plot (219). The coded formula Rowe utters to Mrs Bellairs brings into the text a formulaic narrative that ends only with the repetition of the original utterance. It is as if the text Rowe speaks holds within it a potential narrative that is made manifest by an error in reading and then is withdrawn by a repetition of the original command.

Before Bellairs interprets or reads it, the text, "Don't tell me the past. Tell me the future," stands at the junction of numerous possible readings in the moment of interpretive purity which exists before meanings are closed off. Bellairs's response signals the end of this openness as it determines the narrative's course. That is, instead of Rowe hearing some harmless information and going home, for instance, he is given another coded text which enables him to win the cake. The thriller plot that follows ultimately is both the result of an error and an attempt to redress this error – a point made clear when Hilfe repeats the originally coded text, though in doing so he opens it to another, this time ironic, reading: " 'What made you go and have your fortune told? You had no future' " (219).

Between the two occurrences of the code-text lies the narrative of *The Ministry of Fear*, which acts as a kind of commentary on the code-text since, by the time Hilfe repeats the code, we possess a greater understanding of the statement's context and of the error that led to the original misreading: we cannot, however, close the statement's meaning. In this sense, the novel explicitly represents a process of reading that privileges the role of error and indeterminacy in the creation and continuation of narrative and of commentary.[7] Or, to put the matter another way, every reading of a text is shown to be a misreading or a "misprision," as Harold Bloom would have it, and every interpretation is itself another narrative.

The error that Mrs Bellairs and her fellow conspirators make is the same error Pinkie makes in *Brighton Rock*; they assume that one can produce a text which will be read in only one way. Bellairs reads Rowe's request as the linguistic marker, the signature, of a contact within the Nazi spy ring. But the fact that it is Rowe who utters this particular formula immediately opens it to a second reading that is the more literal expression of his desire to know the future. Even a simple statement raises the possibility of multiple readings when the context of the utterance shifts.

The narrative continually demonstrates the failures of those authors and readers who would seek to limit and control the meanings in texts: Bellairs and the other conspirators are either dead or imprisoned by the novel's end; Rennit's Orthotex detective agency suffers the loss of Jones; and Rowe as the adventure hero who believes in certainty (89) is replaced by Rowe the duplicitous figure of the modern thriller. Those who survive, like Rowe, Anna Hilfe, and the "surrealist" Prentice (158), do so because they recognize a basic uncertainty at the heart of experience and of language. Rowe and Anna at the end of the novel are precariously perched on the "summit" where they must "tread carefully for a lifetime" in the perpetual uncertainty of a world where words stand apart from secure meanings: "He tried tentatively a phrase, 'My dear, my dear, I am so happy,' and heard with infinite tenderness her prompt and guarded reply, 'I am too.' It seemed to him that after all one could exaggerate the value of happiness ..." (221). "Happy," here, has been stripped of its meaning by the novel's final sentence, since neither Rowe nor Anna is genuinely happy. For each, the word is part of an expected response offered according to the rules of the code governing the lovers' discourse. Both Rowe and Anna realize that they *should* say they are happy at their reunion, but neither actually believes in "happiness" for their future together. These two survive because they can accept the illusory, fictional nature of a reality wherein words are divorced from certain meanings.[8]

Scotland Yard's Prentice, despite being a skilled detective, also accepts a fundamental indeterminacy. Responding to Rowe's story of the fair and the cake and the attempt by Poole on Rowe's life, Prentice advises Rowe that " 'life can be very odd. Oh, very odd. You should read more history' " (160). As readers, however, we find that history is explicitly figured in terms of texts and not in terms of a past reality. "The history of Contemporary Society," Rowe dreams, is "in hundreds of volumes, but most of them are sold in cheap editions: *Death in Piccadilly, The Ambassador's Diamonds, The Theft of the Naval Papers, Diplomacy, Seven Days' Leave, The Four Just Men ...*" (66). This conception of history, of course, forms part of the dream's argument that "the world has been remade by William Le Queux" (65), but it also prefigures Rowe's later encounter with history in his discussions with Johns and in the newspapers he sees. As Anna remarks to him:

"It seems so strange," she said. "All these terrible years since 1933 – you've just read about them, that's all. They are history to you. You're fresh. You aren't tired like all the rest of us everywhere."

"1933," he said. "1933. Now 1066, I can give you that easily. And all the kings of England – at least – I'm not sure ... perhaps not all."

"1933 was when Hitler came to power."

"Of course. I remember now. I've read it all over and over again, but the dates don't stick."

"And I suppose the hate doesn't either."

"I haven't any right to talk about these things," he said. "I haven't lived them ..." (116)

For Rowe, as Digby, history is a text he reads in the newspapers that he believes impinges little upon his life – despite the fact that history contains the stuff of thrillers:

On the tray lay always the morning paper. Digby had not been allowed this privilege for some weeks, until the war had been gently broken to him. Now he could lie late in bed, propped comfortably on three pillows, take a look at the news: "Air Raid Casualties this Week are Down to 255," sip his coffee and tap the shell of his boiled egg: then back to the paper – "The Battle of the Atlantic." The eggs were always done exactly right: the white set and the yolk liquid and thick. Back to the paper: "The Admiralty regret to announce ... lost with all hands." There was always enough butter to put a little on the egg ... (119)

Digby does not realize, though the narrative makes it clear, that he is a part of history, of this text, and for him to pretend otherwise is a gross mistake. Digby cannot say, as Rowe discovered earlier, that "it's not my war" (77): Digby must act within the text, within the thriller, because he is a part of that text.

Since the war exists only as a series of texts for Digby, he can gain insights into the true state of affairs that others are incapable of because they are directly involved. At the same time, because Digby is also Rowe, who has, as it were, fallen out of battle and in one sense out of the narrative, he is able to interpret freely these texts and see in them the possibilities of multiple readings. This is particularly evident in his discussion with Johns about both Fifth Columnists and the newspaper's account of questions in parliament concerning some allegedly missing secret plans:

"... there seem to me [Rowe] to be so many holes in the statement."

"It seems quite clear to me."

"The M.P. who asked the question must have been briefed by someone who knew about those plans. Somebody at the conference – or somebody who was concerned in sending or receiving the plans. Nobody else could have known about them. Their existence is admitted by the Minister."

"Yes, yes. That's true."

"It's strange that anyone in that position should spread a canard. And do you notice that in that smooth elusive way politicians have the Minister doesn't, in fact, deny that the plans were missing? He says that they weren't wanted, and that when they were wanted they were there." (121–2)

Rowe's reading reminds Johns of a similar story involving missing plans and leads Johns to suggest that Rowe, who speculated that he might have been a detective before he lost his memory (121), was not a detective but a "detective writer" (123), a comment that not only foregrounds Rowe's engagement with the world as an engagement with texts but also self-reflexively links Rowe's narrative of intrigue with the novel's larger narrative.

As a detective, Rowe stands alongside the novel's other investigators, Rennit and Jones of the Orthotex detective agency and Graves and Prentice of Scotland Yard. Each of these characters exemplifies a different approach to reading texts while also representing different types of fictional detectives found in various forms of detective fiction. Rennit, for instance, seems a parody of the hard-boiled detective portrayed in Hammett's or Chandler's texts. His offices, like those of Spade or Marlowe, possess "an air of abandonment," and Rennit, himself, in hard-boiled fashion, keeps a whisky bottle in his filing cabinet (30). He also tells Rowe, following the detective story's conventions, that "life ... isn't like a detective story" (35). As a detective, he deals mostly in divorce cases and is clearly out of his depth when confronted with Rowe's story.

Despite his bravado and his declared preference for a hard realism, Rennit's view of crime is singularly conservative:

"Life, you [Rowe] know, isn't like a detective story. Murderers are rare people to meet. They belong to a class of their own."

"That's interesting to me."

"They are very, very seldom," Mr Rennit said, "what we call gentlemen. Outside of story-books. You might say that they belong to the lower orders." (35)

Unlike Hilfe, who draws on international events and personal experience to assert that "there's no longer a thing called a criminal class" (46), Rennit's attitude is rooted in nineteenth-century notions of class. While claiming not to be Sherlock Holmes (32), his approach to detection, to reading, is that of the classical detective who believes in the certainty of causal chains leading to and from the origins of a crime. He possesses an "extraordinary … ability to reduce everything to a commonplace level" (34) and admits a preference for "the Straightforward" (35). Rennit considers Rowe's story "odd," but he believes that solving the case involves only "a simple matter of tracing" (39). Like Mrs Bellairs and the conspirators, Rennit and Jones, true to their firm's name, think that texts can be made to yield a single, orthodox meaning. As members of the ironically named Orthotex bureau of inquiry, they are able to ignore differences in their pursuit of an univocal interpretation: " 'I [Rennit] know all the beginnings. I've been in this line of business for thirty years. Thirty years. Every client thinks he's a unique case. He's nothing of the kind. He's just a repetition' " (31). That Rowe's story is radically different from the narratives to which Rennit and Jones are accustomed substantially reduces Orthotex's chances for success: Jones, to his cost, is easily spotted by Hilfe – " 'He [Jones] sticks out a yard' " (49) – a fact that sharply undercuts the efficacy of the agency.

Unlike Rennit, Hilfe finds Rowe's story "fascinating" (44); and, in a sense, the contrast between Rennit's and Hilfe's views represents, in part, the contrast between the ideologies of the classical detective story and of the thriller. Whereas Orthotex stands for certainty and a conservative belief in a criminal class, Hilfe reflects the thriller's ambiguous moral universe in at least three ways: he believes that crime is not the province of a specific class but a pervasive force at all levels of society; he prefers to think of conspiracy as a "game" one can play (45); and he possesses a "nihilistic abandon" that allows him to accept the fundamental uncertainty implicit in the belief that there is no difference between the criminal and non-criminal worlds (48). The war gives each of these beliefs a particularly resonant credence. As Hilfe notes, "There's no longer a thing called a criminal class. *We*

[Willi and Anna Hilfe] can tell you that. There were lots of people in Austria you'd have said couldn't ... well, do the things we saw them do. Cultured people, pleasant people, people you had sat next to at dinner ... in these days it really pays to murder, and when a thing pays it becomes respectable" (46). Anticipating George Steiner's speculations in "Humane Literacy," Greene, through Hilfe's remarks, challenges the humanitarian ethos of Leavis and the Scrutineers who seek a return to a lost, more cultured age. Ultimately, in the modern world of the thriller, Orthotex fails and Rennit himself is obliged to call in the police (74).

The police investigators fare slightly better than Rennit and Jones. Graves is typical of the unimaginative, plodding investigator, such as Lestrade in Doyle's stories, who distrusts the brilliant, eccentric, and Holmesian detective, Prentice. " 'Poor Graves – the passionate crimes of railway porters are his spiritual province. In this branch our interests have to be rather more bizarre. And so he distrusts us – really distrusts us' " (161). Prentice, on the other hand, stands as the master sleuth who, though erratic in his behaviour, seems able to penetrate the deepest of mysteries; however, like Rennit, Prentice is also associated with the pre-First World War era and an Edwardian methodology. He is a figure comparable to Holmes, and the sections of the novel in which Prentice appears are highly reminiscent of aspects of Conan Doyle's stories.

The structure of the Sherlock Holmes stories is paralleled in *The Ministry of Fear*'s narrative structuring of the action of Prentice's investigation. There is an initial interview at which the detective displays his acumen. He then arrives at an hypothesis which he seeks to test either on his own or in the company of a bewildered companion. When this hypothesis is confirmed, the detective offers his companion a partial explanation, which is often given on the way to some confrontation with the criminal. Finally, the detective summarizes the case and explains his conclusions.

For Prentice, Rowe's story represents "a beautiful problem [that] ... could almost [be] put into algebraic terms" (160). As is often the case when Holmes meets his clients, Prentice is able to open his meeting with Rowe by summarizing the circumstances that brought Rowe to him (161–2). The performance is not as startling as some of Holmes's, but, none the less, it is surprising both for Rowe and the reader, who have been unaware to this point of police involvement in the case. Then, as Rowe responds to questions, Prentice forms an hypothesis that, as in Conan Doyle's stories, is kept from both the detective's companion (in this case, Rowe) and the reader until the detective is ready to explain his actions.

Mr Prentice closed his eyes; it was perhaps an affectation, but who could live without affectations?

"Why do you [Prentice] ask about the Regal Court?"

"It's a shot in the dark," Mr Prentice said. "We have so little time."

"Time for what?"

"To find a needle in a haystack." ...

He had dropped his enigmatic statement into the air and was out of the room almost before the complete phrase had formed, his long legs moving stiffly, like stilts. Rowe was left alone with Beavis and the day slowly wore on. (164–5)

Prentice's final comment could easily find its place in Holmes's speech, while the detail of "his long legs moving stiffly, like stilts" recalls both Doyle's descriptions of Holmes ("In height he was rather over six feet, and so excessively lean that he seemed to be considerably taller" [Doyle 20]) and Sidney Paget's illustrations for the Holmes stories.

The text suggests in a number of places that Prentice is modelled on the classical detectives of the late nineteenth and early twentieth century. He is, we are told, "always ready to abandon the particular in favour of the general argument" (162) while yet being attentive to detail. Also, like Holmes in "The Copper Beeches," Prentice responds with derisive bitterness to the beauty of the English countryside, seeing only the potential for monstrous crime taking place under the noses of incompetent county police who are unable to recognize murder when it happens (177). Similarly, Prentice is an affected character possessing the "air of Arthur Balfour, but you felt that he knew it ... He had chosen a physical mould just as a writer chooses a technical form" (164). Here, the mention of Balfour links Prentice to the period before the First World War,[9] while the simile suggests that the "mould" for Prentice is a textual one. Given the numerous indications of Prentice's Holmesian character and the fact that the plot Prentice works to uncover is similar in kind to plots Holmes uncovered in at least three separate stories ("The Second Stain," "The Naval Treaty," and "The Bruce-Partington Plans"), this textual mould is surely that of the master sleuth, typified by Holmes. And, like Holmes, Prentice possesses a faith in rational thought that leads him to assume an air of authority that is at least bordering on arrogance and at most fascist.

As Greene presents him, Prentice exhibits the dark side of the Holmesian type that, though hinted at in Conan Doyle's stories, is there tolerated and even admired as the confident expression of the ability to read into the heart of any mystery. In the world of the 1930s and 1940s, Conan Doyle's perspective, with its underlying ideology of certainty, was no longer tenable. Prentice's authority, accordingly, is allied with a tendency towards fascism that is expressed in a nihilistic urge to efface the past or, in his particular case, the mistakes of the past (178). Elsewhere we see a similar urge in Rowe, who welcomes the destruction of the blitz because it seemingly frees him from his past (22), and in Johns, who describes the temptation of nihilism for idealists as an expression of a desire to erase the past:

"The scrapping of all the old boundaries, the new economic ideas ... the hugeness of the dream. It *is* attractive to men who are not tied – to a particular village or town they don't want to see scrapped. People with unhappy childhoods, progressive people who learn Esperanto,[10] vegetarians who don't like shedding blood."

   "But Hitler seems to be shedding plenty."

   "Yes, but the idealists don't see the blood like you [Rowe] and I do. It's all statistics to them." (120)

Later still, Rowe feels the pull of nihilism when he gazes on the sleeping Hilfe (203); but, unlike Hilfe or the idealistic Forester, Rowe resists this temptation because he is "tied" by both his growing love for Anna and his adolescent faith in pre-First World War adventure-story values.

   Prentice, like Holmes, not only admires those he pursues (159) but also participates in a legally sanctioned brand of authoritarianism that, as in Greene's earlier novels, sharply undercuts distinctions between England, representative of an ideological good, and Nazi Germany, representative of an ideological evil.[11] Like the idealists who Johns says think in terms of statistics, Prentice views the case as an algebraic problem and sees the possible results in terms of numbers:

"It's really serious," Mr Prentice said. "I don't know quite how serious. But you might say that we all depend on it ... You know there are always weaknesses that have to be covered up. If the Germans had known after Dunkirk just how weak ... There are still weaknesses of which if they knew the exact facts ..." This [the ruins of London are being indicated by Prentice] would be nothing to it [the devastation that would result if the Germans are successful in getting the microfilm]. Nothing ... It's worth – oh, a thousand lives to them." (166–7)

Equally indicative of Prentice's authoritarianism is that he threatens both Davis and Rowe with jail if they refuse to cooperate with him (167) and then orders them to help him trap Cost: " 'You had no right to bring me [Davis] into this.'/Mr Prentice turned sharply. 'Oh yes,' he said, 'every right. Nobody's got a right to life these days. My dear chap you are conscripted for your country' " (168). Similarly, Prentice's interrogation of Mrs Bellairs reveals a measure of cruelty and violence that suggests Prentice thinks of himself as above the authority of law:

He said sharply, "Is this your best tea service, ma'am?" wincing ever so slightly at the gaudy Prussian blue.

"Put it down," Mrs Bellairs implored, but he had already smashed the cup against the wall. He explained to his man, "The handles are hollow. We don't know how small these films are. You've got to skin the place."

"You'll suffer for this," Mrs Bellairs said tritely.

"Oh no, ma'am, it's you who'll suffer. Giving information to the enemy is a hanging offence."

"They don't hang women. Not in this war."

"We may hang more people ma'am," Prentice said ... "than the papers tell you about." (176)

In this context, the detective genius, Prentice, shows himself to be a tyrant whose power stems from his capacity to punish rather than from the rule of law.

The suggestions that women are also hanged and that hanging occurs more often than one might realize – two things which imply the use of measures outside the law's prescriptions – seemingly confirm Hilfe's judgment that there is no difference between the societies he and Prentice serve. When trapped by Rowe, Hilfe confesses an adolescent horror of being beaten:[12]

"We don't beat up our prisoners here."

"Oh no?" Hilfe said. "Do you really believe that? Do you think you are so different from us?"

"Yes."

"I wouldn't trust the difference," Hilfe said. "I know what we do to spies. They'll think they can make me talk – they will make me talk." (215)

Hilfe's argument makes us aware of the parallels between Rowe and D. of *The Confidential Agent*; both men must choose a side. In *The Ministry of Fear* Rowe must believe in a difference, which the narrative itself denies, because he finds it "impossible to go through life without trust: that is to be imprisoned in the worst cell of all, oneself" (43). He realizes that communication with anything outside the self – the very process of reading – is only possible through the acknowledgment of difference.

Rennit, too, accepts a fundamental distinction based upon an orthodox belief in there being two classes, one of which is criminal and the other of which is not. His sense of difference is so crudely invoked, however, that it pushes Orthotex into a position wherein differences disappear; that is, within the two classes all experience is much the same. Rennit and Jones cannot deal with Rowe's story because they see it as a repetition of earlier stories, all of which are easily reducible to a simple matter. Their plight is that of those readers or critics who read a text according to a single preconception. As a result of this approach, the text is either reductively assimilated to a preferred paradigm of some sort – romance, tragedy, novel, *Bildungsroman*, lyric, "entertainment," or even literature (to suggest a few labels that can function in this way) – or it is dismissed as a disappointment or unreadable or a failure.

Prentice is in a more difficult position than Rennit since, with Edwardian faith, he would like to believe in the existence of clear differences and in the ability of the reasoning mind to detect and correctly read these differences. In the modern period, however, this is no longer possible; although metaphor may erase difference, the same sign can be read in various ways because its very construction is arbitrary and ambiguous. The situation of wartime, paradoxically because wartime propaganda emphasizes difference, subverts the very structures of difference upon which Prentice relies. Not only are his actions indistinct from those of the enemy against whom he fights, but he is thwarted both by error and by the vicissitudes of experience. He lays a trap for Cost but does not foresee the possibility of Cost's suicide since Prentice, apparently unaware of the fairy tale, prejudicially and erroneously does not associate great courage with tailors (172). Similarly, he arrives too late at Forester's sanatorium because he is forced to rely on the county police despite not having any confidence in them. As well, he cannot anticipate Johns's own investigative activities which lead to the deaths of Forester and Poole. As in Doyle's "The Dancing Men," the detective's knowledge and seeming cleverness cannot prevent circumstance from undermining for the reader the detective's Edwardian faith in the possibility of certainty.

In a situation where one "[doesn't] know who are ... friends and who are ... enemies" (199), the only way a coherent reading of events can be assembled is if, as Prentice does in assembling the story of Rowe, one "[leaves] out the mysteries" (167). But, to omit the mysteries, the items that cannot be accounted for or else cannot fit into the interpretive narrative – however unavoidable such an omission – is to risk the collapse of the interpretive narrative. When Prentice fails at Dr Forester's he can only succumb to a self-annihilating despair and the comfort of anonymity within a larger narrative framework where he, Rowe, Johns, and Jones will be present only as some of the "mysteries" left out; in this sense, they will be denied the difference that makes reading possible when they are subsumed in the larger differential structure of presence and absence: " 'We are beaten ... One must avoid self-importance, you see. In five hundred years' time, to the historian writing the Decline and Fall of the British Empire, this little episode would not exist. There will be plenty of other causes. You and me and poor Jones will not even figure in a footnote. It will be all economics, politics, battles' " (187–8). Because it is a text, as the allusion to Gibbon's work makes clear, such a history will involve an interpretive act that will give way to other interpretations which, since they will look to those things originally omitted, may reassess the importance of Prentice or Rowe or anyone else for that matter; thus, even as it is being offered, the comfort Prentice seeks is denied. If we recall that the record of contemporary history has already been likened to a multivolume canon of thrillers, then Rowe's story, because it is told in a thriller – *The Ministry of Fear* – cannot be erased from the record of that history though it may drop in or out of the canon depending upon the prevailing critical fashion. Although Prentice fails to conclude his investigation successfully, his activities are of crucial importance to Rowe who, because of Prentice, is able to continue his own investigation.

Rowe's detection of both his past and Hilfe is explicitly tied to his ability to read texts. Just as books themselves are given importance in the first part of *The Ministry of Fear*, so is the reading of texts emphasized in the second, making the novel a story of reading. In one sense, Rowe as Digby seems a textually innocent reader, but in another the ideal of a textually innocent reader is illusory. Rowe is never free from the contamination a reader will normally bring to texts. With twenty years of his past effaced, he reads the world in terms of adventure stories written for young boys and adolescents, and so he sees duplicity in the statements of politicians although earlier he could not see a similar duplicity in Hilfe's or Bellairs's words. As well, because he imagines himself to be the hero of an adventure story, he acts heroically when he sneaks into the sick-bay and then, later, challenges Hilfe without the help of the police. In whatever he does, Rowe's actions and his understanding of experience are determined by what he has read.

The importance of the already-read in the creation of coherent readings is underscored by the emphasis the narrative places on Rowe's reading of certain books which he finds in the sanatorium. As is so often the case in Greene's novels, books are a central part of the description of particular settings, and, consequently, they comment on the characters associated with those settings. For instance, Poole's room in the sick-bay contains "a shabby collection – Carlyle's *Heroes and Hero-Worship*, lives of Napoleon and Cromwell, and numbers of little paper-covered books about what to do with Youth, Labour, Europe, God" (138). Here the small library is itself a clue, since it indicates that Poole – already a figure associated with menace and danger – has an interest in autocratic political leaders and self-proclaimed demigods; thus, it is not surprising to the reader that he should be part of Hilfe's network of spies working for Hitler. Rowe also comes across some volumes from Forester's library – Tolstoy's *What I Believe*, Freud's *The Psycho-Analysis of Everyday Life*, and a biography of Rudolf Steiner (131). Since Forester is a psychiatrist, the presence of a volume by Freud is understandable, and the Steiner biography reflects a philosophic idealism on the part of Forester that privileges the role of pure thought. Tolstoy's *What I Believe*, however, is the most important of these three texts for *The Ministry of Fear* since the narrative quotes parts of it.

Thematically, Tolstoy's words offer both an idealistic statement suggesting why Forester betrayed his country and the opportunity for Digby to compare his actions with those of Tolstoy. When he reads Tolstoy, Rowe as Digby realizes the folly of Tolstoy's advocacy of non-resistance in the face of evil and so becomes convinced that he can no longer remain in Forester's care, ignorant of the responsibilities and duties he might have had in the outside world.[13]

But important as Tolstoy's actual text is for the novel on a thematic level, the narrative also stresses how Rowe comes across the specific passages he reads. When he opens Tolstoy, he finds "faint indentations in the margin where pencil marks had been rubbed out" (131). To Rowe, Tolstoy's words possess a nobility because they so aggressively shatter the dogma of patriotism and love of one's country; by contrast, Rowe finds "something ignoble in the attempt to rub out the pencil-mark" (131). As a result of this discovery and inspired by Tolstoy's words, Rowe loses respect for Forester and, consequently, has the courage to challenge him (146), which forces the sequence of events that leads to Rowe leaving the sanatorium for the police. Furthermore, because the marks of erasure are mentioned or discussed in at least five places (131, 135, 146, 184, 195), the narrative invests them with an importance that demands they be considered not for Tolstoy's content in the passages nor for what they tell us about Forester, but for their own status as texts that exist, quite literally, under erasure.

When a man rubs out a pencil-mark he should be careful to see that the line is quite obliterated. For if a secret is to be kept, no precautions are too great. If Dr Forester had not so inefficiently rubbed out the pencil-marks in the margins of Tolstoy's *What I Believe*, Mr Rennit might never have learnt what had happened to Jones, Johns would have remained a hero-worshipper, and it is possible that Major Stone would have slowly wilted into further depths of insanity between the padded hygienic walls of his room in the sick bay. And Digby? Digby might have remained Digby.

For it was the pencil-marks which kept Digby awake and brooding at the end of a day of loneliness and boredom. You couldn't respect a man who dared not hold his opinions openly, and when respect for Dr Forester was gone, a great deal went with it. The noble old face became less convincing: even his qualifications became questionable. (135)

Rowe's act of reading a text that exists only under erasure distinguishes his method of reading from both Rennit's and Prentice's. The marks of erasure represent the invisible traces of the already-read that, like the memories of the past repressed by the Freudian censor in Rowe's mind, stand behind any text.[14] Forester's erased scoring is, on one level, a meta-text – a commentary on Tolstoy's text – since it provides an invisible framework that directs the reader's attention to specific passages and claims for them an importance the rest of the text is not given. On another level, the erasures figure the whole network of prior texts and indeterminate meanings that any text carries with it and that any reader brings to any text. Rowe's experience with Tolstoy's text thus mirrors our own experiences with any text we may encounter. The erasures force Rowe to read Tolstoy in more than one way so that he interprets the marked passages not just as statements of Tolstoy's belief but also as indications of Forester's beliefs and of his own situation as Digby. Rowe sees a reflection of himself in the scored passages, a vision that is made explicit for him and the reader by the commonalities in the descriptions of Tolstoy and of Rowe when the latter glimpses himself in a mirror (133).

As the product of a text himself, Rowe reads in terms of the already-read. This point, too, is underscored later in the description of the bombed city of London to which Rowe returns: "The long train stood darkly along number one platform: the bookstalls closed, the blinds drawn in most of the compartments. It was a novel sight to Rowe and yet an old sight. He had only to see it once like the sight of a bombed street, for it to take up its place imperceptibly among his memories. This was already life as he'd known it" (211). Here, the already-read – Rowe's experience of the war is at this point an experience of texts – stands as the permanent memory trace of other texts within his mind or, to put it another way, within the text that is himself. Like the Derridian trace that exists in the gaps between structures of stimuli and resistance, the already-read is both obliquely indicated in the pun on "novel" and situated in the space between the antithetical senses of "novel" and "old" which, because they exist within a grammatically parallel scheme, are bonded terms describing the same "sight." Although of indeterminate origin, the already-read remains present despite the erasure of Rowe's memory; Rowe still reads in terms of texts.

In this context, the already-read is given an ambiguous status, since it makes texts meaningful by providing the structures that order them into coherent narratives and, therefore, into instruments of power. It is also the reason for misreading, however, since previously developed structures are brought to bear upon a text that is at once both unique within a given historical and linguistic moment and the result of a developmental process that makes use of previous texts. This latter property of the already-read is apparent in the errors of Rennit, who sees every case as a repetition of a previous case, and of Mrs Bellairs, who considers Rowe's request, "Don't tell me the past. Tell me the future," a password because of her previous understanding of the formula.

For Rowe, the already-read is the key to making sense of an otherwise unreadable world; it is the means whereby he understands texts. To attempt to eliminate it or to wish it away, as he wishes "to mislay the events of twenty years" (13), leads only to a position of mystery and confusion, of destructive nihilism (the desire to eliminate the already-read causes Rowe to welcome the destruction of the blitz [22]), where even the most obvious details become incomprehensible. (Rowe, as Digby, must ask Johns to explain the basics of the Second World War to him [113].) As well, Digby's experience demonstrates that the already-read can never be erased – it can only be repressed and so, in this respect, it becomes a condition of writing (Derrida, "Freud" 226). The point is that it is impossible to read objectively as an innocent reader considering a text as an isolated artifact. As Rowe realizes before his memory loss, "books are complicated and contradictory with experience; they are formed out of our own disappointed memories" (89). After his memory loss, Rowe continues to read in terms of the already-read, but now the texts have changed and he reads in terms of the adventure story.

Since the already-read is central to the production of coherent readings, it is also the key to narrative production; and in *The Ministry of Fear* narrative itself is a force capable of having tremendous effects.

Later, in *Our Man in Havana*, Greene shows how fictions have the power to create reality, but in *The Ministry of Fear* – although the same thing is implied through Rowe's acting like a romance-adventure hero – narrative is presented as an mechanism of power. The murder at the seance is a fiction designed to push Rowe out of the picture, to halt his investigation. Rowe responds by writing his own narrative, and, though he thinks "the story ... a terribly thin one" (71), its existence – not its content (since it is not read by anyone) – threatens Hilfe and leads to the attempt on Rowe's life in Travers's hotel room. Later, both Forester (133) and Hilfe (205–6; 216–17) threaten Rowe not with violence but with the story of his past. The novel, in short, presents narrative as a potent weapon because it is the expression of knowledge; the war, as Greene ironically showed in his story "Men At Work," is fought not only with bombs and guns but with texts as well.

Because *The Ministry of Fear* is a book about texts, it is also a book about itself. Rowe, the reader of romantic adventures, stands as both a reader of texts and a text to be read. His investigation, encompassing as it does inquiries into crime and into the self, offers the fullest treatment of Greene's sense of the fictional detective. *The Ministry of Fear* is its author's most ambitious and most complex handling of the materials of detective fiction and of the problem of accommodating a radically sceptical approach to the demands of reading. This novel explores the issues of popular literature, reading, and writing in numerous and complicated ways. It illustrates Greene's own movement from the classical detective story to the modern thriller, and it continues the examination of English society that he began with *Stamboul Train* and *It's a Battlefield*. *The Ministry of Fear* also takes to a greater extreme than any of Greene's other novels the implications of detective fiction as a model for narrative.

From the 1930s on, detective fiction became increasingly important to Greene. Not only is the influence of the detective story and thriller evident in all of his novels, but Greene himself came to see the genre as providing an apt metaphor for the novelist's experience: as Bendrix muses in *The End of the Affair*, "a detective must find it as important as a novelist to amass his trivial material before picking out the right clue" (25), and as Greene reflects in the autobiographical *In Search of a Character*, "the novel is an unknown man and I have to find him" (13). Although *Loser Takes All* may be a cautionary tale warning us against the dangers of too rigid an application of systems (O'Prey 110), most of Greene's novels and a number of his short stories can be profitably read as investigations of reading, of writing, of the power of fictions, and of the boundaries of high culture and popular culture, literature and genre fiction. *The Third Man*, *The End of the Affair*, *The*

Quiet American, Our Man in Havana, A Burnt Out Case, The Honorary Consul, and *The Human Factor*, for instance, all make use of structures and conventions associated with different aspects of detective fiction, sometimes obliquely, as in *The End of the Affair, A Burnt Out Case*, and *The Comedians*, and sometimes more obviously, as in *The Third Man, The Quiet American, Our Man in Havana, The Honorary Consul*, and *The Human Factor*. With the possible exception of *Our Man in Havana*, however, no other novel of Greene's is so playful or so all-encompassing in its treatment of the materials of detective fiction as *The Ministry of Fear*.

7 The End of This Affair: Summing Up

By 1943 Graham Greene's reputation was such that Walter Allen could begin a discussion of Greene's novels by asserting that "it would be generally agreed … that Graham Greene is the leading English male novelist of his generation" (148). Allen's claim was all the more striking in that Greene's work to this point was almost entirely rooted in the popular form of the thriller – a form not much respected by a critical establishment whose tastes and preferences were tied to the experimental discourse of the high modernists. What Greene had done was respond to the crises of the 1930s in such a way as to challenge openly the high-modernist discourse of the previous decade. Central to this project was his use of the material of popular fiction, specifically the thriller, as a means of political and literary interrogation. Inspired by his love for the melodramatic fiction of his boyhood, he sought in his fiction to duplicate and expand on the effects of books by Buchan, Haggard, Stevenson, and others while presenting a political vision compatible with the demands of the 1930s. This meant turning away from the literary experiments of writers such as Woolf, Forster, or Proust and embracing instead an aesthetic that emphasized a renewed form of realism capable of dealing with political and social problems. At the end of his life, Greene explained:

I think to exclude politics from a novel is excluding a whole aspect of life. Virginia Woolf certainly wouldn't have introduced politics [in her novels]. I began to get a little tired of Virginia Woolf, you know. Mrs. Dalloway going shopping up Regent Street and the thoughts which went through her head. I reacted rather against her by being a storyteller. You see, my mother was a cousin of Robert Louis Stevenson and I'd like to think that I've followed in his tradition. I've reacted against the Bloomsbury Circle. (MacArthur D5)

Greene's writing turned to an older model to reflect a continual concern for social justice, which in novels such as *Stamboul Train, It's a Battlefield*, and *England Made Me* frequently emerges in an ironic assessment of English society under capitalism.

Crucial to his social and political critique is the importance Greene places on reading and interpretation. In the 1930s, when high-modernist critics such as the Leavises sought to make literature the province of a cultural élite and treat it as something beyond specific historical, political, and social concerns, Greene and other young writers, such as Auden, Isherwood, and Orwell, tried to broaden the reading public for literature by rediscovering and revitalizing popular forms.[1] In this way literature could, it was hoped, awaken in a large audience not only a sense of a shared cultural heritage but also a sense of social justice and the consequent need for social change. Greene and others saw it as vital that people learn to question the seemingly "natural" state of affairs; people had to be aware of the governing role of the dominant ideology in their lives if they were to resist falling prey to totalitarianism. To this end, he came to see the thriller, a genre explicitly concerned with the reading and interpretation of texts, as best able to investigate and present "the fog-belt of melodrama" inside which "the entire planet gravitates" (Allain 65).

The thriller's structure, based as it is on the two-story structure of the classical detective story, illustrates the interpretive process wherein one text is read and made sense of through the creation of another text. Books such as *A Gun for Sale, Brighton Rock, The Confidential Agent*, and *The Ministry of Fear* encourage a radically sceptical approach to reading that ultimately undermines both the seeming "correctness" of interpretations offered by designated "authorities" (such as politicians, military spokesmen, religious leaders, or literary critics) and the hierarchical structures that maintain those authorities and their political power in their respective realms.

Cognizant of the fact that he cannot substitute his own ideology or interpretations for those he discredits in his texts, Greene adopted a liberal position that locates the authority behind any reading in the individual. Like D. in *The Confidential Agent*, however, we must realize that "heresies" will creep into our particular readings, which consequently can attain only a provisional status since they too can be subjected to the same interpretive rigours as any other reading.

Hence, Greene claimed that he did not fight injustice in his fiction; rather, he expressed a "sense of injustice"; his aim was "not to change things but to give them expression" (Allain 81). Yet the implied argument that one must work to overcome injustice cannot be escaped; as Rowe realizes in *The Ministry of Fear*, "you couldn't let things stay as they were, with the innocent struggling in fear for breath and dying pointlessly" (180).

In using the thriller and in explicitly remarking on this usage through the "entertainment" label, Greene declared himself opposed to those who would simplistically classify literature as high or "serious" art and low or "escapist" work. For Greene, the conditions of aesthetic value arise out of a complex series of relationships between readers and texts and among texts themselves: value cannot be determined by or imposed upon a work by a critical authority outside these relationships. In this way the hierarchy is challenged and individuals are left to think freely for themselves and not to rely upon those who would tell them what is good or bad.

There is no denying that the achievement of these ends demands a great deal of the reader, particularly one who may be more accustomed to a popular fiction that reinforces traditional values by encouraging loyalty to an imperialistic and class-bound social order. Since Greene saw almost all popular fiction as propaganda for the established order, he strove through the late 1920s and early 1930s to restructure the detective story so that it exposed and questioned rather than reinforced the dominant ideology. "Driven back to the 'blood'" (*Reflections* 65), he came to rely, particularly after 1936, on the thriller to provide the organizing structure for his novels. This move allowed him to question traditional structures of authority by expressing the paradoxes inherent in the genre and by recasting the character of the detective so as to strip him of the kind of confident authority that Dupin, Holmes, and Poirot possess. The authority of the latter elevates them above the law and expresses a totalitarian desire for a system of universal surveillance. Lacking such authority, Greene's investigators are deliberately ambiguous while their function is often spread over a number of characters, none of whom is able to discover the truth. In *A Gun for Sale* and *The Ministry of Fear*, respectively, Raven and Rowe are themselves murderers, though of different sorts. In *Brighton Rock*, Ida Arnold is mocked by the narrative and compared unfavourably to the character of Pinkie. In *The Confidential Agent*, D. wanders in confusion, unsure of whom or what to trust. Other investigators are no more successful in their efforts to solve the problems of crime and mystery. The Assistant Commissioner of *It's a Battlefield*, Mather of *A Gun for Sale*, and Prentice of *The*

Ministry of Fear are all representatives of the official police whose pretensions to certainty are exploded: although each shares the methodology of more successful fictional detectives such as Holmes or Dupin, none solves the crime he is investigating. Only Mason in "Murder for the Wrong Reason" uncovers the criminal, but then he, himself, is the guilty party, making him a precursor in Greene's early fiction of Raven and Rowe.

In discrediting the authority of the detective, Greene's novels cast doubt on those of us who would claim to present the true interpretation of an event or text. His thrillers are all investigations of reading and of narrative that locate themselves within the framework of other investigations and other narratives. In this context, no absolutely final conclusions can be drawn, since any interpretation opens only on to further interpretations, which are in themselves further narratives calling for comment.

Notes

CHAPTER ONE

1 Greene suppressed his second and third published novels, *The Name of Action* (1930) and *Rumour at Nightfall* (1931). Neither is part of the collected edition of his works or of the Penguin catalogue.

2 The separation of popular culture from high culture, which I will consider later, has been discussed by numerous commentators. For one of the briefer and more succinct accounts of this divide, see Antony Easthope's chapter, "High Culture/Popular Culture: *Heart of Darkness* and *Tarzan of the Apes*," in his *Literary into Cultural Studies*, 75–103.

3 See, for example, Mary McCarthy's attack, "Graham Greene and the Intelligentsia," or Paul Fussell's review, "Can Graham Greene Write English?"; and John Bayley's "God's Greene."

4 The phrase occurs in Ian A. Hunter's review of the first volume of Norman Sherry's biography of Greene in *The Globe and Mail*, 10 June 1989, C7. Reviewers routinely attached this and similar epithets to Greene, and in the wake of his death such tributes continued to be heard: Jack Kroll of *Newsweek* called Greene "one of the most significant novelists of his time" (75), and Philip Marchand of the *Toronto Star* speculated that Greene "may be remembered as the last great English novelist of the 20th century" (4 April 1991, C1). Also attesting to Greene's reputation in the popular press were comments by Greene's fellow novelists who were quoted in obituaries: Kingsley Amis said that until his death Greene "was our greatest living novelist" (quoted in Allen, "Literary Consul" 65), and William Trevor remarked that Greene "was the best novelist in the English language" (quoted in Coles 23).

5 Although Greene abandoned this distinction, it is still employed by the editors of Penguin books and by a number of critics. For example, McEwen treats *Travels With My Aunt* and *The Human Factor* as entertainments, though Greene called neither of them by this name.

6 "The Basement Room" continues to have its original title and is not designated as an entertainment in collections of Greene's short stories.

7 Studies of Greene's work, for the most part, have been of three general types: surveys of diverse quality and sophistication that present a broad, usually thematic, overview of his writing, exemplified by the work of De Vitis, Kelly, Kulshrestha, McEwen, Miller, O'Prey, Sharrock, and Grahame Smith; more specialized studies, such as those by Stratford, Kurismmootil, Gaston, Salvatore, and Choi, which focus on Greene's religious concerns; and considerations of Greene's relation to cinema, as typified by Falk's and Phillips' books as well as Adamson's *Graham Greene and the Cinema*. Lately, Greene's political attitudes have received substantial attention in Couto's *Graham Greene: On the Frontier–Politics and Religion in the Novels* and in Adamson's *Graham Greene: The Dangerous Edge*. Other studies aim at investigating particular aspects of Greene's work. Among these are Boardman's book on exploration as a theme both in Greene's travel writing and in his fiction, Rai's on Greene's existentialism, and Erdinast-Vulcan's on "Greene's childless fathers." As well, numerous collections of critical essays have appeared, such as those edited by Bloom, Cargas, Evans, Hynes, and Meyers; also noteworthy is Wolfe's *Essays in Graham Greene: an Annual Review*, which first appeared in 1987. In addition, Greene has been the subject of many chapters and articles in countless books and journals: essays by Hoggart, Lewis, Lodge, and Zabel are among the more valuable contributions. Finally, a number of journals have published special Graham Greene issues. See, for example, *MFS* 3 (autumn 1957), *Renascence* 12 (fall 1959), *Literature/Film Quarterly* 2.4 (fall 1974), and *College Literature* 12.1 (1985).

8 Atkins, Evans, McCarthy, Webster, and Woodcock are some of the critics who view the entertainments as light work. While theological issues dominated criticism of Greene's writing in the period following the publication of *The End of the Affair*, Gaston's, Kurismmootil's and, to some extent, Couto's books demonstrate a continuing interest in Greene's religious themes. R.W.B. Lewis's view of the entertainments as rehearsals for the novels which followed them has influenced and is shared by a number of other critics, such as De Vitis (27), Ian Gregor (Lodge/Gregor 164), and McEwen (117), and is in part confirmed by Greene himself in *The Other Man* interviews (148). Lewis does not consider *The End of the Affair* a significant advancement of Greene's treatment of Catholic themes, and so he does not place it within his construction of a trilogy.

9 Evelyn Waugh, Greene's friend and a fellow convert to Catholicism, has offered this explanation, in the critically obscure language of theological metaphor, of the difference between the novels and the entertainments: "Superficially there is no great difference between the two categories .... 'Novels' and 'Entertainments' are both written in the same grim style, both deal mainly with charmless characters, both have a structure of sound, exciting plot. You cannot tell from the skeleton whether the man [Greene] is baptized or not. And that is the difference; the 'novels' have been baptized, held deep under the waters of life" (97).

10 Kelly, Kunkel, Webster, and Wolfe quote all or part of Allott and Farris's description.

11 Discrepancies among statements made at different times raises questions about the veracity of his autobiographical comments. Greene's remarks about himself and his work possess a carefully measured reticence not only about his personal life but also about his thoughts on his own texts. One has the sense that Greene was forever guardedly attempting to guide his critics' judgments of his work, and, when a particular critical opinion was to his liking, he seemed to reinforce it with his own comments. Hence, other than some details about circumstances surrounding the composition of his texts, his comments on his own work, though frequently referred to by critics, say little that other critics had not already made commonplace. Moreover, his comments in *A Sort of Life* or *Ways of Escape* are often marked by a retrospective casting that renders them at odds with earlier statements about his work and so make any statements of intention dubious. (For example, he tells us in *Ways of Escape* that *Stamboul Train* is his first thriller and *A Gun for Sale* his second, which leaves us to wonder about *It's a Battlefield* and *England Made Me*.) That Greene believed in influencing his own literary reputation for the better is apparent not only from his autobiographical writings (especially *A Sort of Life* and *Ways of Escape*) but also from his decision to suppress *The Name of Action* and *Rumour at Nightfall*. (Also evidence of Greene's lack of compunction about suppressing texts for the sake of an author's literary reputation is his decision not to include *The Last Post* in his edition of the works of Ford Madox Ford, which he edited for the Bodley Head.) On Greene's autobiographical writings, see Martin Stannard's "In Search of Himselves: The Autobiographical Writings of Graham Greene" and David Lodge's "What There is to Tell."

12 Lewis's essay "The 'Trilogy' of Graham Greene" has appeared in a number of forms since its first publication in a 1957 issue of *Modern Fiction Studies* (vol. 3, 195–215). Not only did Lewis make it the core of his chapter on Greene in his book *The Picaresque Saint*, but numerous editors, such as Harry J. Cargas, Samuel Hynes, and Harold Bloom, have included Lewis's remarks either in whole or in part in their collections of essays on Greene's work.

13 From 1930 to 1940 Greene published nine novels and two travel books
    (which developed out of trips to Liberia in 1935 and Mexico in 1939),
    completed a biography of Lord Rochester (published in 1974 as *Lord Roch-
    ester's Monkey*), reviewed films from 1935–39 for the *Spectator* and, briefly
    (July 1937–December 1937), for *Night and Day* – of which he was literary
    editor. As well, he wrote hundreds of essays and book reviews in the
    period.

14 Greene's interest in detective fiction, particularly that of the nineteenth
    century, is reflected in his catalogue of Victorian detective fiction published
    in 1966 as *Victorian Detective Stories: A Catalogue of the Collection Made by
    Dorothy Glover and Graham Greene*. He and his brother Hugh also edited
    two related anthologies: *Victorian Villainies* (Harmondsworth: Penguin
    1984) and *The Spy's Bedside Book: An Anthology* (London: Hart Davis 1957).
    (Hugh Greene is responsible as well for the *Rivals of Sherlock Holmes* anthol-
    ogies of short stories.)

15 Ford's distinction is made in *The English Novel*, 83ff. Obviously, something
    of Ford's dualism lies behind Greene's own novel/entertainment distinc-
    tion.

16 Greene suggested that his mention of Bowen was "a little mild baiting of
    the intellectuals"; but, since he added that he chose Bowen because he did
    not "think that the books one reads as an adult influence one as a writer,"
    his selection of her novel for special comment is as good as any other
    choice he might have made from among the books he read in his child-
    hood (Shuttleworth 39).

17 For a discussion of Greene's use of romance in work that appeared from
    1950 to 1973, see Brian Thomas's *An Underground Fate: The Idiom of Romance
    in The Later Fiction of Graham Greene*.

18 Michael Denning sees the thriller's emphasis on the conflict between
    good and evil working in two different ways. There are "magical thrillers
    where there is a clear contest between Good and Evil with a virtuous hero
    defeating an alien and evil villain, and those that we might call existential
    thrillers which play on a dialectic of good and evil overdetermined by
    moral dilemmas, by moves from innocence to experience, and by identity
    crises, the discovery in the double agent that the self may be evil" (34).
    Greene's thrillers are clearly of the "existential" variety.

19 *Journey Without Maps* ostensibly recounts the trip Greene made to Liberia
    in 1935; but, in its insistence on getting beneath the veneer of civilization
    and on the importance of returning to the primitive, it quickly assumes
    the archetypal patterning of a psychological, even metaphysical, explora-
    tion of the self.

20 It is not hard from this vantage-point to see how Greene's fondness for
    melodrama led to his preoccupation with the "seedy," to his Catholic nov-
    els, and to the much discussed issue of his Manichean or perhaps Jansenist

sympathies. This path has been clearly marked both by critics, such as Anthony Burgess, Francis Kunkel and A.J.M. Smith, and by Greene himself, although he always denied these feelings (Couto 212).

21 The hard-boiled detective novel that Chandler and others (Grella, Cawelti, and Stowe, for example) discuss is, as Palmer notes, a type of the thriller. Edmund Wilson links Chandler's work with Greene's and Hitchcock's ("Who Cares" 262). As testimony to Hammett's importance in Britain, Graves and Hodge in *The Long Week-End*, their social history of the inter-war period, judge Hammett to be the only first-rate writer among authors of detective novels (301).

22 See Joseph Bristow's *Empire Boys: Adventures in a Man's World* for a recent treatment of these codes. Janet Batsleer's, Tony Davies', Rebecca O'Rourke's, and Chris Weedon's volume, *Rewriting English: Cultural Politics of Gender and Class*, also considers the question of popular literature in terms of gender.

23 Comments by Orwell support Martin Green's reading of the period's literary history. In "Boy's Weeklies" Orwell stresses the influence of Kipling's work, singling out *Stalkey and Co.* (1899) for special notice. His essay "Good Bad Books" notes the proliferation of subgenres in the period between 1880 and 1920; and "Bookshop Memories" (1936) confirms the gender of most readers of adventure stories: Orwell notes that the average novel – "the ordinary, good-bad, Galsworthy-and-water stuff which is the norm of the English novel – seems to exist only for women. Men read either the novels it is possible to respect, or detective stories. But their consumption of detective stories is terrific" (244). This linking of inferior fiction and women readers reflects, as studies by Huyssen, Melman, and Trotter show, one of modernism's persistent prejudices. A related discussion is Morris Dickstein's "Popular Fiction and Critical Values: The Novel as a Challenge to Literary History," which locates *Robinson Crusoe* at an originating point in a tradition of popular fiction and remarks upon the book's influence.

24 Gabriel Josipovici suggests that "the urge to recapture the much more real pleasures and terrors of childhood colours all he [Greene] writes" (120). V.S. Pritchett has also remarked with respect to Greene's ambivalence about childhood authors that the "misanthropy of Greene often reads as if it were a resentment of the deceit of books for boys and a rancour against the loss of the richly populated solitude of childhood" (82). The charge of misanthropy has often been levelled at Greene, particularly by early critics such as Sean O'Faolain, who is perhaps the most emphatic in this regard.

25 As pointed out, the nature and sincerity of this commitment to the cause of the workers is certainly questionable for a number of writers. For a lucid and stimulating discussion of how the literary intelligensia reshape or "rewrite" the Left, see John Carey's *The Intellectuals and the Masses: Pride*

and Prejudice Among the Literary Intelligensia, 1880–1939, especially the chapter "Rewriting the Masses," 23–45.

26 David Thomson notes that the political concepts of Left and Right were relatively recent developments in British politics, having emerged only in the later 1920s (116–18).

27 In the Couto interview, Greene playfully responds to the suggestion that he has romanticised the left: "Maybe I do. But I don't think I romanticise the Communists. I have a certain sympathy and there's a link between Communism and Catholicism, the Curia and the Politburo. But there's not much of the real Communism left; it's become State Capitalism. In any case I'd rather romanticise the Left than romanticise the Right as Evelyn Waugh did" (211–12).

28 Greene's desire for destruction is not unique among writers. As Carey points out, the "ardour for extinction" is a common, one might almost say fashionably polemical, feature of the "intellectually superior" (12), whatever their politics, and is frequently expressed by such apocalyptic prophets of the early twentieth century as Nietzsche, Wells, Lawrence, and Yeats. Greene's view seems to arise out of a sense of religious failure and an acute awareness of where the crises of the 1930s were leading. As well, it appears similar to Orwell's: "Only revolution can save England, that has been obvious for years, but now the revolution has started, and it may proceed quite quickly if only we can keep Hitler out. Within two years, maybe a year ... we shall see changes that will surprise the idiots who have no foresight. I dare say the London gutters will have to run with blood. All right, let them, if it is necessary" ("My Country" 538).

29 Terry Eagleton quotes an 1885 letter Engels wrote to novelist Minna Kautsky: "A socialist-based novel fully achieves its purpose ... if by conscientiously describing the real mutual relations, breaking down conventional illusions about them, it shatters the optimism of the bourgeois world, instils doubt as to the eternal character of the bourgeois world, although the author does not offer any definite solution or does not even line up openly on any particular side" (*Marxism* 46). Leftist critics in the 1930s felt that literature had to concern itself with two things: the working class and the portrayal of reality. Anthony Blunt argued that "the true revolutionary art of today will be realistic" because realistic art "most closely represents the ideas of the rising class" (quoted in Symons, *Thirties* 97). A. Calder-Marshall followed Engels in stating that "the most important function of the revolutionary novelist, to my mind, is to portray the whole scene as it is" (*Left Review* 2.16: 876), while Ralph Fox similarly declared: "The revolutionary task of literature to-day is to restore its great tradition, to break the bonds of subjectivism and narrow specialization, to bring the creative writer face to face with his only important task, that of winning the knowledge of truth, of reality" (37).

30 See, for example, Hugh Walpole, *A Letter to a Modern Novelist.*

31 Lukács's "The Ideology of Modernism" (1956), though not a product of the 1930s, is perhaps the best-known statement of this position.

32 See Edgell Rickword, "Straws for the Wary: Antecedents to Fascism," for a contemporary's discussion of the link between the moderns and fascism. John Harrison's *The Reactionaries* and John Carey's *The Intellectuals and the Masses: Pride and Prejudice Among the Literary Intelligensia, 1880–1939* are also of interest here.

33 Woolf herself, however, was not unaware of the weaknesses such an approach implied. In her essay "How It Strikes a Contemporary" (1923), she complains of the failures of contemporary writing: "The most sincere of them [our contemporaries] will only tell us what it is that happens to himself. They cannot make a world, because they are not free of other human beings. They cannot tell stories because they do not believe that stories are true. They cannot generalize. They depend on their senses and emotions, whose testimony is trustworthy, rather than on their intellects whose message is obscure. And they have perforce to deny themselves the use of some of the most powerful and some of the most exquisite of the weapons of their craft" (239).

34 Watson places the Bloomsbury group (the Woolfs, Maynard Keynes, Strachey, Forster, Russell) on the Left in his tally of political allegiance among writers in the inter-war period (87–8). Quentin Bell notes that Woolf's relationship with some of the younger left-wing writers – Spender, Day Lewis, Isherwood – was "easy, friendly and cordially appreciative," despite the fact that they "must also have known that ... her prose could never be an effective vehicle for conveying political ideas"; none the less, "her attitude to politics was a kind that they found sympathetic" (186).

35 In poetry, this same conviction manifests itself in the idiom of the "Audenesque" (a term Greene used in a film review [*PD* 53]), which, among other things, is characterized by the use of concrete images and details that are emphasized by the definite article. Such a technique clearly draws relations between the reader's experience of the world and the world of the poem. For a full discussion of the "Audenesque," including Greene's relation to it, see Bergonzi's *Reading the Thirties*, especially 39–65.

36 This was Stephen Spender's judgment as well in his pamphlet "The New Realism" (1939): "There is a tendency for artists today to turn outwards to reality, because the phase of experimenting in form has proved sterile. If you like, the artist is simply in search of inspiration, having discovered that inspiration depends on there being some common ground of understanding between him and his audience about the nature of reality and on a demand from that audience for what he creates" (quoted in Lodge, *Modes* 190).

37 "The true bearers of ideology in art are the very forms, rather than the abstractable content, of the work itself" (Eagleton, *Marxism* 24).

38 The phrase "fantastic realities" is Christopher Isherwood's (Foreword 34).

39 Mass Observation's statement of purpose, "Poetic Description and Mass Observation," emphasizes the goal of transforming subjective opinion into objective statement through a process of defamiliarization. Subjective reports "become objective because the subjectivity of the observer is one of the facts under observation ... MASS OBSERVATION is a technique for obtaining objective statements about human behaviour ... Poetically, the statements are also useful. They produce a poetry which is not, as at present, restricted to a handful of esoteric performers. The immediate effect of MASS OBSERVATION is to de-value considerably the status of the 'poet.' ... In taking up the rôle of observer, each person becomes like Courbet at his easel ... The process of observing raises him from subjectivity to objectivity. What has become unnoticed through familiarity is raised into consciousness again" (3). The Mass Observation project is briefly elucidated in Julian Symons's *The Thirties*, 110–16. See also Stephen Spender's comment, quoted above in note 36.

40 Orwell, too, saw fiction as contaminated with liberal-bourgeois ideology: "*All* fiction from the novels in the mushrooming libraries downwards is censored in the interests of the ruling class" ("Boy's Weeklies" 203). Brecht is similarly aware of the ideology of traditional realism: "Even the realistic mode of writing, of which literature provides many very different examples, bears the stamp of the way it was employed, when and by which class, down to its smallest details" (81); consequently, realism, as a concept, must be cleansed ("Popularity and Realism").

41 For a discussion of this point, see Stuart Laing's essay "Presenting 'Things as They Are': John Sommerfield's *May Day.*"

42 Ortega calls the assumption that all men are equal a "profound injustice" ("Dehumanization" 7). In *The Revolt of the Masses* (1930), he writes that "the greatest crisis that can afflict peoples, nations, civilizations ... [is] the rebellion of the masses" (*Revolt* 11), which is the inevitable result of the spread of liberal democracy coupled with scientific and techno-industrial advances (*Revolt* 56). Robert Graves and Laura Riding see democracy as equally destructive for literature: "The populace now exercises a more tyrannical influence over English writers than ever before. This is due to a mistranslation of the democratic principle, that everyone has not only the right, but the obligation, to be responsible for himself, into a statement of historical achievement: that everyone has equal capability with everyone else" ("Poetry and Politics" 273). John Carey, in an excellent and highly lucid study of modernism's relations to mass culture, argues that modernist literature and art sought to exclude the newly educated (semi-educated) and "preserve the intellectual's seclusion from the mass" (vii).

43 On the concern for the state of high culture in the 1930s, see Frank Glover-smith's "Defining Culture: J.C. Powys, Clive Bell, R.H. Tawney and T.S. Eliot."

44 Q.D. Leavis, who was hostile to all forms of popular art, was also critical of any practice that made literature available to the general public: circu-lating libraries (9), books at Woolworth's (14), the Book Society (23), book clubs (37), cheap paperbacks (152), and serialization in the popular press (152, 177–8). Yet not all modernist writers condemned all forms of "escap-ist" art. Eliot, as Chinitz argues, had a deep affection for the culture of the music-hall, detective stories, the Marx brothers, and sensationalized tab-loid accounts of murder. Ellen E. Berry sees Gertrude Stein as equally un-comfortable with "the great divide" between high culture and popular culture. Joyce, too, should be added to the list of writers and artists who shared this discomfort.

45 "The temptation to accept the cheap and easy pleasures offered by the cinema, the circulating library, the magazine, the newspaper, the dance-hall, and the loud-speaker is too much for almost everyone. To refrain would be to exercise a severer self-discipline than even the strongest minded are likely to practise, for only the unusually self-disciplined can fight against their environment and only the unusually self-aware could perceive the necessity of doing so" (225). Needless to say, for Leavis the highbrow cult of detective fiction showed how strong the temptation was to adopt the easy, that is, the popular, attitude (200).

46 Indeed, the view that mass culture is dangerous can be traced back to antiquity. See Patrick Brantlinger, *Bread and Circuses*, and Alan Swinge-wood, *The Myth of Mass Culture*, for discussions of the history of the mass-culture critique. For a general discussion of the critique, see Herbert J. Gans, *Popular Culture and High Culture*. Other useful discussions are found in C.W.E. Bigsby's "The Politics of Popular Culture," Peter Miles and Malcolm Smith's *Cinema, Literature and Society*, Antony Easthope's *Literary into Cultural Studies*, and Harriett Hawkins's *Classics and Trash: Traditions and Taboos in High Literature and Popular Modern Genres*.

47 Dickstein's comments on the role of critics in this regard are interesting: "The coming of modernism sharpened the split between high and popu-lar fiction by emphasizing originality, difficulty, and experimentation and devaluing the formulaic, stereotypical elements which modern mass culture shares with the folk cultures of the past. It also led to a distrust of storytelling ... But the writers themselves rarely heeded this split, and al-ways borrowed freely from every part of the cultural spectrum. Only the critics, sociologists, and literary historians drew sharp boundaries, routin-izing the imaginative" (64–5). On the entrenchment of modernist assump-tions within the academy, see Bruce Robbins, "Modernism in History, Modernism in Power", 237–9.

48 See David Trotter's essay "A Horse Is Being Beaten: Modernism and Popular Fiction" for a reading of the subversive aspects of popular fiction.

49 "The Elizabethan drama was aimed at a public which wanted *entertainment* of a crude sort, but would *stand* a good deal of poetry; our problem should be to take a form of entertainment, and subject it to the process which would leave it a form of art" (*The Sacred Wood* 70). See David Chinitz's "T.S. Eliot and the Cultural Divide" for a discussion of Eliot's favourable response to popular culture, especially in the 1920s.

50 De Tocqueville summarized these characteristics in "Literary Characteristics of Democratic Times," chapter 13 of the second volume of *Democracy in America* (58–63). A relevant passage is quoted in Sharrock (21).

51 Fred D. Crawford's *'Mixing Memory and Desire': "The Waste Land" and British Novels* examines the influence of Eliot's poem on a number of British novelists, including Greene (103–23). Crawford suggests that Greene's entertainments contain more frequent allusions to *The Waste Land* than do the novels (119), which, he says, attempt to solve the waste-land dilemma (123).

52 In *The Other Man* Greene admits the negative influence on these novels of his reading in the 1920s (130). Sharrock offers a good critique of Greene's early prose style with reference to *The Man Within* (43–5).

53 Swinnerton is also mentioned in *A Sort of Life* (151). The review appeared in *The Evening News* (20 November 1931), 10, under the title "People We All Know." Stratford notes that it was not as "scathing" as Greene remembered, nor was it a "very perceptive piece of criticism" (*Faith*, 105 and 116). Sherry quotes many of Swinnerton's comments in his biography of Greene (396).

54 Henry James's "The Art of Fiction" makes it clear that the success of any novel depends upon its ability to produce "the illusion of life" and that this is "the beginning and end of the art of the novelist" (35–6).

55 See Greene's essays on James in *Collected Essays* ("Henry James: The Private Universe" [1936], 21–34; "Henry James: The Religious Aspect" [1933], 34–44; "*The Portrait of a Lady*" [1947], 44–50; "The Plays of Henry James" [1950], 50–5) and in *The Portable Graham Greene* ("The Lesson of the Master" [1935], 541–3). Ford and Conrad are also discussed in many places in *Collected Essays* but most specifically in "Ford Madox Ford" (1939 and 1962), 121–30; "The Dark Backward: A Footnote" (1935), 55–60; "Remembering Mr. Jones" (1937), 138–40; and "The Domestic Background" (1935), 140–2. (The first two of these are on Ford, the last two on Conrad.) Greene also edited the Bodley Head's four-volume edition of Ford's work (1962).

56 In "The Art of Fiction" (1884), James writes: "The air of reality (solidity of specification) [resulting from fidelity to exactness or 'truth of detail'] seems … to be the supreme virtue of a novel" (35).

57 One might argue that James's innovation of the *ficelle* allowed for the presentation of a character's consciousness without shifting the plane of reality in the narrative. That is, the *ficelle* (such as Miss Gostrey in *The Ambassadors*) allows for a naturalized presentation of consciousness that cannot distort the reality of the visible world presented in the novel.

58 The phrase is from John Mair's review of *The Confidential Agent* in the *New Statesman* (18 [23 September 1939], 432; Cassis 20). It is also quoted on the back of the Penguin edition of the novel.

59 Later, Greene elaborated on his position: "I think that an artist who wants his art to be part of his life should welcome the chance of showing people ways of working with enjoyment ..." (Gilliatt 49).

60 See *Fiction and the Reading Public*, 46, 51, 53, 286–7.

61 This view has been reiterated by Arnold Weinstein in *Vision and Response in Modern Fiction* ("all novels are mystery stories and all novels both describe and engender the acquisition of knowledge" [15]) and by James Guetti in "Aggressive Reading: Detective Fiction and Realistic Narrative" ("all verbal form ... occurs on the grid of a detective story" [154]).

62 On detective fiction's role in the deterioration of rigid cultural distinctions, see Dipple (130–1), Tani, and Berry's consideration of Gertrude Stein (179–83). Stowe suggests that "detective fiction shares with demagoguery the capacity to mesmerize, but it also shares with Brecht's art, and Chaplin's, the ability to arouse critical awareness, to 'alienate' its reader from its own plot, characters, and apparent generic assumptions" ("Convention" 589). Jon Thompson's *Fiction, Crime, and Empire: Clues to Modernity and Postmodernity* appeared too late for me to take account of his comments. It is gratifying to see how closely this reading of modernism and of the emergence of detective fiction corresponds to my own; however, Thompson's survey of the genre doesn't discuss Greene's work in any substantial way.

CHAPTER TWO

1 Greene later claimed to have presented the meeting "unfairly" (*SL* 98) and to have had no real knowledge of Communist Party meetings. For the scene in *It's a Battlefield*, he relied on his experience of the one such meeting that he did attend in Paris in 1923 (*WE* 28). However inaccurate Greene's presentation was, it did influence Christopher Isherwood's own depiction of a similar scene in *Mr. Norris Changes Trains* (1935) (Hynes, *Auden* 179).

2 Auden, "XXX" ("Sir, no man's enemy ..."), *Poems* (London: Faber 1930), 79; reprinted *English Auden* 36.

3 A passage from "The Virtue of Disloyalty" is perhaps relevant here: "It has always been in the interests of the State to poison the psychological wells, to encourage cat-calls, to restrict human sympathy. It makes government

easier when the people shout Galilean, Papist, Fascist, Communist. Isn't it the story-teller's task to act as the devil's advocate, to elicit sympathy and a measure of understanding for those who lie outside the boundaries of State approval? The writer is driven by his own vocation to be a protestant in a Catholic society, a catholic in a Protestant one, to see the virtues of the capitalist in a Communist society, of the communist in a Capitalist state. Thomas Paine wrote, 'We must guard even our enemies against injustice.' … the writer should always be ready to change sides at the drop of a hat. He stands for the victims, and the victims change. Loyalty confines you to accepted opinions: loyalty forbids you to comprehend sympathetically your dissident fellows; but disloyalty encourages you to roam through any human mind: it gives the novelist an extra dimension of understanding" (609).

4 The same point is made in *It's a Battlefield* when Mrs Coney, after finding out that Jim Drover is a communist, denounces communists, fiercely denies that she is of the same class as Milly and Jim Drover, and refuses to help Milly by signing the petition for a reprieve (99). Similarly, in *The Confidential Agent*, Mrs Bennett, one of the citizens of the impoverished mining community of Benditch, boasts that she and her husband "Don't mix with *their* kind … Socialists" (164).

5 The connection between popular culture and the feminine has been discussed by a number of critics. See Janet Batsleer *et al.*, *Rewriting English: Cultural Politics of Gender and Class*, Billie Melman's *Women and the Popular Imagination in the Twenties: Flappers and Nymphs*, and Andreas Huyssen's *After the Great Divide: Modernism, Mass Culture, Postmodernism*, especially his third chapter, "Mass Culture as Woman: Modernism's Other," 44–62. Orwell's comments from "Bookshop Memories, quoted in note 22, are again exemplary.

6 The same kind of pairing of the popular with the feminine can be detected in the character of Ida Arnold who, though not the monster Mabel Warren is, can claim her as a textual antecedent.

7 The inclusion of Charles Reade (1814–84) alongside Shakespeare and Chaucer is certainly a piece of irony on Greene's part. Reade's literary reputation is hardly as secure as that of either of the others. An author who was often conspicuous in his preoccupation with social problems – as in, for instance, *It's Never Too Late to Mend* – Reade enjoyed popular and critical success with *The Cloister and the Hearth* (1861). Although Reade seems the perfect author for Savory to mention since the two are made to bear a temperamental similarity, Savory's assurance that Reade will live exposes both Savory's critical fallibility and his misplaced hope that his work, too, might survive.

8 An ironic allusion here to F. Scott Fitzgerald's *The Great Gatsby* ("So we beat on, boats against the current, borne back ceaselessly into the past") is

revealing of how we are to see Savory. In his lifetime Fitzgerald never matched the success he had with *This Side of Paradise* (1920) and was considered a writer who had squandered his talents. It is possible that Greene wants us to think of Savory in a this way.

9 In his essays Greene notes the dangers of early success ("Fame falls like a dead hand on an author's shoulder, and it is well for him when it falls only in later life" [*CE* 80]) and condemns authors who are too concerned with "the public life" (*CE* 142). As well, essays on Arnold Bennett ("The Public Life" [1936]) and A.E.W. Mason ("Journey Into Success" [1952]) (*CE* 142 and 161) also reflect Greene's sense that popular success can be damaging to aesthetic aims.

10 On the spy as a figure for the writer, see William M. Chase's "Spies and God's Spies: Greene's Espionage Fiction," especially 159–61.

11 Greene also observed that the influence of film is one of the causes of a difference that exists between nineteenth- and twentieth-century writing: "The Victorians described things statically. We describe things in film terms. The decor isn't separated from the action" (Gilliatt 50; Allain 132–3 makes the same point). Beginning with V.S. Pritchett's review of *It's a Battlefield*, a number of Greene's critics have remarked upon the influence of the cinema in his work. See, for example, Waugh 97–8, Sharrock 45–51, and G. Smith 204–15 as well as the books of Phillips, Falk, and Adamson. Greene has suggested to Phillips that *It's a Battlefield* was his only attempt to write in cinematic terms ("GG: On the Screen" 169), though, unlike *Stamboul Train*, which fulfilled his hopes of it being made into a movie, *It's a Battlefield* was never filmed.

12 Greene's mention of his acquaintance with Pudovkin's essays on montage, which were published in *Close Up* (1927–33), appears in *Ways of Escape* (46).

13 Greene also invokes Brooke's poem in *A Gun for Sale* in reference to Calkin, who desires the return of war. The same cannot be said of Anthony, but the allusion whenever it occurs in Greene's work is clearly intended to suggest a prelapsarian innocence and naïvete that is located in the years before 1914.

14 The sky-writing at the novel's end also makes the criminal nature of capitalism clear: "Krogh's" becomes "rogh's" (=rogues) as the "K" fades while the "s" is drawn (206). Elsewhere, Greene employs the phrase "honour among thieves" in relation to businessmen. (See, for example, *Stamboul Train* 154, *England Made Me* 206, and *The Confidential Agent* 63.)

15 *Pericles* has seldom been considered one of Shakespeare's major works. In 1914 Lytton Strachey called it a "miserable archaic fragment," and in 1930 E.K. Chambers "spoke of it as the corrupt product of mixed authorship" (Michaels xii). (Strachey's review is item 4, page 4, and Chambers' is item 399, page 138, in Nancy C. Michael's *"Pericles": An Annotated Bibliography*

[New York and London: Garland Publishing 1987].) Such comments as these suggest that we are to see Hammarsten's preference for *Pericles* as counter to opinions of the play in the period and as another instance of the reader's attention being drawn to a supposedly minor work.

16 Lockhart, as Davidge notes, is best known for his *Memoirs of the Life of Sir Walter Scott* (published in eight volumes, 1837–38); his *Spanish Ballads* (1823), also referred to by Davidge (96), is a work of translation. Some of Horne's work was republished in the decade before *England Made Me*: *The New Spirit of the Age* (1844; reprinted 1925), *Orion* (1843; reprinted 1928), *The Good Natured Bear* (1846; reprinted 1927), *The London Doll* (1852; reprinted 1922), and *King Penguin* (1848; reprinted 1925). The last three of these are children's stories that continued to be popular in the 1930s. Horne, however, was considered "a talent that early wrote itself out" (*British Authors of the Nineteenth Century* 309). Alexander Smith, a poet and essayist, is thought to have been ruined by early success. Initially compared by critics with Keats and Tennyson in 1853, his career floundered amid accusations of plagiarism. His *Edwin of Deira* (1861) was an epic poem with chivalry as its theme. Unfortunately, parts of Tennyson's *Idylls of the King* had already begun to appear, heightening the attack on Smith as a plagiarist.

Each of the authors Greene mentions – Lookhart, Horne, and Smith – is now considered a relatively minor figure, and all three have close ties to the popular literature of the nineteenth century, despite their attempts to be taken as "serious" writers.

CHAPTER THREE

1 John Bayley and Stephen Hynes both see all of Greene's novels as thrillers, while A.J.M. Smith and Ian Gregor refer to Greene's books as "theological thrillers."

2 See Julian Symons's *Bloody Murder: From Detective Story to Crime Novel*, 13–16, 162ff. On "shocker" as a British term, see Buchan's "Letter to Thomas Arthur Nelson," which is his dedication to *The Thirty-Nine Steps* (1915), vi. According to the *OED*, both "thriller" and "shocker" are first used as generic descriptions at about the same time, 1889–90.

3 Here, for purposes of clarity, "detective fiction" will be the umbrella term for the genre under which all possible subforms such as the classical detective story, or "whodunit?," the hard-boiled detective story, the police procedural, the spy novel, the suspense novel, the thriller, and so on can be grouped. Although "mystery" is also commonly used in this capacity, the older use of the term identifies those works that evince a strong reliance on a sense, whether borne out or not, of a supernatural occurrence – even if the seemingly supernatural is later explained as natural – for the tale to

be effective. Hence, plays such as *Abraham and Issac* and *The Second Shepherd's Play* are referred to as "mystery plays," while the title of a Gothic novel such as Radcliffe's *The Mysteries of Udolpho* can suggest that this novel, too, is a mystery.

4 Thus, in *The Orators* (1932) figures such as Poirot and Holmes take their places in a ritualized liturgy as they are appealed to in the refrains of prayers: "O Poirot deliver us ... O Holmes deliver us" (67).

5 Greene does praise the evocation of a specific time and place in the film, *Sherlock Holmes* (*PD* 274), which is consistent with his view of Conan Doyle's work in general. See, for example, his introduction to *The Sign of Four* (Pan Books 1973; reprinted as *Reflections* 289–92) or his review of Hesketh Pearson's biography of Conan Doyle entitled, "The Poker-Face" (*CE* 119–21).

6 In an essay on Henry James, "The Lesson of the Master" (1935), Greene remarked: "Life is violent and art has to reflect that violence" (541).

7 William Le Queux (1864–1927), a journalist and British Secret Service agent, became a prolific writer of spy stories. Many, such as *The Great War in England in 1897* (1893) and *The Invasion of 1910* (1905), aimed to publicize the need for British preparedness for war.

8 Hays, Zabel, and Robson all take Rowe's remarks as Greene's justification for writing thrillers. McCarthy (229) and McEwen (118–19) find the suggestion that life is like a thriller problematic.

9 In *A Sort of Life* Greene does not mention the story's title, but Wobbe's bibliography of Greene's work lists *The Empty Chair* as the manuscript of a detective story (dated 1926) in the collection of the Humanities Research Center at Austin, Texas (Wobbe 312). As no other detective story is listed prior to 1929, this manuscript is more than likely the story Greene recalls in *A Sort of Life*. Sherry also reports that Greene wrote the first four chapters of a "shocker" called *Queen's Pawn* in 1926 as well; however, all trace of this manuscript has been lost (310).

10 For another account of the detective story as a story of reading, see Clive Bloom's "Reading and Death: Considering Detective Fiction in the Nineteenth Century," in *The Occult Experience and the New Criticism: Daemonism, Sexuality, and the Hidden in Literature*, 80–9.

11 Todorov takes this cue from the French novelist Butor, but Chandler had already noted as much in his notebooks: "In its essence the crime story is simple. It consists of two stories. One is known to the criminal and to the author himself. It is usually simple, consisting chiefly of the commission of a murder and the criminal's attempts to cover up after it ... The other story is the story which is told. It is capable of great elaboration and should, when finished, be complete in itself. It is necessary, however, to connect the two stories throughout the book. This is done by allowing a bit, here and there, of the hidden story to appear" (*Notebooks* 42).

12 Knox's "Detective Story Decalogue" (1928) and Van Dine's "Twenty Rules for Writing Detective Stories" (1946) are both reprinted in *The Art of the Mystery Story*, ed. Howard Haycraft, 189–96.

13 Holmes, too, found significance in silence, omission, and absence. Christie's passage recalls a well-known example of Holmes's method in "Silver Blaze":

> "Is there any other point to which you would wish to draw my [Watson's] attention?"
> "To the curious incident of the dog in the night-time."
> "The dog did nothing in the night-time."
> "That was the curious incident," remarked Sherlock Holmes. (347)

Similarly, in *The Valley of Fear* Holmes finds it suggestive that there should be nothing incriminating in Professor Moriarty's rooms (776).

14 These two codes are tied to the irreversible sequence of events in a narrative and so are easily identified with the text's readerly qualities. The other three codes Barthes identifies – the semantic, the symbolic, and the cultural – extend the text's plurality and reinforce its writerly qualities. Yet none of the codes functions independently of the others.

15 Peter Brooks, in *Reading for the Plot*, recasts this tension in psychoanalytic terms as a struggle between the forces of eros and thanatos in the text.

16 "Every action sequence that occurs in a detective novel between a crime and its solution delays for a time that solution even when it appears logically required by it. Down to the level of a sentence, all telling involves the postponing of an end simply because articulate speech is linear and expresses itself in the dimension of time" (Porter 41).

17 Brooks notes Miller's point that *diegesis*, Plato's term "to designate the narrative of events – the summary of action, as opposed to its imitative reproduction, or *mimesis* – suggests in its etymology that narrative is the retracing of a line already drawn" (Brooks 338 note 9; Miller "Ethics of Reading," 25).

18 In "The Adventure of Charles Augustus Milverton," Holmes and Watson, having broken into Milverton's house, witness his killing and, instead of apprehending the murderer, elect to remain silent as to the killer's identity: "I [Holmes] think there are certain crimes which the law cannot touch, and which therefore, to an extent, justify private revenge" (582). Similarly, in "The Abbey Grange," Holmes confides: "Once or twice in my career I feel that I have done more real harm by my discovery of the criminal than ever done by his crime. I have learned caution now, and I had rather play tricks with the law of England that with my own conscience" (646).

19 The Op makes this particularly clear in *Red Harvest*, where he describes himself as going "blood-simple like the natives" (142) and "getting a rear

[a thrill] out of planning deaths" (145). Interestingly, Doyle also expressed this kind of sentiment in his attempt at something like hard-boiled fiction in the second half of *The Valley of Fear* (1915): Edwards, the Pinkerton detective sent to investigate corruption in a trade union, says to McGinty, the man he is after, "Maybe they will say that I was as bad as you. They can say what they like, so long as I get you" (863).

20 The similarities between the two situations go much farther than this. For instance, both the Queen and the Minister D___ sought to conceal the letter by not concealing it, that is, by leaving it in the open in the hope that the obviousness of its presence would protect it from searching eyes. Lacan elaborates further similarities by seeing a triangular structure surrounding each theft of the letter. In the first, the King stands unseeing while the Minister D___ steals the letter under the Queen's gaze. In the second, the police stand in the position of the unseeing King (they have failed to find the letter) while Dupin assumes the Minister D___'s role in the original theft, leaving the Minister D___ to stand in the position of the Queen (the Minister D___ does not see that Dupin took the letter but this knowledge will be forthcoming to him) (Lacan 32). There is much more to Lacan's reading of "The Purloined Letter," but I do not intend to enter into the critical fray that his reading has inspired. Interested parties should consult Muller and Richardson's *The Purloined Poe* for discussions of "The Purloined Letter" relating to Lacan's seminar.

21 In *A Gun for Sale* Raven's past includes working for a Brighton race gang: the murder of Kite is one of the things he confesses to Anne.

22 One could, of course, reverse this point and say that the criminal's story is interrupted by the story of the investigation. As well, it is interesting that Pinkie, like Ida, struggles with an enigma which in his case is the question of Ida's identity, a problem that he and his followers turn to frequently in the text (for example, 100, 196, 232). (The enigma Ida struggles with is, of course, the mystery of Hale's death.) In this way, too, the stories of the investigation and of the investigated are inverted.

23 A more recent illustration of Brooks's point is found in the novels of Ross Macdonald, which frequently problematize the detective's search for the cause of a crime by locating it in a series of events that occurred well before the actual crime. Lew Archer's inquiry moves along an ill-defined path into the past and, ultimately, into myth as Macdonald's narratives evoke the story of another inquirer, Oedipus.

24 François Eugene Vidocq (1775–1857), a thief, convict, and jailbreaker among other things, used his knowledge of the Parisian underworld to become a successful thief-taker as one of the first agents of the Sûreté. His *Memoires*, published in 1829, offer dramatic and bizarre accounts of his adventures. Émile Gaboriau (1833–73) began writing daily instalments of lurid fiction for newspapers in 1859 and then went on to write a number

of novels, many of them dealing with crime and its detection. Both Vidocq and Gaboriau are credited with having a formative influence on the genre. Poe read Vidocq and, though Vidocq is only mentioned by name towards the end of "The Murders in the Rue Morgue," a good deal of Poe's opinion of Vidocq is expressed in the character of the Prefect G___ in "The Purloined Letter" (Haycraft, *Murder for Pleasure* 25; see also Symons, *Bloody Murder* 27–56 for Vidocq's and Gaboriau's roles in the development of the genre).

25 Todorov points out that any distinction between a sign (narrative) and its interpretation must be made with caution, since "signs, like their interpretation, are *narratives*. The narrative of an adventure signifies another narrative; the spatio-temporal coordinates of the episode change but its very nature does not" (*Poetics* 123; Todorov's emphasis). This point is easily illustrated with reference to detective fiction. In the Sherlock Holmes stories, and this is particularly true of *A Study in Scarlet* (1887), *The Sign of the Four* (1890), and *The Valley of Fear* (1915), an initial narrative becomes the basis of a second narrative, which serves to interpret or explain the earlier account. Similarly, the short stories frequently open with the visit of a client who relates his story to Holmes. Holmes acts on the basis of his reading of the client's narrative and so a second narrative, Watson's, is occasioned by the first in order to explain it. Epigrammatically, "The narrative is always a signifier; it signifies another narrative" (*Poetics* 125).

26 A similar relationship of mutual dependence exists between the characters of the detective and the criminal. Stephano Tani, noting that Dupin's narrator/companion has "the fancy of a double Dupin – the creative and the resolvent" ("Murders in the Rue Morgue" 533), suggests that this duality is expressed in the pairing of Dupin and the criminal Minister D___ in "The Purloined Letter": "Each depends upon the other for his existence. As Dupin conjures up fanciful possibilities – ultimately the murderer personality – the murderer, in effect, 'invents' the detective who must necessarily follow (and chase) the murderer; in other words, the detective exists – is made possible – because the murderer exists. The criminal is simply 'creative'; the detective both stifles and, ironically, *realizes* the criminal's creativity by bringing to light the full nature of the criminal act and then imposing on the criminal the detective's 'resolvent' power, defusing creative anarchy with common-sense morality" (6). Tani argues, and the relationship between Holmes and Moriarty seems to bear him out, that one of two principles of the genre developed by Poe is that the two fundamental terms of the conflict in the detective story (the detective and the criminal) function as doubles of each other, with each being the negation of the other (15). (See also Hoffman, 122–30.)

27 The power of fictive endings has been well explored by Kermode in *The Sense of an Ending*: "Men, like poets, rush 'into the middest,' *in medias res*,

when they are born; they also die *in mediis rebus*, and to make sense of their span they need fictive concords with origins and ends, such as give meaning to lives and poems" (7). The final ordering of the detective provides the necessary "fictive concord" which charges all that has gone before with "significant duration", that is, with meaning (45).

28 Peirce distinguished the frequently confounded terms of induction and abduction (or hypothesis, as he called it earlier in his career) in the following way: "By induction, we conclude that facts, similar to observed facts, are true in cases not examined. By hypothesis, we conclude the existence of a fact quite different from anything observed, from which, according to known laws, something observed would necessarily result. The former is reasoning from particulars to the general law; the latter, from effect to cause" (136). For discussions of Peirce's theory of abduction as it relates to the methods of Dupin and Holmes, see *The Sign of Three – Dupin, Holmes, Peirce*, ed. Umberto Eco and Thomas A. Sebeok; and Kathleen Gregory Klein and Joseph Keller's "Deductive Detective Fiction: The Self-Destructive Genre."

29 Daniel Kempton has made the point that "in Poe, the detective (the hero of the intellect) is always prejudiced, committed beforehand to a particular course of investigation and a particular line of argument" (7–8).

30 There is always difference involved in repetition. As Miller tells us, "even an exact repetition is never the same, if only because it is the second and not the first. The second constitutes the first, after the fact, as an origin, as a model or archetype. The second, the repetition, is the origin of the originality of the first" ("Ariadne's Thread" 66–7).

31 Derrida's discussion of Freud's permanent memory trace in "Freud and the Scene of Writing" echoes Barthes's sense that origin disappears in structures of repetition: "The text is not conceivable in an originary or modified form of presence. The unconscious text is already a weave of pure traces, differences in which meaning and force are united – a text nowhere present, consisting of archives which are *always already* transcriptions. Originary points. *Everything begins with reproduction.* Always already: repositories of a meaning which was never present, whose signified presence is always reconstituted by deferral ... belatedly ..." ("Freud" 211; my emphasis). For Derrida, and he attributes this realization to Freud, the concept of primariness – of there being an original impression made in memory – is a "theoretical fiction," "for repetition does not *happen to* an initial impression; its possibility is already there, in the resistance offered *the first time* by the psychical neurones. Resistance itself is possible only if the opposition of forces [between resistance and stimulation] lasts and is repeated at the beginning. It is the very idea of a *first time* which becomes enigmatic" ("Freud" 202; Derrida's emphasis). To move from these insights into Freud's texts to Barthes's perception of

literary production is easily done given the notion of the "already-written."

32 Barthes defines ideology as "what is repeated and *consistent*" (*Roland Barthes* 104; Barthes's emphasis). It is the whole structure of unconscious mechanisms – of ideas, values, feelings – that binds disparate elements separated by wealth, class, race, sex, or creed into a common society. Ideology is the process that transforms a particular distribution of power, choices, or directions into appearing natural or normal, or into appearing as "common sense" or the best thing to do in a given circumstance (Chambers 210). An extended definition can be found in Raymond Williams's *Keywords: A Vocabulary of Culture and Society*, 126–30.

33 Robert Daniel says of Poe's detective that "Dupin is a sort of secular god … the most enduring religious substitute in the imagination of what has been called A Century of Hero-Worship" (104).

34 See Foucault's study, *Discipline and Punish: The Birth of the Prison* 67–9.

35 For descriptions of those elements that make up the formulas of the classical detective novel and of the hard-boiled detective novel, see Dorothy Sayers' "Introduction to *The Omnibus of Crime*," George Grella's "The Formal Detective Novel" and "The Hard-Boiled Detective Novel," and John G. Cawelti's *Adventure, Mystery, and Romance*, chapters 4 and 6.

36 See Peter J. Rabinowitz's "Rats Behind the Wainscoting: Politics, Convention, and Chandler's *The Big Sleep*" for a discussion of Eddie Mars in the novel.

37 The hard-boiled detective's sense of impotence is well illustrated near the end of Hammett's *Red Harvest* (1929) by the Op's comments made to Willson, the wealthy publisher who hired the Op to rid Personville ("Poisonville") of the criminal gangs dominating municipal politics: "You'll have your city back, all nice and clean and ready to go to the dogs again" (187). Similarly, the Op's remarks at the end of "$106,000 Blood Money" also suggest his impotence: " 'I'm going to take a couple of weeks off,' I said from the door. I felt tired, washed out" (458).

CHAPTER FOUR

1 In *In Search of a Character* Greene comments on the importance of initials for his characters (63).

2 This same link is apparent in *A Gun for Sale* when Raven confesses to Anne while the two are hiding in the railway shed (124). The importance of psychoanalysis in and for Greene's work is beyond the purview of this study. Roland A. Pierloot has recently offered a thoroughly detailed account, *Psychoanalytic Patterns in the Work of Graham Greene*, for those interested in this area of study.

3 The same awareness is visible in *It's a Battlefield* when Milly insists that Conder write out his promise to give her publicity (she has just got Mrs Coney's signature on a petition for the reprieve of Jim Drover), and he replies, "Writing a thing doesn't make it any more true. You're talking to a man who knows" (104). Here it is Milly who assumes a connection between writing and truth. (The same is true of Mrs Coney, who fears signing anything: "If you sign things ... you don't know what you let yourself in for" [98].) Conder, however, finds lies most effective in catching attention (85), and, consequently, he strips writing of veracity.

4 See, for instance, Arthur Calder-Marshall's early assessment of Greene's work, "The Works of Graham Greene," 373.

5 Dates for comments from Greene's diary are given in Sherry's biography. Those passages relevant to the genesis of *It's a Battlefield* are found on pages 457–8.

6 Greene commented on the importance of dreams for himself and his work in a number of places. See, for instance, *A Sort of Life*, 73. Of particular interest is his dream, described on page 75, of being pursued by a sinister figure. Recently, parts of a dream-diary Greene kept have been published under the title *A World of My Own*.

7 In that the city is often foregrounded in *It's a Battlefield*, Roger Sharrock detects the influence of Virginia Woolf's *Mrs. Dalloway* (67–8). If this is the case, however, Greene is surely reacting against Woolf's novel since, as we have seen, his sense of the how the external world is to be represented in fiction is quite different from Woolf's.

8 Greene's debt to Conrad's novel has been remarked upon and discussed by a number of critics, among them Kenneth Allott and Miriam Farris (87–9), Norman Sherry (457), and Lynne Cheney.

9 This tendency for the detective to assume the functions of judge and jury in hard-boiled fiction is clearly exemplified in the title of Mickey Spillane's first novel, *I, the Jury*; in this novel, however, Mike Hammer's pursuit of justice, like Conrad Drover's pursuit in *It's a Battlefield*, is clouded by a morally dubious desire for personal revenge.

10 For instance, the assistant commissioner's housekeeper, Mrs Simpson, agrees with the courts: " 'I'd like to see 'em [murderers] all strung up and finished with' " (76–7).

CHAPTER FIVE

1 Greene claims that he was under no illusions that *It's a Battlefield* would be popular (*WE* 27); however, given that he deliberately wrote the book with the screen in mind (Allain 146) during "a time of great financial anxiety" (*WE* 26), it seems unlikely that he did not hope in 1934 that the

book would be successful. (Sherry, too, reports that Greene hoped the book would sell well [456].) Greene also seems to have hoped for *England Made Me*'s success, since he spoke of it as "a modern adventure story" similar to *Stamboul Train* (Shuttleworth 33).

2 The waste lands seen from trains are described in *The Confidential Agent* (159–60), where the names of mining villages offer ironic commentary on Depression society in both Wales and the northern parts of England. Brighton's occult world is well evoked in *Brighton Rock*, as Ida uses a ouija board and Cubitt gets his fortune told from a mechanical machine. Slough has been immortalized in John Betjeman's 1937 poem "Slough," whose first stanza reads: "Come, friendly bombs, and fall on Slough/It isn't fit for humans now,/There isn't grass to graze a cow/Swarm over, Death!" Here, violence is not only expected but prayed for. Similarly, in *The Lawless Roads* Greene suggests the need for violence as a tool of purgation (224).

3 *The Tenth Man*, published in 1985 but probably written in 1944 when Greene was under contract at MGM, is also set in this period.

4 Greene later stated, "I don't think that Pinkie was guilty of mortal sin because his actions were not committed in defiance of God, but arose out of the conditions to which he had been born" (Allain 158–9).

5 Greene's preface to *The Third Man* makes the point that "the film, in fact, is better than the story because it is the finished state of the story" (10).

6 In linking the armaments industry to the coming of the next war, Greene is reflecting a position, commonly held in the 1930s, which grew out of the belief that the arms industry was responsible for the First World War. See Ivan Melada's "Graham Greene and the Munitions Makers: The Historical Context of *A Gun for Sale*" and *Guns for Sale: War and Capitalism in English Literature, 1851–1939*. The link between war and financial prosperity is also made clear in a discussion among the policemen in *A Gun for Sale*:

> "You can't expect people to buy gas masks at twenty-five bob a time, but we're having a raid the day after tomorrow with smoke bombs from Hanlow aerodrome, and anyone found in the street without a mask will be carted off by ambulance to the General Hospital. So anyone who's too busy to stop indoors will have to buy a mask. Midland Steel are supplying all their people with masks, so it'll be business as usual there."
>
> "Kind of blackmail," the superintendent said. "Stay in or buy a mask. The transport companies have spent a pretty penny on masks." (71)

7 Raven tells Anne that he once killed a race-course gangster named "Battling Kite" (*GS* 127), and in *Brighton Rock* a gang leader named Kite was killed by Colleoni's mob. Hence, Greene draws a relationship in the later novel between Colleoni, the wealthy gangster of *Brighton Rock*, and Sir Marcus of *A Gun for Sale*.

8 It is perhaps an indication of Poe's influence on *A Gun for Sale* that Mather, like the narrator of "The Man in the Crowd," prefers to search for his clues in crowds (86), while Raven, too, stays in "the most crowded streets" so as not to feel conspicuous (88).

9 Mather's narrow belief that events on the continent will not affect England is shared by Bates, the union leader in *The Confidential Agent*, who asks D., "What's this [the fact that coal will be sold to the fascists in D.'s country] got to do with me?" (168). Similarly, in *The Ministry of Fear* Rowe decides at one point to give up his investigation, concluding: "It's nothing to do with me: it's their war, not mine … It's not my war" (77); but as Rowe comes to realize, "the world is a small cramped place" (89). Each of these novels reflects the limitations of such readings while also offering a critique of British isolationist sentiment.

10 In *It's a Battlefield* and *The Power and the Glory* characters are identified by their functions: the Assistant Commissioner, the Priest, and the Lieutenant, for example.

11 Mather's story becomes a variation of Raven's story. Significantly, Mather has points in common with Raven: both endure the suicide of a family member, and both feel a desperate need to belong and be a part of a wider context: Mather fulfils this desire as a member of the police force; Raven, however, is unable to find the fulfilment that comes with being part of a community.

12 The question of locating the narrative's origins becomes even more complex when we consider the beast fable of the cat and the fox that Anne tells to Raven. Although the text does not explicitly comment on Anne's fable, it seems clear that we are to link the participants in the fable – the cat, the fox, and the dogs – with characters in the novel; thus, *A Gun for Sale* again acknowledges its status as a reinscription of a much earlier narrative.

13 Again, references to popular, nearly forgotten authors dot Greene's text. Edgar Wallace's work, as we have already noted, was hugely popular and much admired by Greene. Netta Syrett, now largely unknown, wrote a number of very popular books, some of which were for and about children; her name, then, takes on an ironic significance in the context of Greene's account of Pinkie, who is referred to as "the Boy" throughout *Brighton Rock*, for Syrett "delight[ed] to take for her plot-idea the eccentric or the child of genius faced with the unexpectedness of life" (H. Williams 467). Syrett also possessed a keen interest in psychical phenomena (Lester 92–3). *The Good Companions* (1929), by J.B. Priestley, and *Sorrell and Son* (1925), by Warwick Deeping, were both tremendously popular and reassuring novels. Greene was often critical of Priestley, whom he satirized in *Stamboul Train*, though he paid him tribute for his role as a BBC commentator in the aftermath of Dunkirk (*Reflections* 87–9).

Deeping's novel dealt with the plight of the Great War's veterans and an emerging sense of class conflict. Both novels are referred to in a number of places in *Brighton Rock*. At the book's end, Ida returns home to find that "Warwick Deeping wasn't in a bookshelf and *The Good Companions* was on its side" (244).

14   Francis L. Kunkel (107), James Hall (116), and Paul O'Prey (73) all are critical of Ida's blatantly secular outlook, while R.W.B. Lewis (243), Richard Kelly (41), and Hall (116) are three of many critics who think of Pinkie as a tragic figure. There is, indeed, no shortage of evidence for reading Pinkie as satanic. He grew up in a Brighton slum ironically called Paradise Piece, but the place has been demolished, and he is unable to return to it. Descriptions of him also suggest obscure infernal origins. Of particular importance are references to his eyes as "ageless" (23), "touched with the annihilating eternity from which he had come" (21). Other details also contribute to a sense of Pinkie as evil incarnate: his birth is not registered anywhere (166) and his phone number is, significantly, "Three sixes" (48). Allusions to Marlowe's *Dr. Faustus* reinforce the implication that Pinkie is an inhabitant of hell.

15   In a sense, Rose's helplessness before Pinkie's evil is completely logical in that, if we think of her is a figure of absolute "Good," she cannot, by her nature, condemn or punish. As Pinkie is surprised to realize, her goodness completes his evil: the two of them "[live] in the same country, [speak] the same language, [come] together like old friends, [feel] the same completion" (127). Again we venture into Greene's potentially Manichean vision: "the world ... lay there always, the ravaged and disputed territory between two eternities" (139).

16   See, for example, Elizabeth Davis (23), Kunkel (109), O'Prey (71), Roger Sharrock (86ff.), Philip Stratford (72), Harvey Curtis Webster (101), and Morton Dauwen Zabel (36).

17   Eliot's remarks are based on *Revelation* 3: 14–16 and read as follows: "So far as we are human, what we do must be either evil or good; so far as we do evil or good, we are human; and it is better, in a paradoxical way, to do evil than to do nothing: at least, we exist. It is true to say that the glory of man is his capacity for salvation; it is also true to say that his glory is his capacity for damnation" (183). In this context, "damnation itself is an immediate form of salvation – of salvation from the ennui of modern life because it at last gives some significance to living" (181). In the essay, "Frederick Rolfe: Edwardian Inferno," Greene writes: "The greatest saints have been men with more than a normal capacity for evil, and the most vicious men have sometimes narrowly evaded sanctity" (*CE* 131).

18   Colley Cibber was poet laureate from 1730 to 1757 and is generally considered one of the worst poets to hold the post. (He is attacked by Pope in *The Dunciad*.) That Greene echoes the name of an author, particularly an

author who is perhaps better known for his satiric portrait in Pope's *Dunciad* than for his own work, again foregrounds questions of textuality in the opening pages of *Brighton Rock*.

19 See also David G. Wright's "Greene's *Brighton Rock*" (*Explicator* 41.4), 52–3, for a similar conclusion.

20 Aside from Pinkie, Hale, and Spicer, who all die in the course of the novel, various young women are mentioned periodically as the casualties of Brighton's poverty and crime: Peggy Baron, scarred with vitriol (47); Violet Crow, "violated and buried under the West Pier" (142); Annie Collins, suicide on the rail tracks (165); and Molly Carthew, also a suicide (199). As well, the *News of the World*, which Pinkie reads, bears the headline, "Assault on Schoolgirl in Epping Forest" (200). Rose, who is tempted to suicide by Pinkie, typifies the experience of Brighton's poor, young women.

21 What this does is force a reconsideration at the end of the novel of the whole problem of Ida's moral inferiority when placed alongside the religious sense of Pinkie and Rose. In this light it is perhaps significant that it is the priest who suggests that Ida may have been right (246).

22 Reference is also made in a discussion between D. and L. to "Z.'s pictures" (29). Of course, by using letters to identify characters, Greene is able to avoid revealing his characters' nationality – a move that probably has its origins in his desire both to present the story in terms of a general situation not unique to any one nation and to avoid possible libel suits.

23 Greene did not respond to the *Left Review*'s "Authors Take Sides" campaign, and he much later stated that he could support neither side in the conflict (Couto 208). His contemporary statement on the crisis is made indirectly in his essay "The Apostles Intervene" (*CE* 230–4), where he is critical of the "hysterical partisans" who responded to the "Authors Take Sides" campaign with "the sweeping statements, the safe marble gestures, the self-importance of our own 'thirties" (230–1).

24 D. differs from Dr Bellows, the inventor of the Entrenationo Language and founder of the Entrenationo Language Centre. Bellows's dream of a universal language is based on the mistaken notion that differences between languages, not difference within language, create misunderstanding and conflict. Bellows assumes that language and texts can be interpreted only in one way, and that misunderstandings and conflicts would be avoided if everyone read in the same way. As D. realizes, however, Bellows fails because reading is not so straightforward a process. (Rennet, in *The Ministry of Fear*, finds this as well.) Where Bellows's dream collapses is in his inability to recognize that differences in meaning can emerge within the same language or even within the same word.

CHAPTER SIX

1 Allott and Farris (194), Bergonzi (*Wartime* 30), Lodge ("GG" 105),
McEwen (121), Spurling (37), Webster (113), and Woodcock (126, 137)
all tend to condemn *The Ministry of Fear*. Allott and Farris discuss the
novel in terms of Greene incorporating a "greater incoherence" into the
"loosely knocked-up narrative," which results in "a certain ungainli-
ness" and a rather "ramshackle look" (194); although, in fairness, they
also praise Greene's "fertility of invention, the pinpointing of detail, the
reality of the ungrotesque characters … and the confidence with which
Greene drives the narrative forward at high speed when the emphasis is
on action" (194) – all of this, they find, has had an "exhilarating effect on
Greene's style" (194). Other critics, such as G. Smith (41), Couto (105),
De Vitis (38), Lewis (240), and Wolfe (101, 121), praise the book, although in De Vitis's and Lewis's cases it is a qualified praise. Sherry is
more enthusiastic, claiming that it is "by any standards a remarkable
novel, the best novel about the blitz written during the Second World
War" (2. 148).

2 Seen from another perspective, the "external events in the story are mainly
reflecting and not determining [Rowe's] inner evolution" (Pierloot 85). For
a psychoanalytical reading of the novel emphasizing Rowe's "inner journey," see Pierloot, 85–99.

3 Panek briefly enumerates a number of the texts that are alluded to in
Greene's novel (123).

4 Wolfe applauds Greene's portrayal of the psychological conditions of
wartime England (102), while A.J.M. Smith calls the book "a kind of
Kafkaesque parable of … wartime" (27).

5 Greene said that he read Yonge's novel in 1916 or so and that he added
the epigraphs to the chapters of *The Ministry of Fear* when he revised the
book after the Second World War (*SL* 38).

6 Indeed, one might see the killing of his wife as the expression of a desire
to take heroic action; that is, in practising euthanasia, Rowe courageously
violates social conventions.

7 Implicitly, any detective story figures this same process, since only error
allows the narrative to continue. When the detective is free from error, he
or she announces his or her final reading, which traditionally closes the
narrative. If the detective cannot be free of error, the text will fail to provide a satisfying sense of closure, although, as is the case with *Trent's Last
Case*, this does not preclude the narrative from ending.

8 The scene is the linguistic counterpart to the scene at the end of *Rumour At
Nightfall* where Chase and Monti gaze upon the body of the dead Crane,
whose identity is confused by the superimposition of the face of Caveda
in the photograph that lies upon Crane's face.

9 Arthur Balfour served as a Conservative prime minister from 1902 to 1905 and as foreign secretary from 1916 to 1919. Early in his career he earned the nickname "Bloody Balfour" because of his severity in suppressing insurrection in Ireland, and so he is perhaps a suitable figure for Prentice to be compared to.

10 The reference to "progressive people who learn Esperanto" recalls the fascist idealists, such as K., of the Entrenationo Language Centre in *The Confidential Agent*.

11 Johns notes as well that he would not be surprised if the British also made use of a "Ministry of Fear" (121) – a point that further obliterates sharp distinctions between the two sides. It is somewhat paradoxical that Greene should have praised J.B. Priestley in 1940 for supplying the British with an ideology: "He gave us the idea of the two orders, the Nazi and our own in simple terms, as moving as poetry" (*Reflections* 88). What appealed to Greene, however, was not so much the simple ideological polarities that Priestley outlined – such polarities are never accepted in Greene's fiction – but Priestley's call for social change after the war: "Surely it was a sign of something that the BBC should allow a speaker to refer to the old false peace, 'the defeat of goodwill,' to appeal openly for a new order in England after the war" (88).

12 Hilfe resembles Davis in *A Gun for Sale*, Pinkie in *Brighton Rock*, and K. in *The Confidential Agent* – all of whom dread having the violence they so easily participate in turned upon themselves.

13 Tolstoy's words and Rowe's response to them are curiously ambiguous. The passages from Tolstoy that Forester had marked emphasize the individual's duty to stand apart from nationalistic or religious causes. Forester's erasures, then, suggest that he no longer accepts this position and so has given himself over to the fascist cause. On the other hand, Rowe's response is similar in that he too cannot stand apart and, like Forester, he chooses a side. In one way, the inclusion of Tolstoy's position can be seen as an ironic jab at the apolitical writers of high modernism, especially the Bloomsbury group. The title of Tolstoy's essay "What I Believe" and the name of Dr Forester seem calculated to recall E.M. Forster's 1939 essay of the same title. Indeed, Forster's essay expresses views remarkably similar to Tolstoy's; Forster not only says he would betray his country before he would betray his friends (76) but he also claims that he would "look the other way" when confronted by violent aggression (79). For Greene, however, the positions of Tolstoy and Forster must have been attractive, since his views, expressed in the 1948 exchange "Why Do I Write?" and in his 1969 lecture/essay "The Virtue of Disloyalty" (to say nothing of his yet to be unravelled place in the Kim Philby affair), follow those of Tolstoy and Forester in several points. I think that we have to agree with Rowland Smith that the views Greene

held in 1948 are quite different from those he professed in 1942–43 and earlier (Smith 104–5).

14 This same process is at work in *A Gun for Sale*, since Raven confirms his identification of Anne's purse by seeing the marks where her initials had once been. Raven, too, reads a text that is figuratively erased; and, for him, the result is the retracing of an old experience (*GS* 90–2).

CHAPTER SEVEN

1 Greene's work was ignored by *Scrutiny* until 1952 when F.N. Lees's "Graham Greene: A Comment" appeared. Needless to say, Lees was highly critical of Greene's work, accusing him of "regrettable sentimental[ity]" in the thrillers (32), "bad, showy, shallow writing" in *The Power and the Glory* (35), and "unsureness of technique" in *The Heart of the Matter* (38).

Bibliography

Adamson, Judith. *Graham Greene and Cinema*. Norman, Okla.: Pilgrim Books 1984.

– *Graham Greene: The Dangerous Edge – Where Art and Politics Meet*. London: Macmillan 1990.

Adorno, Theodor, and Max Horkheimer. "Enlightenment as Mass Deception." 1938. *Dialectic of Enlightenment*. Tr. John Cumming. New York: Herder and Herder 1972 (120–67).

Allain, Marie-Françoise. *The Other Man: Conversations with Graham Greene by Marie-Françoise Allain*. 1981. Tr. Guido Walman. London, Sydney, Toronto: Bodley Head 1983.

Allen, Glen. "The Literary Consul: Graham Greene was a Sublime Storyteller." *Maclean's* 104.15 (15 April 1991): 65.

Allen, Walter. "The Novels of Graham Greene." *Penguin New Writing*. No. 18. Harmondsworth: Penguin 1943. Nendeln Liechtenstein: Kraus Reprint 1970. 148–60.

Alley, Kenneth D. "*A Gun For Sale*: Graham Greene's Reflection of Moral Chaos." *Essays in Literature* 5.2 (fall 1978): 175–85.

Allott, Kenneth and Miriam Farris. *The Art of Graham Greene*. 1951. New York: Russell and Russell 1963.

Arnold, Matthew. *Culture and Anarchy*. 1869. Ed. J. Dover Wilson. Cambridge: Cambridge University Press 1969.

Atkins, John. *Graham Greene*. London: John Calder 1957.

Auden, W.H. *The English Auden: Poems, Essays and Dramatic Writings 1927–1939*. Ed. Edward Mendelson. 1977. London: Faber 1986.

– "The Guilty Vicarage." 1938. *The Dyer's Hand and Other Essays*. London: Faber 1963 (146–58).

- "The Heresy of Our Time." Hynes, *Graham Greene* 93–4.
- "Honour." 1934. *The Old School: Essays by Divers Hands.* Ed. Graham Greene. Oxford: Oxford University Press 1984 (1–12).
- Introduction to *The Poet's Tongue*. 1935. *English Auden* 327–30.
- *New Year Letter.* 1940. *Collected Longer Poems.* New York: Vintage 1975 (77–130).
- *The Orators: An English Study.* 1932. *English Auden* 59–110.
- "Poetry, Poets, and Taste." *The Highway* (December 1936). Rpt. *English Auden* 358–60.
- Review of *Culture and Environment* by F.R. Leavis and Denys Thompson, *How to Teach Reading* by F.R. Leavis, and *How Many Children Had Lady Macbeth?* by L.C. Knights. *The Twentieth Century* (May 1933). Rpt. *English Auden* 317–18.
Auerbach, Erich. *Mimesis: The Representation of Reality in Western Literature.* 1946. Trans. Willard R. Trask. 1953. Princeton: Princeton University Press 1974.
Aydelotte, William O. "The Detective Story as a Historical Source." *The Yale Review* 39 (1949): 76–95.
Barthes, Roland. "Criticism as Language." 1963. *The Critical Moment: Essays on the Nature of Literature.* Ed. *Times Literary Supplement.* London: Faber 1964 (123–9).
- "The Death of the Author." 1968. *Image-Music-Text* Essays Selected and Translated by Stephen Heath. Glasgow: Fontana 1977 (142–8).
- "From Work to Text." 1971. *Image-Music-Text* 155–64.
- *The Grain of the Voice: Interviews 1962–1980.* 1981. Trans. Linda Coverdale. New York: Hill and Wang 1985.
- "Introduction to the Structural Analysis of Narrative." 1966. *The Semiotic Challenge.* Trans. Richard Howard. New York: Hill and Wang 1988 (95–135).
- *The Pleasure of the Text.* 1973. Trans. Richard Miller. New York: Hill and Wang 1975.
- *Roland Barthes By Roland Barthes.* 1975. Trans. Richard Howard. New York: Hill and Wang 1984.
- *S/Z: An Essay.* 1970. Trans. Richard Miller. New York: Hill and Wang 1974.
- "The Sequences of Action." 1969. *The Semiotic Challenge* 136–48.
- *Writing Degree Zero.* 1953. Trans. Annette Lavers and Colin Smith. New York: Hill and Wang 1977.
Batsleer, Janet, Tony Davies, Rebecca O'Rourke, and Chris Weedon. *Rewriting English: Cultural Politics of Gender and Class.* New Accents. London and New York: Methuen 1985.
Bayley, John. "God's Greene." Review of *The Captain and the Enemy* by Graham Greene, *Graham Greene* by Neil McEwen, and *A Reader's Guide to Graham Greene* by Paul O'Prey. *New York Review of Books* 16 March 1989: 3–4.
Bell, Quentin. *Virginia Woolf: A Biography.* Vol. 2. New York: Harcourt, Brace, Jovanovich 1972.

Belsey, Catherine. *Critical Practice.* New Accents. London and New York: Methuen 1980.

– "Re-Reading the Great Tradition." *Re-Reading English.* Ed. Peter Widdowson. New Accents. London and New York: Methuen 1982 (121–35).

Bentley, E.C. *Trent's Last Case.* 1913. New York: Harper and Row 1978.

Bergonzi, Bernard. *Reading the Thirties: Texts and Contexts.* London: Macmillan 1978.

– *Wartime and Aftermath: English Literature and Its Background 1939–1960.* Oxford and New York: Oxford University Press 1993.

Berman, Russell A. "Modernism, Fascism, and the Institution of Literature." *Modernism: Challenges and Perspectives.* Ed. Monique Chefdor, Ricardo Quinones, and Albert Wachtel. Urbana and Chicago: University of Illinois Press 1986 (94–102).

Berry, Ellen E. "Modernism/Mass Culture/Postmodernism: The Case of Gertrude Stein." Dettmar 167–90.

Betjeman, John. "Slough." Skelton 74.

Bigsby, C.W.E. "The Politics of Popular Culture." *Approaches to Popular Culture.* Ed. C.W.E. Bigsby. London: Edwin Arnold 1976 (3–26).

Bloom, Clive. *The Occult Experience and the New Criticism: Daemonism, Sexuality, and the Hidden in Literature.* Brighton, Sussex: Harvester; Totowa, N.J.: Barnes and Noble 1986.

Bloom, Harold. *The Anxiety of Influence.* Oxford: Oxford University Press 1973.

– ed. *Graham Greene.* Modern Critical Views. New York, New Haven, Philadelphia: Chelsea House 1987.

– Introduction. Bloom, *Graham Greene* 1–8.

Boardman, Gwenn R. *Graham Greene: The Aesthetics of Exploration.* Gainesville: University of Florida Press 1971.

Bottomore Tom. *The Frankfurt School.* Key Sociologists. London and New York: Tavistock 1984.

Bradbury, Malcolm. "Virginia Woolf and Ford Madox Ford: Two Styles of Modernity." *Possibilities.* Oxford, London, New York: Oxford University Press 1973 (121–39).

Brantlinger, Patrick. *Bread and Circuses: Theories of Mass Culture as Social Decay.* Ithaca: Cornell University Press 1983.

Brecht, Bertolt. "Popularity and Realism," *Aesthetics and Politics.* Trans. and ed. Ronald Taylor. London: NLB [New Left Books] 1977.

Bristow, Joseph. *Empire Boys: Adventures in a Man's World.* Reading Popular Narrative. London: Harper Collins 1991.

British Authors of the Nineteenth Century. Eds. Stanley J. Kunitz and Howard Haycraft. 1936. New York: H.W. Wilson 1964.

Brooks, Peter. *Reading for the Plot: Design and Intention in Narrative.* 1984. New York: Vintage 1985.

Brown, Dennis. *The Modernist Self in Twentieth Century English Literature: A Study in Self-Fragmentation.* New York: St Martin's 1989.

Buchan, John. *The Thirty-Nine Steps*. 1915. London and Sydney: Pan 1978.

Burgess, Anthony. "Monsieur Greene of Antibes." *But Do Blondes Prefer Gentlemen? "Homage to Quert Yuiop" and Other Writings*. New York, Toronto, St. Louis: McGraw-Hill 1986 (20–5).

Burstall, Christopher. "Graham Greene Takes the Orient Express." *Listener* 80 (21 November 1968): 672–7.

Caesar, Adrian. *Dividing Lines: Poetry, Class and Ideology in the 1930s*. Manchester and New York: Manchester University Press 1991.

Calder-Marshall, Arthur. "The Works of Graham Greene." *Horizon* 1 (May 1940): 367–75.

Carey, John. *The Intellectuals and the Masses: Pride and Prejudice Among the Literary Intelligensia, 1880–1939*. London: Faber 1992.

Cargas, Harry J., ed. *Graham Greene*. The Christian Critic Series. St Louis, Mo: B. Herder, n.d.

Cassis, A.F. *Graham Greene: An Annotated Bibliography of Criticism*. Scarecrow Author Bibliographies 55. Metuchen, N.J. and London: The Scarecrow Press 1981.

Cawelti, John G. *Adventure, Mystery, and Romance: Formula Stories as Art and Popular Culture*. Chicago and London: University of Chicago Press 1976.

– and Bruce A. Rosenberg. *The Spy Story*. Chicago and London: University of Chicago 1987 (chapter 5, "At a Crossroads: Eric Ambler and Graham Greene," 101–24, is Rosenberg's.)

Chambers, Iain. *Popular Culture: The Metropolitan Experience*. Studies in Communication. New York: Methuen 1986.

Chandler, Raymond. *The Big Sleep*. 1939. New York: Vintage 1976.

– Introduction. 1950. *Trouble is My Business*. New York: Ballantine 1973 (vii–xi).

– *The Notebooks of Raymond Chandler*. Ed. Frank MacShane. London: Weidenfeld and Nicholson 1976.

– *Raymond Chandler Speaking*. Ed. Dorothy Gardiner and Kathrine Sorley Walker. London: Hamish Hamilton 1962.

– *Selected Letters of Raymond Chandler*. Ed. Frank MacShane. New York: Columbia University Press 1981.

– "The Simple Art of Murder: An Essay." 1944. *The Simple Art of Murder*. New York: Ballantine 1980 (1–21).

Chase, William M. "Spies and God's Spies: Greene's Espionage Fiction." Meyers 156–80.

Cheney, Lynne. "Joseph Conrad's *The Secret Agent* and Graham Greene's *It's a Battlefield*: A Study in Structural Meaning." *MFS* 16.2 (September 1970): 117–32.

Chesterton, G.K. "A Defence of Detective Stories." *The Defendant*. London: Dent 1901 (157–62).

Chinitz, David. "T.S. Eliot and the Cultural Divide." *PMLA* 110.2 (March 1995): 236–47.

Choi, Jae-Suck. *Greene and Unamuno: Two Pilgrims to La Mancha.* American University Studies Series III: Comparative Literature, vol. 35. New York, Bern, Frankfurt au Main, Paris: Peter Lang 1990.

Christie, Agatha. *The ABC Murders.* 1936. New York: Pocket Books 1977.

– *Cards on the Table.* 1936. New York: Dell 1974.

– *Murder on the Orient Express.* 1934. New York: Pocket Books 1976.

– *The Murder of Roger Ackroyd.* 1926. New York: Pocket Books [1939].

Christopher, J.R. "A Detective Searches for a Clue to *The Heart of the Matter.*" *The Armchair Detective* 4.1 (October 1970): 32.

Clark, Jon *et al.*, eds. *Culture and Crisis in Britain in the 30s.* London: Lawrence and Wishart 1979.

Cockburn, Claud. *Bestseller: The Books that Everyone Read 1900–1939.* London: Sidgwick and Jackson 1972.

Coles, Joanna. "End of the Affair for Graham Greene." *Guardian Weekly* 14 April 1991: 23.

Collins, Wilkie. *The Moonstone.* 1868. Ed. J.I.M. Stewart. Harmondsworth: Penguin 1971.

Connolly, Cyril. "Deductions From Detectives." 1931. *The Evening Colonnade.* London: David Bruce and Watson 1973 (490–5).

– *Enemies of Promise.* 1938. Harmondsworth: Penguin 1979.

Conrad, Joseph. Preface to *The Nigger of the "Narcissus".* 1897. *Joseph Conrad on Fiction.* Ed. Walter F. Wright. Lincoln: University of Nebraska Press 1964: 160–4.

Couto, Maria. *Graham Greene: On the Frontier – Politics and Religion in the Novels.* New York: St Martin's 1988.

Crawford, Fred D. "Graham Greene: Heaps of Broken Images," *Mixing Memory and Desire: "The Waste Land" and British Novels.* University Park, Penn., and London: Pennsylvania State University Press 1982 (103–23).

Culler, Jonathan. *Barthes.* Fontana Modern Masters. Glasgow: Fontana 1983.

– "Story and Discourse in the Analysis of Narrative." *The Pursuit of Signs: Semiotics, Literature, Deconstruction.* Ithaca: Cornell University Press 1981 (169–87).

– *Structuralist Poetics: Structuralism, Linguistics, and the Study of Literature.* 1975. London: Routledge and Kegan Paul 1983.

Cunningham, Valentine. *British Writers of the Thirties.* Oxford and New York: Oxford University Press 1988.

– "Neutral?: 1930s Writers and Taking Sides." Gloversmith 45–69.

Daniel, Robert. "Poe's Detective God." *Twentieth Century Interpretations of Poe's Tales: A Collection of Critical Essays.* Ed. William L. Howarth. Englewood Cliffs, N.J.: Prentice-Hall 1971: 103–10.

Davis, Elizabeth. *Graham Greene: The Artist as Critic.* Fredericton: York Press 1984.

Denning, Michael. *Cover Stories: Narrative and Ideology in the British Spy Thriller.* London and New York: Routledge and Kegan Paul 1987.

Derrida, Jacques. "Freud and the Scene of Writing." *Writing and Difference.* Trans. Alan Bass. Chicago: University of Chicago Press 1978 (196–231).

– "The Law of Genre." *On Narrative.* Ed. W.J.T. Mitchell. Chicago and London: University of Chicago Press 1981 (51–78).

"Detection Club Oath, The." Haycraft, *Art of the Mystery* 197–9.

Dettmar, Kevin J.H., ed. *Rereading the New: A Backward Glance at Modernism.* Ann Arbor: University of Michigan Press 1992.

De Vitis, A.A. *Graham Greene.* Rev. ed. Twayne's English Authors Series 3. Boston: Twayne 1986.

Dickstein, Morris. "Popular Fiction and Critical Values: The Novel as a Challenge to Literary History." *Reconstructing American Literary History.* Harvard English Studies 13. Ed. Sacvan Bercovitch. Cambridge, Mass.: Harvard University Press 1966 (29–66).

Dipple, Elizabeth. *The Unresolvable Plot: Reading Contemporary Fiction.* New York and London: Routledge, Chapman and Hall 1988.

Donaghy, Henry J. *Graham Greene: An Introduction to His Writings.* Amsterdam: Rodopi 1983.

– *Conversations with Graham Greene.* Literary Conversation Series. Jackson and London: University Press of Mississippi 1992.

Donoghue, Denis. "Graham Greene, Autobiographer." *England, Their England: Commentaries on English Language and Literature.* New York: Alfred A. Knopf 1988 (323–31).

Doyle, Arthur Conan. *The Complete Sherlock Holmes.* 2 vols. Garden City, N.Y.: Doubleday 1930.

Eagleton, Terry. *Literary Theory: An Introduction.* Minnesota: University of Minnesota Press 1983.

– *Marxism and Literary Criticism.* London: Methuen 1976.

Easthope, Antony. *Literary into Cultural Studies.* London and New York: Routledge 1991.

Eco, Umberto, and Thomas A. Sebeok, eds. *The Sign of Three: Dupin, Holmes, Peirce.* 1983. Bloomington and Indianapolis: Indiana University Press 1988.

Eliot, T.S. "Baudelaire." 1930. *Selected Prose.* Ed. John Hayward. Harmondsworth: Penguin 1963 (174–84).

– *Christianity and Culture: "The Idea of a Christian Society" and "Notes Towards The Definition of Culture."* 1940 and 1949. New York: Harcourt, Brace, Jovanovich 1968.

– "The Metaphysical Poets." 1921. *Selected Essays.* New York: Harcourt, Brace 1950 (241–50).

– Review of *The Beast With Five Fingers* by W.F. Harvey. *Criterion* 8.10 (September 1928): 175–6.

– *The Sacred Wood.* 1920. London: Methuen 1969.

- "Wilkie Collins and Dickens." *Selected Essays*. London and Boston: Faber 1980 (460–70).

Erdinast-Vulcan, Daphna. *Graham Greene's Childless Fathers*. London: Macmillan 1988.

Evans, Robert O., ed. *Graham Greene: Some Critical Considerations*. 1963. Lexington: University of Kentucky Press 1967.

- Introduction. Evans v–xv.

Falk, Quentin. *Travels in Greeneland: The Cinema of Graham Greene*. London, Melbourne, New York: Quartet 1984.

Ford, Boris, ed. *The Modern Age*. The Pelican Guide to English Literature, vol. 7. 1961. Harmondsworth: Pelican 1972.

Ford, Ford Madox. "The Detective Novel." 1938. *The Ford Madox Ford Reader*. Ed. Sondra J. Stang. Foreward by Graham Greene. Manchester: Carcanet Press 1986 (285–7).

- *The English Novel*. Philadelphia and London: Lippincott 1929.

Forster, E.M. "English Prose Between 1918 and 1939." 1944. *Two Cheers for Democracy* (277–89).

- "What I Believe." 1939. *Two Cheers for Democracy*. 1951. Harmondsworth: Penguin 1974 (75–84).

Foucault, Michel. *Discipline and Punish: The Birth of the Prison*. 1975. Trans. Alan Sheridan. New York: Vintage 1979.

Fowler, Alastair. *Kinds of Literature: An Introduction to the Theory of Genres and Modes*. Cambridge, Mass.: Harvard University Press 1982.

Fox, Ralph. *The Novel and the People*. 1937. London: Laurence and Wishart 1979.

Fraser, G.S. *The Modern Writer and His World: Continuity and Innovation in Twentieth-Century Literature*. 1953. New York and Washington: Frederick A. Praeger 1965.

Frye, Northrop. *The Secular Scripture: A Study of the Structure of Romance*. 1976. Cambridge, Mass.: Harvard University Press 1982.

Fussell, Paul. "Can Graham Greene Write English?" *The Boy Scout Handbook and Other Observations*. Oxford and New York: Oxford University Press 1982 (95–100).

- *The Great War and Modern Memory*. 1975. Oxford, London, and New York: Oxford University Press 1977.

- *Wartime: Understanding and Behavior in the Second World War*. 1989. New York and Oxford: Oxford University Press 1990.

Gans, Herbert J. *Popular Culture and High Culture*. New York: Basic Books 1974.

Gaston, George M.A. *The Pursuit of Salvation: A Critical Guide to the Novels of Graham Greene*. Troy, N.Y.: Whitsun 1984.

Gilliatt, Penelope. "Profiles: The Dangerous Edge." *The New Yorker* 55 (26 March 1979): 43–50.

Gloversmith, Frank, ed. *Class Culture and Social Change: A New View of the 1930s*. Sussex: Harvester 1980.

Gorra, Michael. *The English Novel at Mid-Century: From the Leaning Tower*. London: Macmillan 1990.

"Graham Greene: The Man Within." *TLS* (17 September 1971): 1101–2. Rpt. Hynes, *Graham Greene* 8–16.

Gransden, K.W. "Graham Greene's Rhetoric." *Essays in Criticism* 31.1 (Jan. 1981): 41–60.

Graves, Robert, and Alan Hodge. *The Long Week-End: A Social History of Great Britain 1918–1939*. 1940. New York: Norton 1963.

Graves, Robert, and Laura Riding. "Poetry and Politics." *The Common Asphodel: Collected Essays on Poetry*. 1949. New York: Haskell House 1970 (273–83).

Green, Martin. *Dreams of Adventure, Deeds of Empire*. New York: Basic Books 1979.

– *The English Novel in the Twentieth Century: The Doom of Empire*. London, Melbourne and Henley: Routledge and Kegan Paul 1984.

Greene, Graham. *The Bear Fell Free*. London: Grayson and Grayson 1935. Rpt. Folcroft Press 1970.

– *Brighton Rock*. 1938. Harmondsworth: Penguin 1988.

– *British Dramatists*. London: William Collins 1942.

– *Collected Essays*. 1969. Harmondsworth: Penguin 1981.

– Comments made as part of a tribute to Auden. *New Verse* Nov. 1937; rpt. New York: Kraus 1966: 29–30.

– *The Confidential Agent*. 1939. Harmondsworth: Penguin 1980.

– *The End of the Affair*. 1951. Harmondsworth: Penguin 1980.

– *England Made Me*. 1935. Harmondsworth: Penguin 1981.

– *A Gun for Sale*. 1936. Harmondsworth: Penguin 1984.

– *In Search of a Character: Two African Journals*. 1961. Harmondsworth: Penguin 1980.

– *It's a Battlefield*. 1934. Harmondsworth: Penguin 1980.

– *Journey Without Maps*. 1936. Harmondsworth: Penguin 1983.

– *"The Last Word" and Other Stories*. Toronto: Lester and Orpen Dennys 1990.

– *The Lawless Roads*. 1939. Harmondsworth: Penguin 1979.

– "The Lesson of the Master." 1935. *Portable* 541–3.

– *The Ministry of Fear*. 1943. Harmondsworth: Penguin 1982.

– "Murder for the Wrong Reason: An Unusual Thriller in Three Installments." *The Graphic* 126 (5, 12, 19 October 1929). Rpt. *"The Last Word" and Other Stories*: 110–37.

– *Our Man in Havana*. 1958. Harmondsworth: Penguin 1977.

– *The Pleasure Dome: Collected Film Criticism 1935–1940*. Ed. John Russell Taylor. 1972. Oxford, New York, Toronto, Melbourne: Oxford University Press 1980.

- *The Portable Graham Greene.* Ed. Philip Stratford. New York: Viking 1973.
- Preface to *Victorian Detective Stories: A Catalogue of the Collection Made by Dorothy Glover and Graham Greene.* London: Bodley Head 1966 (vii–viii).
- *Reflections.* Selected and introduced by Judith Adamson. Toronto: Lester and Orpen Dennys 1990.
- *Rumour at Nightfall.* New York: Doubleday 1932.
- "The Seed Cake and the Love Lady." *Life and Letters* 10.56 (August 1934): 517–24.
- *A Sort of Life.* 1971. Harmondsworth: Penguin 1974.
- *Stamboul Train.* 1932. Harmondsworth: Penguin 1979.
- *"The Third Man" and "The Fallen Idol."* 1950. Harmondsworth: Penguin 1973.
- *Travels With My Aunt.* 1969. Harmondsworth: Penguin 1977.
- "The Virtue of Disloyalty." *Portable* 606–10.
- *Ways of Escape.* 1980. Harmondsworth: Penguin 1981.
- "While Waiting For a War." *Granta* 17 (Autumn 1985): 11–32.
- *A World of My Own: A Dream Diary.* Toronto: Alfred A. Knopf 1992.
- *Yours etc.: Letters to the Press 1945–1989.* Selected and Introduced by Christopher Hawtree. Toronto: Lester and Orpen Dennys 1989.
Grella, George. "The Formal Detective Novel." Winks 84–102.
- "The Hard-Boiled Detective Novel." Winks 103–20.
Guetti, James. "Aggressive Reading: Detective Fiction and Realistic Narrative." *Raritan* 2.1 (summer 1982): 133–54.
Hall, James. *The Lunatic Giant in the Drawing Room: The British and American Novel Since 1930.* Bloomington: Indiana University Press 1968.
Hall, Stuart, and Paddy Whannel. *The Popular Arts.* 1964. Boston: Beacon Press 1967.
Hammett, Dashiell. *The Dain Curse.* 1929. New York: Vintage 1972.
- *Red Harvest.* 1929. New York: Vintage 1972.
- "$106,000, Blood Money." *The Big Knockover: Selected Stories and Short Novels.* Ed. Lillian Hellman. New York: Vintage 1972 (412–58).
Harper, Ralph. *The World of the Thriller.* 1969. Baltimore and London: Johns Hopkins University Press 1974.
Harrison, J.F.C. *The Common People: A History from the Norman Conquest to the Present.* London: Flamingo (Fontana) 1984.
Harrison, John. *The Reactionaries.* New York: Schocken 1967.
Hartman, Geoffrey. "Literature High and Low: The Case of the Mystery Story." Most and Stowe 210–19.
Hawkins, Harriett. *Classics and Trash: Traditions and Taboos in High Literature and Popular Modern Genres.* Toronto and Buffalo: Univesity of Toronto Press 1990.
Haycraft, Howard, ed. *The Art of the Mystery Story.* New York: Grosset and Dunlap 1947.

– *Murder for Pleasure: The Life and Times of the Detective Story.* 1941. New York: Carroll and Graf 1984.

Hays, H.R. "A Defense of the Thriller." *Partisan Review* 12 (1945): 135–7.

Henderson, Philip. *The Novel Today: Studies in Contemporary Attitudes.* London: Bodley Head 1936.

Hoggart, Richard. "The Force of Caricature." Hynes, *Graham Greene* 79–92.

– "Mass Communications in Britain." Ford, *Modern Age* 442–57.

Howarth, Patrick. *Play Up and Play the Game: The Heroes of Popular Fiction.* London: Eyre Methuen 1973.

Howe, Irving. *Decline of the New.* New York: Harcourt, Brace 1970.

Hühn, Peter. "The Detective as Reader: Narrativity and Reading Concepts in Detective Fiction." *MFS* 33.3 (autumn 1987): 451–66.

Hunter, Ian A. "A Sinner's Soul, An Angel's Words." Review of *The Life of Graham Greene* by Norman Sherry. *Globe and Mail* (10 June 1989): C7.

Hutcheon, Linda. *Narcissistic Narrative: The Metafictional Paradox.* 1980. New York and London: Methuen 1984.

Hutchinson, Peter. *Games Authors Play.* London and New York: Methuen 1983.

Huyssen, Andreas. *After the Great Divide: Modernism, Mass Culture, Postmodernism.* Bloomington and Indianapolis: Indiana University Press 1986.

Hynes, Samuel. *The Auden Generation: Literature and Politics in England in the 1930s.* 1976. Princeton, N.J.: Princeton University Press 1982.

– ed. *Graham Greene: A Collection of Critical Essays.* Twentieth Century Views. Englewood Cliffs: Prentice-Hall 1973.

– Introduction. Hynes, *Graham Greene* 1–7.

Iser, Wolfgang. "The Reading Process: A Phenomonological Approach." *The Implied Reader: Patterns of Communication in Prose Fiction From Bunyan to Beckett.* 1972. Baltimore and London: Johns Hopkins University Press 1978 (274–94).

Isherwood, Christopher. Foreword to *The Railway Accident and Other Stories* by Edward Upward. Harmondsworth: Penguin 1972.

– *Goodbye to Berlin.* 1939. Bungay, Suffolk: Triad/Granada 1979.

– *Lions and Shadows: An Education in the Twenties.* Norfolk, Conn.: New Directions 1947.

James, Henry. From "Alphonse Daudet." 1883. *Theory of Fiction: Henry James* (93–4).

– "The Art of Fiction." 1884. *Theory of Fiction: Henry James.* Ed. James E. Miller. Lincoln: University of Nebraska Press 1972 (27–44).

James, P.D. "The Art of the Detective Novel." *Journal of the Royal Society of Arts* 133 (August 1985): 637–49.

Jameson, Fredric. *The Political Unconscious: Narrative as a Socially Symbolic Act.* 1981. Ithaca: Cornell University Press 1983.

Johnstone, Richard. *The Will to Believe: Novelists of the Nineteen Thirties.* 1982. Oxford and New York: Oxford University Press 1984.

Josipovici, Gabriel. "The Heart of the Matter." *The Mirror of Criticism: Selected Reviews, 1977–82*. Sussex: Harvester; Totowa, N.J.: Barnes and Noble 1983 (118–27).

Kelly, Richard. *Graham Greene*. New York: Fredrick Ungar 1984.

Kempton, Daniel. "The Gold/Goole/Ghoul Bug." *ESQ* 33.1 (1987): 1–19.

Kermode, Frank. *The Art of Telling: Essays on Fiction*. 1971–1983. Cambridge, Mass.: Harvard University Press 1983.

– *The Genesis of Secrecy: On the Interpretation of Narrative*. 1979. Cambridge, Mass.: Harvard University Press 1982.

– *History and Value*. The Clarendon Lectures and the Northcliffe Lectures. 1987. Oxford: Clarendon Press 1988.

– "The House of Fiction: Interviews with Seven English Novelists." *Partisan Review* 30 (1963): 61–82.

– *The Sense of an Ending: Studies in the Theory of Fiction*. 1967. Oxford, London, New York: Oxford University Press 1981.

King, James. "In the Lost Boyhood of Judas: Graham Greene's Early Novels of Hell." *Dalhousie Review* 49 (1969–70): 229–36.

Klein, Kathleen Gregory and Joseph Keller. "Deductive Detective Fiction: The Self-Destructive Genre." *Genre* 19 (1986): 155–72.

Knight, Stephen. *Form and Ideology in Crime Fiction*. Bloomington: Indiana University Press 1980.

Knights, L.C. and Donald Culver. "*Scrutiny*: A Manifesto." *Scrutiny* 1.1 (May 1932). Rpt. *The Importance of "Scrutiny": Selections from "Scrutiny: A Quarterly Review", 1932–48*. Ed. Eric Bentley. New York: George W. Stewart 1948 (1–5).

Knox, Ronald A. "A Detective Story Decalogue." Haycraft, *Art of the Mystery* 194–6; rpt. Winks 200–2.

Kroll, Jack. "Map of Greeneland." *Newsweek* 117.15 (15 April 1991): 75.

Kulshrestha, J. P. *Graham Greene: The Novelist*. Delhi, Bombay, Calcutta, Madras: Macmillan of India 1977.

Kunkel, Francis L. *The Labyrinthian Ways of Graham Greene*. 1960. Mamaroneck, N.Y.: Paul P. Appel 1973.

Kurismmootil, K.C. Joseph, s.j. *Heaven and Hell on Earth: An Appreciation of Five Novels of Graham Greene*. Chicago: Loyola University Press 1982.

Laing, Stuart. "Presenting 'Things as They Are': John Sommerfield's *May Day* and Mass Observation." Gloversmith 142–60.

Lambert, Gavin. "The Double Agent: Graham Greene." *The Dangerous Edge: An Inquiry into the Lives of Nine Masters of Suspense*. New York: Grossman-Viking 1976 (132–70).

Leavis, F.R. *Mass Civilization and Minority Culture*. Cambridge: Minority Press 1930. Rpt. Folcroft Press 1969.

– "'*Scrutiny*': A Retrospect." August 1962. *Literary Taste, Culture, and Mass Communication*. Vol. 13. Ed. Peter Davison, Rolf Meyersohn, and Edward

Sils. Cambridge: Chawyck-Healey; Teaneck, N.J.: Somerset House 1978 (85–100).

Leavis, Q.D. *Fiction and the Reading Public*. 1932. London: Chatto and Windus 1965.

Lees, F.N. "Graham Greene: A Comment." *Scrutiny* 19 (1952–53): 31–42.

Lester, John A., Jr. *Journey Through Despair 1880–1914: Transformations in British Literary Culture*. Princeton, N.J.: Princeton University Press 1968.

Levenson, Michael. *Modernism and the Fate of Individuality: Character and Novelistic Form from Conrad to Woolf*. Cambridge: Cambridge University Press 1991.

Levine, Lawrence W. *Highbrow/Lowbrow: The Emergence of Cultural Hierarchy in America*. Cambridge, Mass.: Harvard University Press 1988.

Lewis, R.W.B. "Graham Greene: The Religious Affair." *The Picaresque Saint: Representative Figures in Contemporary Fiction*. Philadelphia and New York: Lipponcott 1959 (220–74).

Lodge, David. "Behind the Smoke Screen" and "The Lives of Graham Greene." Two-part review of *The Life of Graham Greene, vol. 2, 1939–1955* by Norman Sherry, *Graham Greene: The Man Within* by Michael Shelden, *Graham Greene: Three Lives* by Anthony Mockler, *Graham Greene: Friend and Brother* by Leopoldo Duran, *Reflections* by Graham Greene, selected and introduced by Judith Adamson, *A World of My Own: A Dream Diary* by Graham Greene, and *The Graham Greene Film Reader: Reviews, Essays, Interviews, and Film Stories*, ed. by David Parkinson. *New York Review of Books* 8 June 1995: 61–67; 22 June 1995: 25–8.

– *Graham Greene*. Columbia Essays on Modern Writers 17. New York: Columbia University Press 1966. Rpt. as "Graham Greene." *The Novelist at the Crossroads and Other Essays on Fiction and Criticism*. 1971. London and New York: Ark Paperbacks 1986 (87–118). Rpt. and updated in *Six Contemporary British Novelists*. Ed. George Stade. New York: Columbia University Press 1976 (1–56).

– and Ian Gregor. "Graham Greene." *The English Novel*. London: Sussex 1976 (155–71).

– "The Language of Modernist Fiction: Metaphor and Metonomy." *Modernism*. Pelican Guides to European Literature. 1976. Ed. Malcom Bradbury and James McFarlane. Harmondsworth: Penguin 1981 (481–96).

– "Modernism, Antimodernism and Postmodernism." *Working With Structuralism: Essays and Reviews on Nineteenth- and Twentieth-Century Literature*. 1981. London, Boston and Henley: Ark Paperbacks 1986 (3–16).

– *The Modes of Modern Writing: Metaphor, Metonymy, and the Typology of Modern Literature*. 1977. Chicago: University of Chicago Press 1988.

– "What There Is To Tell." 1980. *Write On: Occasional Essays 1965–1985*. London: Secker and Warburg 1986 (125–30).

Lukács, Georg. "The Ideology of Modernism." *Realism in Our Time: Literature and the Class Struggle.* 1956. Trans. John and Necke Mander. New York: Harper and Row 1971 (17–46).

MacArthur, James R. "To the Heart of the Master." *Globe and Mail.* 19 Jan. 1991: D5.

MacCabe, Colin. *James Joyce and the Revolution of the Word.* London: Macmillan 1978.

– "Realism and the Cinema: Notes on Some Brechtian Theses." *Tracking the Signifier – Theoretical Essays: Film, Linguistics, Literature.* Minneapolis: University of Minnesota Press 1985 (33–57).

Macdonald, Ross. "The Writer as Detective Hero." Winks 179–87.

Macleod, Norman. " 'This strange, rather sad story': The Reflexive Design of Graham Greene's *The Third Man.*" *Dalhousie Review* 63.2 (summer 1983): 217–41.

Malamet, Elliott. "The World Remade: The Art of Detection in the Fiction of Graham Greene." *Diss.* University of Toronto 1990.

"Man of Mystery: The Enigma of Graham Greene." *Listener* 102 (4 October 1979): 441–3.

Mandel, Ernest. *Delightful Murder: A Social History of the Crime Story.* London and Sydney: Pluto Press 1984.

Marchand, Philip. "Graham Greene lived a novel life." *Toronto Star.* 4 April 1991: C1.

Marcus, Stephen. "Dashiell Hammett." Most and Stowe 197–209.

Margolies, David. "*Left Review* and Left Literary Theory." Clark *et al.* (67–82).

Martin, Graham. "Novelists of Three Decades: Evelyn Waugh, Graham Greene, C.P. Snow." Ford, *Modern Age* 394–414.

Mass Observation. "Poetic Description and Mass-Observation." *New Verse* Feb.-Mar. 1937; rpt. New York: Kraus 1966: 1–6.

Matthews, J. Brander. "Poe and the Detective Story." *The Recognition of Edgar Allan Poe: Selected Criticism Since 1829.* Ed. Eric W. Carlson. Ann Arbor: University of Michigan Press 1966 (82–94).

Maurois, André. "Graham Greene." Trans. Mary Ilford. *Points of View from Kipling to Graham Greene.* Trans. Hamish Miles and Mary Ilford. New York: Frederick Ungar 1968 (383–409).

McCabe, Cameron. *The Face on the Cutting-Room Floor.* 1937. Harmondsworth: Penguin 1986.

McCarthy, Mary. "Graham Greene and the Intelligensia." *Partisan Review* 11 (1944): 228–30.

McDiarmid, Lucy. *Saving Civilization: Yeats, Eliot, and Auden Between the Wars.* Cambridge: Cambridge University Press 1984.

McDonald, James L. "Graham Greene: A Reconsideration." *Arizona Quarterly* 27.3 (autumn 1971): 197–210.

McEwen, Neil. *Graham Greene*. Macmillan Modern Novelists. London: Macmillan 1988.

Melada, Ivan. "Graham Greene and the Munitions Makers: The Historical Context of *A Gun for Sale*." *Studies in the Novel* 13.3 (fall 1981): 303–21.

– *Guns for Sale: War and Capitalism in English Literature, 1851–1939*. Jefferson and London: McFarland 1983.

Melman, Billie. *Women and the Popular Imagination in the Twenties: Flappers and Nymphs*. New York: St Martin's 1988.

Menikoff, Barry. "Modernist in Search of an Audience: Graham Greene in the Thirties." *Writers of the Old School: British Novelists of the 1930s*. Ed. Rosemary M. Colt and Janice Rossen. London: Macmillan 1992 (85–102).

Mercer, Colin. "Complicit Pleasures." *Popular Culture and Social Relations*. Ed. Tony Bennett, Colin Mercer, and Janet Woollacott. Philadelphia: Open University Press 1986 (50–68).

Meyers, Jeffrey, ed. *Graham Greene: A Revaluation. New Essays*. New York: St Martin's 1990.

Miles, Peter, and Malcolm Smith. *Cinema, Literature and Society: Elite and Mass Culture in Interwar Britain*. London, New York, and Sidney: Croom Helm 1987.

Miller, D.A. *The Novel and the Police*. Berkeley: University of California Press 1988.

Miller, J. Hillis. "Ariadne's Thread: Repetition and the Narrative Line." *Critical Inquiry* 3.1 (autumn 1976): 57–77.

– "The Ethics of Reading: Vast Gaps and Parting Hours." *American Criticism in the Poststructuralist Age*. Ed. Ira Konigsberg. Michigan Studies in the Humanities. Ann Arbor, Mich.: University of Michigan Press 1981.

– *Fiction and Repetition: Seven English Novels*. Cambridge, Mass.: Harvard University Press 1982.

Miller, R.H. *Understanding Graham Greene*. Columbia, S.C.: University of South Carolina Press 1990.

Milne, A.A. *The Red House Mystery*. 1922. New York: Dell 1984.

Milton, John. *Paradise Lost. Complete Prose and Major Prose*. Ed. Merritt Y. Hughes. New York: Odyssey Press 1957 (173–469).

Most, Glenn W. "The Hippocratic Smile: John Le Carré and the Traditions of the Detective Novel." Most and Stowe 341–65.

– and William W. Stowe, eds. *The Poetics of Murder: Detective Fiction and Literary Theory*. San Diego, New York, London: Harcourt Brace Jovanovich 1983.

Muir, Edwin. Review of *Brighton Rock*. *Listener* 20 (21 July 1938): 153. Rpt. in *The Truth of Imagination: Some Uncollected Reviews and Essays by Edwin Muir*. Ed. P.H. Butter. Aberdeen: Aberdeen University Press 1988 (75–6).

Muller, John P., and William J. Richardson, eds. *The Purloined Poe: Lacan, Derrida, and Psychoanalytic Reading*. Baltimore and London: Johns Hopkins University Press 1988.

Murch, A.E. *The Development of the Detective Novel*. London: Peter Owen 1958.

Nehring, Neil. "Revolt into Style: Graham Greene Meets the Sex Pistols." *PMLA* 106.2 (March 1991): 222–37.

O'Donnell, Donat. "Graham Greene." *Chimera* 5.4 (summer 1947): 18–30.

O'Faolain, Sean. "Graham Greene: 'I Suffer, therefore, I am.'" *The Vanishing Hero: Studies in Novelists of the Twenties*. London: Eyre and Spottiswoode 1956 (71–97).

O'Prey, Paul. *A Reader's Guide to Graham Greene*. Worcester: Thames and Hudson 1988.

Ortega y Gasset, José. "The Dehumanization of Art." 1925. Trans. Helene Weyl. *"The Dehumanization of Art" and Other Essays on Art, Culture, and Literature*. Princeton, N.J.: Princeton University Press 1972 (3–54).

– *The Revolt of the Masses*. 1930. Trans. Anonymous. New York: Norton 1957.

Orwell, George. "Bookshop Memories." 1936. *Collected Essays, Journalism and Letters of George Orwell*. Vol. 1. Ed. Sonia Orwell and Ian Angus. London: Secker and Warburg 1968 (242–6).

– "Boy's Weeklies." 1939. *CEJL* vol. 1: 175–203.

– "Good Bad Books." 1945. *CEJL* vol. 2: 19–22.

– "Inside the Whale." 1940. *CEJL* vol. 1: 493–527.

– Letter to T.R. Fyvel. 15 April 1949. *CEJL* vol. 4: 496–7.

– "My Country Right or Left." 1940. *CEJL* vol. 1: 535–40.

– "The Sanctified Sinner." Hynes, *Graham Greene* 105–9.

– "Writers and Leviathan." 1948. *CEJL* vol. 4: 407–14.

Palmer, Jerry. "Thrillers." *Popular Fiction and Social Change*. Ed. Christopher Pawling. London: Macmillan 1984 (76–98).

– *Thrillers*. London: Edward Arnold 1978.

Pandit, P.N. *The Novels of Graham Greene: A Thematic Study in the Impact of Childhood on Adult Life*. New Delhi: Prestige Books 1989.

Panek, LeRoy L. *The Special Branch: The British Spy Novel 1890–1980*. Bowling Green, Ohio: Bowling Green University Press 1981.

Peirce, Charles S. "Deduction, Induction and Hypothesis." 1878. *Essays in the Philosophy of Science*. Ed. Vincent Tomas. New York, Indianapolis: Bobbs-Merrill 1957 (126–43).

– "The Logic of Abduction." 1901 and 1903. *Essays* 235–55.

Phillips, Gene D. *Graham Greene: The Films of His Fiction*. Studies in Culture and Communication. New York and London: Teachers College Press 1974.

– "Graham Greene: On the Screen." Hynes, *Graham Greene* 168–75.

Pierloot, Roland A. *Psychoanalytic Patterns in the Work of Graham Greene*. Psychoanalysis and Culture 5. Amsterdam and Atlanta, Ga.: Rodopi 1994.

Poe, Edgar Allan. *The Collected Works of Edgar Allan Poe*. Vols. 2 and 3. Ed. Thomas Ollive Mabbott. Cambridge, Mass.: Harvard University Press 1978.

– "The Man of the Crowd." *Collected Works* 505–18.

- "The Murders in the Rue Morgue." *Collected Works* 521–74.
- "The Mystery of Marie Roget." *Collected Works* 715–88.
- "The Purloined Letter." *Collected Works* 972–97.
Porter, Dennis. *The Pursuit of Crime: Art and Ideology in Detective Fiction.* New Haven and London: Yale University Press 1981.
Pritchett, V. S. "Graham Greene: Disloyalties." *The Tale-Bearers: Essays on English, American and Other Writers.* London: Chatto and Windus 1980 (78–91).
Pryce-Jones, David. *Graham Greene.* 1963. Writers and Critics. Edinburgh: Oliver and Boyd 1973.
Rabinowitz, Peter J. "End Sinister: Neat Closure as Disruptive Force." *Reading Narrative: Form, Ethics, Ideology.* Columbus: Ohio State University Press 1989 (120–31).
- "Rats behind the Wainscoting: Politics, Convention, and Chandler's *The Big Sleep.*" *TSLL* 22.2 (summer 1980): 225–45.
Rai, Gangeshwar. *Graham Greene: An Existential Approach.* New Delhi: Associated Publ. House 1983.
Rama Rao, V.V.B. *Graham Greene's Comic Vision.* New Delhi: Reliance Publish House 1990.
Revelation. Holy Bible. King James Version. Nashville: Holman Bible Publishers 1979.
Richards, I.A. *Principles of Literary Criticism.* 1925. New York: Harcourt, Brace and World, n.d.
Rickword, Edgell. "A Political Pamphlet." *Literature in Society* 80–92.
- "Straws for the Wary: Antecedents to Fascism." *Left Review* 1.1 (October 1934): 19–24. Rpt. *Literature in Society: Essays and Opinions, vol. 2 1931–1978.* Ed. Alan Young. Manchester: Carcanet New Press 1978 (39–45).
Robbins, Bruce. "Modernism in History, Modernism in Power." *Modernism Reconsidered.* Ed. Richard Kiely. Harvard English Studies 11. Cambridge, Mass. and London: Harvard University Press 1983 (229–45).
Roberts, Michael, ed. *New Country: Prose and Poetry by the Authors of "New Signatures."* London: Hogarth Press 1933.
- Preface. Roberts 9–21.
Robson, W.W. *Modern English Writers.* London, Oxford, New York: Oxford University Press 1970 (138–41).
Routh, Michael. " 'Kolley Kibber' – Newspaper Promotion in *Brighton Rock.*" *College Literature* 12.1 (1985): 80–4.
Salvatore, Anne T. *Greene and Kierkegaard: The Discourse of Belief.* Tuscaloosa and London: University of Alabama Press 1988.
Sartre, Jean-Paul. *What is Literature?* 1948. Trans. Bernard Frechtman. London: Methuen 1981.
Sayers, Dorothy L. Introduction to *The Omnibus of Crime.* Winks 53–83.
Scott, Carolyn. "The Urban Romance: A Study of Graham Greene's Thrillers." Cargas 1–28.

Sharrock, Roger. *Saints, Sinners and Comedians: The Novels of Graham Greene.* Tunbridge Wells, Kent: Burns and Oates; Notre Dame, Indiana: University of Notre Dame Press 1984.

Sherry, Norman. *The Life of Graham Greene 1904–1939.* Vol. 1. Toronto: Lester and Orpen Dennys 1989.

– *The Life of Graham Greene 1939–1955.* Vol. 2. London: Jonathan Cape 1994.

"Shocker." Review of *The End of the Affair* by Graham Greene. *Time* 58.18 (29 October 1951): 62–7.

Shuttleworth, Martin, and Simon Raven. "The Art of Fiction: Graham Greene." *The Paris Review* 1 (autumn 1953): 24–41. Rpt. Hynes, *Graham Greene* 154–67.

Silverstein, Marc. "After the Fall: The World of Graham Greene's Thrillers." *Novel: A Forum on Fiction* 22.1 (fall 1988): 24–44.

Skelton, Robin. Introduction. Skelton 13–41.

– ed. *Poetry of the Thirties.* 1964. Harmondsworth: Penguin 1985.

Smith, A.J.M. "Graham Greene's Theological Thrillers." *Queen's Quarterly* 68 (Spring 1961): 15–33.

Smith, Barbara Herrnstein. *Contingencies of Value: Alternative Perspectives for Critical Theory.* Cambridge, Mass. and London: Harvard University Press 1988.

Smith, Grahame. *The Achievement of Graham Greene.* Sussex: Harvester; Totowa, N.J.: Barnes and Noble 1986.

Smith, Rowland. "A People's War in Greeneland: Heroic Virtue and Communal Effort in the Wartime Tales." Meyers 104–30.

Snee, Carole. "Working-Class Literature or Proletarian Writing?" Clark *et al.* (165–91).

Spender, Stephen. "Poetry and Revolution." Roberts 62–71.

– "The Theme of Political Orthodoxy in the 'Thirties." *The Creative Element: A Study of Vision, Despair and Orthodoxy Among Some Modern Writers.* New York: British Books Center 1954 (140–58).

– *The 30's and After: Poetry, Politics, People, 1930's–1970's.* New York: Random House 1978.

Spurling, John. *Graham Greene.* Contemporary Writers. Ed. Malcolm Bradbury and Christopher Bigsby. London and New York: Methuen 1983.

Stannard, Martin. "In Search of Himselves: The Autobiographical Writings of Graham Greene." *Prose Studies* 8 (1985): 139–55.

Steiner, George. "Humane Literacy." 1963. *Language and Silence.* New York: Atheneum 1967 (3–11).

Stevenson, Randall. *The British Novel Since the Thirties: An Introduction.* London: B. T. Batesford 1986.

Stowe, William W. "Critical Investigations: Convention and Ideology in Detective Fiction." *TSLL* 31.4 (winter 1989): 570–91.

– "From Semiotics to Hermeutics: Modes of Detection in Doyle and Chandler." Most and Stowe 366–83.

– "Popular Fiction as Liberal Art." *College English* 48 (November 1986): 646–63.

Stratford, Philip. *Faith and Fiction: Creative Process in Greene and Mauriac.* 1964. Notre Dame and London: University of Notre Dame Press 1967.

– "Graham Greene: Master of Melodrama." *Tamarack Review* 19 (1961): 67–86.

– "Unlocking the Potting Shed." *Kenyon Review* 24 (1962): 129–43.

Sturrock, John. "Roland Barthes." *Structuralism and Since: From Lévi-Strauss to Derrida.* Ed. and introduction John Sturrock. Oxford, New York, London: Oxford University Press 1979 (52–80).

Swingewood, Alan. *The Myth of Mass Culture.* London: Macmillan 1977.

Symons, Julian. *Mortal Consequences.* London: Faber; New York: Harper and Row 1972. Rev. and updated as *Bloody Murder: From the Detective Story to the Crime Novel.* Harmondsworth: Penguin; New York: Viking 1985.

– *The Thirties: A Dream Resolved.* Westport, Conn.: Greenwood Press 1960.

Tani, Stefano. *The Doomed Detective: The Contribution of the Detective Novel to Postmodern American and Italian Fiction.* Carbondale and Edwardsville: Southern Illinois University Press 1984.

Thomas, Brian. *An Underground Fate: The Idiom of Romance in the Later Novels of Graham Greene.* Athens and London: University of Georgia Press 1988.

Thompson, Jon. *Fiction, Crime, and Empire: Clues to Modernity and Postmodernism.* Urbana and Chicago: University of Illinois Press 1993.

Thomson, David. *England in the Twentieth Century.* Pelican History of England 9. 1965. Harmondsworth: Penguin 1981.

de Tocqueville, Alexis. *Democracy in America.* Vol. 2. New York: Vintage 1960.

Todorov, Tzvetan. *The Fantastic: A Structural Approach to a Literary Genre.* 1970. Trans. Richard Howard. 1973. Ithaca: Cornell University Press 1980.

– *Genres in Discourse.* 1978. Trans. Catherine Porter. Cambridge: Cambridge University Press 1990.

– *The Poetics of Prose.* 1971. Trans. Richard Howard. Ithaca: Cornell University Press 1977.

Turnell, Martin. "Graham Greene: The Man Within." *Ramparts* 4 (1965): 54–64.

Van Dine, S.S., [W. H. Wright]. "Twenty Rules for Writing Detective Stories." Haycraft, *Art of the Mystery* 189–93.

Walpole, Hugh. *A Letter to a Modern Novelist.* London: Hogarth Press 1932. Rpt. Folcroft Library 1970.

Watson, George. *Politics and Literature in Modern Britain.* London: Macmillan 1977.

Watt, Ian. *The Rise of the Novel: Studies in Defoe, Richardson and Fielding.* 1957. Harmondsworth: Penguin 1981.

Waugh, Evelyn. "Felix Culpa?" Hynes, *Graham Greene* 95–102.

Webster, Harvey Curtis. "The World of Graham Greene." Evans 1–24. Rpt. as "Graham Greene: Stoical Catholic." *After the Trauma: Representative British Novelists Since 1920.* Lexington: University Press of Kentucky 1970 (97–123).

Weinstein, Arnold L. *Vision and Response in Modern Fiction*. Ithaca and London: Cornell University Press 1974.

Why Do I Write? An Exchange of Views Between Elizabeth Bowen, Graham Greene, and V.S. Pritchett. London: Percival Marshall 1948.

Widdowson, Peter. "Between the Acts? English Fiction in the Thirties." Clark *et al.* (133–64).

Wilding, Michael. "Literary Critics and Mass Media Culture." *Dissent* 18 (1966). Rpt. *Literary Taste, Culture, and Mass Communications*. Vol. 13: 173–6.

Williams, Harold. *Modern English Writers: Being a Study of Imaginative Literature 1890–1914*. 1918. London: Sidgwick and Jackson 1925.

Williams, Raymond. *The Country and The City*. 1973. St Albans: Paladin (Granada) 1975.

– *Culture and Society 1780–1950*. 1958. Harmondsworth: Penguin 1984.

– *Keywords: A Vocabulary of Culture and Society*. Glasgow: Fontana/Croom Helm 1976.

Wilson, Edmund. *Axel's Castle: A Study in the Imaginative Literature of 1870–1930*. 1931. New York: Scribner's 1959.

– "Who Cares Who Killed Roger Ackroyd?" 1945. *Classics and Commercials: A Literary Chronicle of the Forties*. London: W.H. Allen 1951 (257–65).

– "Why Do People Read Detective Stories?" 1944. *Classics and Commercials* 231–7.

Winks, Robin, ed. *Detective Fiction: A Collection of Critical Essays*. 1980. Woodstock, Vermont: Countryman Press – A Foul Play Press Book 1988.

Wobbe, R.A. *Graham Greene: A Bibliography and Guide to Research*. New York and London: Garland 1979.

Wolfe, Peter, ed. *Essays in Graham Greene: an Annual Review*. Vol. 1. Greenwood, Fla.: Penkeville 1987.

– *Graham Greene: The Entertainer*. Carbondale and Edwardsville: Southern Illinois Univerity Press; London and Amsterdam: Feffer and Simons 1972.

Woodcock, George. *The Writer and Politics*. London: Porcupine Press 1948. Rpt. Folcroft Press 1970.

Woolf, Virginia. "How It Strikes a Contemporary." *The Common Reader, First Series*. 1925. Ed. Andrew McNeillie. New York, San Diego, London: Harcourt, Brace, Jovanovich 1984 (231–41).

– "The Leaning Tower." 1940. *Collected Essays*. Vol. 2. London: Hogarth Press 1966 (162–81).

– "Mr. Bennett and Mrs. Brown." 1924. *"The Captain's Death Bed" and Other Essays*. London: Hogarth Press 1950 (90–111).

– "Modern Fiction." 1919. *The Common Reader, First Series*. Ed. Andrew McNeillie (146–54).

– *A Writer's Diary*. Ed. Leonard Woolf. 1953. St Albans: Triad/Panther 1978.

Worpole, Ken. *Dockers and Detectives – Popular Reading: Popular Writing*. London: Verso 1983.

Wright, David G. "Greene's *Brighton Rock.*" *Explicator* 41.4 (summer 1983): 52–3.

Wyndham, Francis. *Graham Greene.* Writers and Their Work 67. London, New York, Toronto: Longmans, Green 1955.

Zabel, Morton Dauwen. "The Best and Worst." Hynes, *Graham Greene* 30–48.

Index